Sometime in Africa

Recollections of a Whirl-Wind Trek
Across the African Continent

Neil B. Dukas

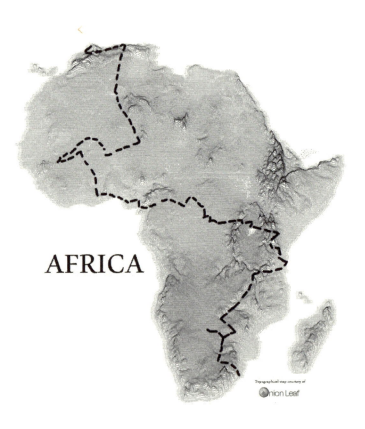

Sometime in Africa

Recollections of a Whirl-Wind Trek Across the African Continent

Neil B. Dukas

KALADAR BOOKS ♦ SAN FRANCISCO

Copyright © Neil Bernard Dukas, 2022

All rights reserved. No part of this publication may be reproduced, stored in a retrieval system, or transmitted in any form or by any means—electronic, mechanical, photocopy, recording, or any other—except brief quotations in printed reviews, without the prior permission of the author.

Sometime in Africa : Recollections of a Whirl-Wind Trek Across the African Continent

Library of Congress Control Number: 2022935887

ISBN 9780983192985

ebook ISBN 9780578397832

Published by KALADAR BOOKS —San Francisco

www.kaladarbooks.com

POD by arrangement with Kindle Direct Publishing, May 1, 2022

Library of Congress Cataloging-in-Publication Data

Names: Dukas, Neil Bernard., author.
Title: Sometime in Africa : recollections of a whirl-wind trek across the African Continent / Neil Bernard Dukas.
Description: San Francisco : Kaladar Books, 2022. | Includes photographs and route maps.
Identifiers: LCCN 2022935887 | ISBN 9780983192985 (paperback)| ISBN 9780983192992 (hardcover) | ISBN 9780578397832 (ebook)
Subjects: LCSH : Dukas, Neil Bernard., 1959– | Authors, English– 21st century. | Africa–Description and travel. | BISAC : TRAVEL / Africa / General.
Classification: LCC DT7-12.25.DU 2022 | BISAC TRV002000 | MDS (DDC) 916.0432 DUK.

LC record available at https://lccn.loc.gov/2022935887

Preface

IN 1983, I SET OUT FOR AFRICA and a five-month journey across the entire continent "from top to bottom" (over 14,000 miles)—all the way from Ceuta and the Pillars of Hercules on the Alboran Sea to Durban, South Africa (plus the preliminary overland passage through England, France, and Spain). It was, as you may have guessed, a memorable trip.

My intent here is not to romanticize what occurred or to tout the adventure. Rather, I have endeavored to convey a sense of the experience as I interpreted it at the time with the odd reflection thrown in, relying on personal letters and journal entries for source material. Where I did not clearly record my thoughts, I have done my best to recall things as well as memory serves. In such cases, I apologize if I have mangled the occasional detail.

This story, it should be noted, is written from the perspective of someone who had neither qualification nor expertise on setting out, merely curiosity. Like all memoirs, it is written from my own perspective—in this instance, a White (Canadian/American) interloper amongst a group of interlopers just passing through. Consequently, it is an admittedly superficial view of Africa as there was no time or opportunity to absorb the eidos of an entire continent. I might add that I was twenty-four at the time, imbued with all the drives and biases of a technically unattached male on leave from the (Canadian) military. Which is to say, I still had a lot to learn.

For a variety of reasons, which I think will become fast apparent, trekking across Africa from north to south was not a common undertaking at the time. Thirty-eight-plus years have elapsed since the events depicted. The world today is a much different place. Attitudes and social mores, including my own, have transformed, possibly for the better. Communications have undergone a veritable revolution. In general, our understanding of a great many subjects is enhanced. This remains, nonetheless, my impression of the experience.

Apart from what little you may discern of Africa in the day and the people touched upon, it is, when all is said and done, a cautionary tale. For any reader contemplating similar "adventure travel" on the fly, I must emphasize that it is only by sheer luck and the generosity of others that I survive to share these memories.

Aside from its cathartic value, if there is any real "purpose" to sharing this account, it is, I suppose, a chance to allow the reader to indulge in a bit of useful introspection. This is one of those stories where the reader, from the safety of a comfortable armchair, has the opportunity to ask oneself, "what would I have done in the same or similar circumstances?" The answers, if you're honest, may surprise you.

Neil B. Dukas
Kingston, Ontario, Canada
March 25, 2022

"MY TRIP" – JOURNAL No. 1

"DO YOU REALIZE WE'RE PUSHING A PIG AND A PYGMY IN A PICKUP?" It was one of Sara's better alliterations. Absurd on the face of it, but astonishingly accurate.

You'd think advancing years would dim the memories of my brief time in Africa, but in my dreams I can still hear the sound of drums drifting over tangled jungle and see the dense star-filled sky over undulating desert sands. My recollections are reinforced by rough notes scrawled in three compact traveler's journals, their covers mottled by mold after sitting for years unprotected in a damp trunk.[1] Looking back, I was clearly at the mercy of whichever prevailing wind happened to be buffeting me along with only a general sense of purpose and intended direction.

My plane arrived at London Gatwick at 10 in the morning, November 18, 1983. I took the train to Victoria Station, then made my way to the Tracks Africa office on Abingdon Road. I was the last member of the "expedition" to check in, which meant I was the final person to receive any last-minute instructions. From the Tracks office, I hightailed it over to the Hospital of Tropical Medicine hoping to pick up a prescription for Maloprim, the one anti-malarial I couldn't obtain in Canada. I was concerned that I had no effective prophylactic for the parts of Africa where malaria was resistant to Chloroquine (notably, Kenya,

---

[1] "My Trip," travel journal 956, designed and printed by Buffalo-Eastcantra Inc., Saint-Laurent, Québec, circa 1971.

Tanzania, and Zaire). To my chagrin, I was informed that no doctor in the United Kingdom would prescribe it to a patient they didn't know, and abruptly turned away.

The author's three Buffalo brand travel journals, black, red, and brown. Each journal included sections to record itineraries, places visited, personal contacts, maps of the world, international time zones, and how to use your wristwatch as a compass

Disappointed, I rang up a childhood friend that had recently moved to France on an internship and, coincidentally, was visiting with family in London. We arranged to meet at Victoria Station. Mike and I attended junior high school together in a middle-class suburb of Toronto. He was of Anglo-French extraction and though born in Morocco held a British passport. As a kid, he had a penchant for pellet guns, dirt bikes, and kung-fu movies, and that's how I tended to remember him. So, I was taken aback when he arrived in a bespoke suit from Savile Row, silk tie, swanky Parisienne messenger bag, and polished leather loafers without socks. He had, moreover, reverted to the name given to him at birth, and I was now, apparently, to address my old friend as "Michel."

Sitting next to one another at a nearby sandwich shop dressed in well-worn khakis, gear stacked beside me, it must have looked to passers-by as if a London financier had taken pity on a luckless drifter. We spent some time catching up in the course of which I discovered that Michel was pining for the girl he'd left behind in Toronto, and yet feeling a bit guilty about it for he had not remained faithful to her. He would be a different man, he assured me, when he returned home, loyal to a fault. He was "in love." I thought about my girlfriend, Edi, and our fresh separation and wondered if I too would emerge from this experience with a similar sense of guilt. I had no intention of being untrue to her, but neither, for his part, had Michel. Discovering that I wasn't scheduled to head out for another three days, my friend called his aunt and uncle and asked if they could put me up, which they were evidently pleased to do.

Michel's uncle, George, and aunt, Ninette, welcomed me into their home like one of the family. George and Ninette, as it turned out, were estranged, but shared the same home "for estate-related reasons." Still, they seemed to get along reasonably well and didn't necessarily avoid one another. George was a virtual clone of Michel's father, Leslie, but the two men couldn't have been more opposite in character. While Leslie was the sort of man to lay his cape down over a puddle to let a lady pass unharmed, George would think nothing of wheeling about to ogle a pretty girl with a licentious whistle thrown in for good measure. To be fair to George, British society at the time, steeped in Benny Hill culture, didn't exactly condemn this sort of behavior. A parallel British tabloid to the Toronto Sun with a similar readership featured a completely topless "Sunshine Girl" on page three.[2] Topless women, to my great amazement, even appeared in British television ads. I couldn't resist asking the English women on our expedition, once I had the chance, what they made of this and was shocked to find that without exception they found it "harmless" and even symbolic of the

---

[2] The practice ended in 2015.

"women's lib" movement. I couldn't decide whether they were being liberal minded or unconsciously sexist. One thing was certain, they thought Torontonians (by extrapolation, Canadians) to be "a bunch of prudes."

Nonetheless, George could be extremely generous. He took time to go with me the next day to Barnet Hospital where we waited together for more than two hours to see a physician about getting me the prescription I needed, only to be once again rebuffed. Ninette was so incensed that the National Health Service would be willing to let anyone travel to Africa without adequate protection against malaria that she called her personal physician on the phone to express, rather vehemently, her feelings on the matter. I wasn't privy to her doctor's side of the conversation so I can only wonder what he made of this unexpected assault on his profession. Needless to say, he agreed to prescribe the Maloprim. I could relax on the matter.

That evening, Michel and I decided to do some sightseeing. After graduating from high school, I took a year off, in a manner of speaking, to train as a vehicle technician with the Canadian military and followed that up with a backpacking trip across Britain. So, I'd seen a little of London already. Michel let on that he'd never been to Soho, the city's famed red-light district, and that decided our destination. Other than curiosity, we were only out for a little entertainment, and consequently behaved ourselves. Even so, we were out much longer than we intended and missed the last Underground train home. It was a long but pleasant walk through the night back to George and Ninette's home in West Finchley. We talked at length about our hopes and ambitions and speculated on what adventures life still had in store for us.

Michel queried me on why I was so intent on traveling across Africa. It was a reasonable question. I had just completed an undergraduate degree in political studies at Queen's University in Kingston, majoring in international relations. To my mind and education, Africa was poised and ready for a makeover, to blossom after decades of instability and underdevelopment. Again, this was 1983. The future looked bright. The "New Africa," already showing signs of emergence, would feature prosperous cities, farms, industries, modern highways, schools, and peaceful domestic intercourse akin to other more "developed" (i.e., Western) political economies.

One of my goals was to experience some fragment of the developing world first-hand, preferably a place on the verge of transformation, like Africa. I wanted also to see things through my own eyes. My professors, middle-aged White males, with rare exception, were competent and well-intentioned scholars, but when all was said and done, academics down to their socks. They did their best to impart an understanding of global society and political economy, but their teaching was necessarily limited and heavily filtered, if only because of the learning environment. Queen's, and the little city of Kingston, were, at the time, both very White and, frankly, very bourgeois. Instinctively, I knew that my education was incomplete, although neither the university nor my professors ever went out of their way to stress that particular point.

I'd minored unofficially in classical studies at Queen's studying roman art and archaeology, and so, relished the idea of visiting sites like Thamugadi (Timgad) in Algeria. Timbuktu also held a certain allure. I was familiar, of course, with the old saw "from here to Timbuktu," a common metaphor for travel to any distant or outlandish spot. The ancient city exemplified travel to a faraway and unattainable place. That was enough to pique my interest.

I'd be leaving something in this discussion out if I didn't mention that I was a huge fan of Humphrey Bogart. The African Queen was an all-time favorite, combining great story telling, history, and geography, not to mention acting, directing, and cinematography. Charlie Allnut—Bogart's slightly depraved but endearing character in the film—was a Canadian, like me. Every time I watched The African Queen,

I felt an inexplicable desire to see the Ulanga River for myself. I had every intention of doing so, if the opportunity presented itself.

I slept in the next day, started to pack, and then went with Michel to Belgravia where I tried to get in touch with family of my own (cousins on my father's side). I was unable to connect with them, but we were able to stop at a chemist to pick up my hard-earned anti-malaria prescription. Back at the house, I telephoned my parents one last time before heading off.

Edi was focused by this time on her graduate research, so, as agreed, I didn't attempt to call her. Letters would suffice going forward. Since we'd first met, some five years previously, I'd gone off on training for two or three months at a time with the Reserves, but this trip, we understood, would be a true test of our relationship. How would we feel about each other when I returned? We talked about it openly and honestly and said our goodbyes, both agreeing that it would be interesting to see if absence indeed makes the heart grow fonder. I gave her the rough itinerary provided by Tracks, emphasizing that if she wrote a letter addressed to me "poste restante" ahead of my expected arrival at any given destination, her letter would be waiting there for me. She assured me that she would write, and often.

I finished packing, deciding to leave the inner layer of my arctic sleeping bag with George and Ninette. It was bulky and seemed to me a ridiculous thing on sober second thought to haul across Africa, of all places. George and Ninette agreed to mail it back to me when I returned to Canada.

I had to be out of the house by 4:30 in the morning to join the expedition, so I thanked Michel and his aunt and uncle for taking such good care of me and went to bed early, anxious about the morning. When the alarm went off, I gathered my things and let myself out of the house while it was still dark outside, then caught the train to Kensington.

For some mysterious reason, our point of rendezvous was not the Tracks Africa office on Abingdon Road, but the sidewalk ("pavement") in front of Ryman Stationary on High Street. Our conveyance not yet arrived, two other members of the expedition were standing about, cigarettes to their lips, bags propped against the wall. We exchanged pleasantries as the other members slowly filtered in. The truck or "lorry"—our expedition home for the next four and a half months—pulled up just as the sun was peeking out, causing a stir. The vehicle (license number HLM977N) was a retired British Army Bedford painted hot pink with deep blue trim to clearly differentiate it from its prior service, "The Pink Pig" scrawled tongue-in-cheek across the hood or "bonnet" for added measure.

Marston mats, perforated steel planks for traction, were hooked on either side of the truck, hinting at the adventure to come. Atop the cab was a bracket for holding camping equipment. A square metal frame sat atop the bed covered in a royal blue waterproof tarp that included pliable transparent vinyl windows with interior night flaps. On either side of the tailgate, were racks for water and spare petrol. An open trailer with tarp was hitched at the back to carry our bags, gas canisters for cooking, and other necessities. Probably the most remarkable aspect of The Pig was how the interior bed had been adapted for two columns of forward-facing repurposed airplane seats, one column on either side of the center aisle, making for an exceptional degree of comfort, although there wasn't much in the way of legroom.

We helped George and Malcolm from Tracks load our bags on the trailer and then stood off to one side, doing our best not to block the sidewalk as they organized their paperwork. A few of our expedition recognized the opportunity to take photographs, myself included. An odd thing happened then. A respectably dressed middle-aged Black woman, shouted at one of us as she passed, "Did you take my picture?" We were all of us taken aback. It wasn't so much a matter of privacy, apparently, as a concern that the camera might have captured her soul, as the woman explained it.

We were momentarily speechless. Such thinking never entered our minds. I can't remember who her ire and suspicion were specifically directed at, but whomever it was, assured her that the focus of our attention was the truck and the members of our expedition, not her or any other passers-by. She continued on her way, muttering unhappily under her breath. The incident soured our mood and caused us all to wonder if taking photographs in Africa might prove more problematic than we ever anticipated.

In all, our expedition consisted of 18 members plus the Tracks Africa "leader" slash co-driver, George, and a driver slash mechanic, Malcolm. Malcolm had a kind disposition and a thick East End accent, or something akin to that. He reminded me of a typical corporal or junior sergeant in the British Army. He was recently divorced and was downhearted about not seeing his young son. He enjoyed his beer and smoked pot a little too often for my taste, given his responsibilities, but we learned, to our great relief, that he was a very capable mechanic. George, the supposed brains of our operation, bore a resemblance to Ringo Starr. He seemed on introduction level-headed and conscientious, but I soon discovered he had an eye for the women. Either Tracks had no policy against fraternizing with the clientele, or he simply didn't give a toss. "Consenting adults," and all that.

There were any number of different ways to characterize our group, by age, sex, marital status, relationship, or occupation, but nationality seemed the most obvious method. So we went around in a circle introducing ourselves by first name and country: "Inger, Denmark," "Rick, New Zealand," "Lila, England," "Ronnie, Canada," "Andy, England," "Kristine, France," "Lynn, Australia," "Gail, Australia," myself, "Canada," "Mark, New Zealand," "Barry, Australia," "Jim, Australia," "Julie, England," "Christine, England," "Elaine, England," and "Alison, England." Two members of the expedition would be joining us in Paris: Bernard a French national, and his partner, Hazel, a New Zealand expat. That made: 1 Dane, 2 French, 4 Aussies, 6 Brits, 3 Kiwis, and 2 Canucks, although the connection to some of the stated nationalities was tentative at best, me no less. Both George and Malcom were English, bringing our expedition total to 20. Eleven women and nine men. As we finished rhyming off our names and nationalities there was a spontaneous and audible sigh of relief. In near unison the group spurted out, "Thank God, no Americans!" In fact, I was a dual US-Canadian national by birth, but opted, given the circumstances, to keep that minor detail to myself.

Ronnie, my fellow 'Canuck,' was a trained nurse, who we were, frankly, very happy to have along, presuming her skills could come in handy. Yet, it's fair to say many of us found her bedside manner difficult to take. But more on that later. Jim and Barry were both veterinarians. Barry, a gentle soft-spoken man, reminded me on introduction of so many of my elementary school teachers. He turned out to be a bit of an animal as far as his personal habits were concerned and scarry addicted to weed. Jim, a burly fellow, aside from being a gifted musician, had a keen and irrepressible wit that frequently got him into trouble with the officials we encountered along the way.

Chris and Julie were physiotherapists with plans to work for three months in Uganda after the trip. It didn't take long to realize Jim and Julie had eyes for one another. Julie impressed me as a particularly sensible woman, moreover, always pleasant and free with a kind word. I could only imagine she found Jim's brash (dare I say "Australian"?) manners an enjoyable change from English fare. Her colleague and traveling companion, Chris, was a full-figured young woman with an alluring smile. I'm not sure that the men in our party looked much beyond that and, not surprisingly, seemed to gravitate to her, volunteering for the same tasks.

I never had much interaction with Chris. She seemed nice enough, but perhaps not entirely in tune with her feelings. One evening early on, she announced at dinner that she'd come to Africa to see the sights and wanted all the men in our party to know that she wasn't interested in a relationship. It wasn't too long after that she took up with Rick. It should be said he was probably closest in age and temperament to her and that pairing up like this had the practical effect of putting an end, at last, to the relentless competition for her attentions.

A New Zealand sheep farmer, Rick was a likeable and uncomplicated guy, but a bit too reckless for his own good. He'd come down with hepatitis while traveling through India the prior spring and it wouldn't have surprised me if he came down with it again this trip. He rarely washed, didn't wear shoes if he could help it, and ate anything without thought or question.

Elaina was an excellent artist, but a bit of a loner. Sometimes she would say things that made me wonder if she was all there, if you catch my meaning. Watching Harry Potter movies many years later, I was reminded of her in the character of Luna Lovegood, albeit some years older. Of all the women in our party I found her the most attractive, quite frankly, but in a distant sort of way. She eventually gravitated to Malcolm and I thought they made a fitting couple.

Alison was of French-English extraction and up to the time she joined our expedition had been teaching English in Spain. I enjoyed her company, reminding me of so many of my classmates in the political studies program at Queen's, drawn to other people's liberation movements and causes.

Since there were two women with homophone names on the expedition, Christine and Kristine, we elected to call the one from England "Chris" and the one from France "Kristine" to help differentiate between the two. Kristine was a graduate student, articulate, and stereotypically obsessed with all things food. She joined the expedition with her boyfriend, a laid-back, blonde, blue-eyed Englishman named Andy. Andy was fluent in French, sang, and played the guitar like a pro. He was a respectable photographer to boot. Andy was about the nicest most charming fellow you could imagine, but his penchant for wine and hashish dismayed me.

Then there was Gail and Lynnette (or "Lynn"), a couple of funny, crude, outspoken women who made a living as occasional cooks in the Australian outback and then spent their hard-earned dollars traveling the world. Gail and Lynn were no youngsters in comparison to the rest of us. I initially worried that they might find the rough going difficult, and yet, they did so with great humor and fortitude.

Inger was our youngest member, not yet twenty-one. A tall, svelte, Danish girl, who spoke perfect, if accented, English. She was our expedition ingénue, so to speak, and we were all instinctively protective of her. After getting to know her, I dare say Inger was quite capable of looking after herself.

Ronnie, as I mentioned, was the other Canadian in our party, although you wouldn't have guessed it from her slightly abrasive personality—loud, opinionated, and worst of all, a compulsive talker. She quickly got on everyone's nerves. Fortunately, she had an exceptional work ethic, pulling more than her fair share of camp duties, so no one went out of their way to complain about her, or at least resisted the temptation.

After an awkward introduction (more about this later), I was befriended by Lila, "an older woman" from my utterly self-absorbed perspective. In fact, Lila was probably no more than ten years older than me, which would have made her all of thirty-four or thirty-five at the time. I never did discover her actual age. She'd been married and, I assumed, divorced and that was enough in my twenty-four-year-old brain to peg her as an older woman. Although she looked nothing like Edi (petite, while Edi was athletic), she seemed to have a similar manner and temperament—spirited, protective of her independence, and determined in everything she did.

I don't mean to convey any harsh criticism of my fellow travelers. I was certainly no saint and would prove to be a difficult enough companion. In fact, it is surprising just how well we got along divvying up chores and the like when it came round to it, not to mention traveling all crammed together in the back of The Pig for hours at a time. The casual attitude towards drugs worried me more than anything. I seemed to be the maverick in that respect. At a practical level, I imagined that if we were ever searched by police and their stashes discovered, I would be deemed guilty by association and was under no misapprehension concerning the character of an Algerian prison. I guess I also struggled with the notion that a group of individuals intent upon a trip of this nature would seek an artificial high. I reflected upon this point in a letter to Edi, "Perhaps it is because, behind all this adventure and excitement there is something vaguely depressing about the state of the world—the imbalances and inequities" (sent from Fez, December 5, 1983).

If it isn't obvious, we were all of us, without exception, Caucasian, that is to say, White, with attendant ramifications that I hadn't even considered before heading out. Moreover, none of us were terribly knowledgeable about Africa, including the hired hands from Tracks. I can also say, in retrospect, that I should have paid much more attention to the fine print in the Tracks Africa brochure:

> **The total cost per person has been reduced substantially for this once in a lifetime trip since we will be treading on new territory as much as each and every participant. However, you will have the satisfaction of knowing there is an experienced driver on board, as well as an excellent back-up service from base should an unexpected contingency arise.**

In my blind resolve to see only the upside of the proposed excursion, I completely failed to foresee the implications of offering an essentially at-cost trip across the heart of Africa to anyone who cared to join. One by one and unbeknownst to me, like ill-fated moths to a flame, our roster filled with individuals intent upon the adventure of a lifetime, but, in too many cases, without a penny to rub together beyond the initiation fee. This would have serious consequences for all concerned down the road. And if I'd read the words more carefully, I might have realized early on that having an "experienced driver on board" was veiled speech masking the fact that the driver was capable but unfamiliar with Africa. When Tracks stated "we will be treading on new territory as much as each and every participant" they meant it, quite literally. Malcolm had a finite amount of experience driving through parts of northern Algeria above the Sahara, and that was it. The sum total of George's experience was leading tour groups in Morocco.

The first thing George had us do was pair-up. Our accommodations were old-style two-man A-frame tents, so those of us that were not already in couples had to find a tent-mate. After a few moments of awkward negotiations, I was paired with Mark, a lean yet sturdy six-foot-three agrochemical student from New Zealand. Mark could be headstrong and overbearing at times, but I liked him well enough. Poor Lila was paired with Ronnie.

Once we were paired, we loaded into The Pig and settled in, much as one might do on entering an airplane with unreserved seating. Since there were no overhead bins, any immediate needs had to be kept in tote bags beneath the seat in front or under our feet. George did a head count and confirmed that our first destination was Paris. It would be another ten years before completion of the Euro Tunnel, a seemingly impossible engineering feat, so we would travel to France via the Dover-Calais Ferry.

The expedition leader then spelled out for us a few crucial details. Our proposed itinerary would take us overland across fourteen countries in North, West, and East Africa, not including the "preliminary" transit through England, France, and Spain. We would have to break ourselves into alternating teams, one for cooking, one for washing, and one for shopping, as needed. With respect to shopping, he had one more point of administration. There was a gas stove and bulk food supplies on board which could be supplemented at any time with funds from the kitty that we were all expected to contribute to as our journey progressed, in total, about $200 US each. The food kitty, explained George, was our responsibility to manage. We needed to elect someone for the task. Jim had some experience along these lines and was a willing volunteer. There being no objection, he was unanimously elected to the post of "chief accountant." If we needed anything along the way, we had only to bang on the small window behind the cab to get our drivers' attention. With the preliminaries concluded, George smacked his hands together enthusiastically. "Any last questions?"

Stepping off the truck at 7:30 a.m. on November 21, 1983, he closed the tailgate and fastened the tarp, joining Malcolm up front. We heard the gears engage and felt the truck move forward. Africa was still a long way off, but the excitement was palpable.

The conversation was animated to begin with. I for one had never seen the Cliffs of Dover and found the ferry crossing altogether thrilling, The Herald of Free Enterprise being the largest vessel I'd ever sailed on, up to that point. We were issued transit visas on arrival in France and quickly got back on the road.

As the day wore on the temperature dropped unexpectedly and dramatically. The banter died down. It was all we could do to keep from freezing in the back of the truck. The smart thing to do would have been to pull out our sleeping bags during a rest stop, but that would have entailed unpacking the trailer and no one, least of all George, wanted to spend time doing that. We arrived in Paris late afternoon, chilled to the bone, and moved into a campground in the Bois de Boulogne on the east bank of the Upper Seine.

The "Bois" was one of two forested appendages tacked onto the capital, like the pseudopods of an amoeba. Half of us set up the tents while the other half worked at cooking up a hot meal. Unfamiliar with what was available and how things were stored, the whole process took much longer than it might otherwise have. That first cup of hot tea was ecstasy and followed-up with a very commendable vegetable stew. About half the group, as it turned out, were vegetarian, but had no objection to adding meat to whatever was on the menu after putting aside their portion. We evidently had some good cooks among us. It boded well for the rest of the trip.

That afternoon, we were joined by the final two members of our expedition, Bernard and Hazel. Bernard, struck me as having just stepped out of the Paris Latin Quarter, a beatnik from a time gone by. A piano tuner by trade, he was fiercely proud of being French and reticent to speak English when a hand or facial gesture could suffice. His partner, Hazel, a New Zealand ex-pat and massage parlor operator, was a vivacious free spirit who never minced words.

Camped next to us, was another overland group from a competing adventure travel firm, Guerba Expeditions, on their way back from North Africa. Some of our party went straight off to explore the city. Others, hung about the camp to socialize with the Guerba group or to hit the sack early. Feeling the onset of a cold, I was among the latter, looking forward to a good night's sleep. But it was not to be. We were awakened in the dead of night by shouts, shrill whistles, and dogs barking. We stuck our heads out of the tent flaps to investigate and were stunned to see a long line of gendarmes advancing across the campground. In due course, they passed us by with a few words of instruction and a quick glance inside each tent. We wondered, of course, what was up. The Bois de Boulogne was known as a hub for prostitution, but that seemed an unlikely explanation for so large an effort. The scuttlebutt about the camp the following morning was that a policeman had been murdered in the wood across the road, but I never read or heard a news report to validate the story.

The police were still poking about while we breakfasted on bacon and eggs. George collected our passports and went off to obtain visas for Algeria and Upper Volta, or Haute-Volta in French. The country changed its name to Burkina Faso about nine months later. I'd managed on my own to obtain visas for Algeria, Niger, and South Africa (my intended final destination) from their respective embassies in Ottawa before departing Canada.

Feeling better and with nothing much else to do, I hopped the Paris Metro together with Mark and Rick and went shopping at Les Halles, a brutal steel, glass, and concrete courtyard complex which, at the time, epitomized the 1970s notion of futuristic architecture. The buskers on the Metro were a different breed than I was used to, one putting on a puppet show for commuters and another entertaining us with Spanish guitar melodies. I exchanged a few pounds sterling for French francs and purchased three rolls of toilet paper and a couple of bottles of water purification tablets.

On the way back to the campsite we learned just how large a hub the Bois de Boulogne was for prostitution. Even though the weather was bitter cold, "the ladies" were out in force, clad in thigh length fur coats with only a swimsuit or nothing at all underneath. I suppose Mark, Rick, and I looked like prospective clients on the prowl. Several flashed us as we walked by, their idea of advertising, I suppose.

At the campsite, we learned that the embassy staff needed at least four more days to consult with their higher ups in Upper Volta before issuing our visas. The camping fees for the Bois de Boulogne were too steep to warrant our hanging about, so the decision was made to move camp the following day. George opted to "camp out" in the embassy waiting room with a good book, hoping that his presence would motivate authorities to speed up the process. I was assigned dishwashing duties that evening, which proved easy enough working with a team. After supper, George and Malcolm treated us to a nighttime tour of Paris in The Pig. Even in the dark, the Paris skyline, edged in soft lamplight, was a wonderful sight to behold. I caught my first glimpse of the Eiffel Tower, Champs-Élysées, and Arc de Triomphe. That night, before going to bed, I started the anti-malarial regime that would carry me through the duration of the trip by taking my first Chloroquine tablets.

The following morning, we packed up and drove to Chémery, a three-hour drive south of Paris, where George had arranged for all of us to sleep together on the floor in a large hall within the Château de Chémery. Remodeled in the 16th century, the château stood or stands on 12th century foundations. The owner, Axel, was a down-to-earth fellow who seemed thrilled to have us as guests, even though Malcolm bumped the château's ancient perimeter wall while trying to squeeze The Pig through the narrow courtyard gate.

The château was a long way from being ready to host actual tourists, but we were happy not to have to spend another night in tents as the temperature continued to drop. At the center of the hall was a huge cedar table, fashioned from one discrete piece of wood, the last remaining table from a set of eight—the others consumed as firewood during various trying times in French history.

We soon discovered the Château de Chémery possessed an astonishing and incongruous secret. After we'd settled in, we were ushered upstairs to a darkened room where, to our immense astonishment, there was a "symphonie automaton." European aristocrats in the 18th century were fond of such devices, wind-up mechanical forebearers of the Audio-Animatronics you find today at a Disney theme park. This particular automaton was the brainchild of a young couple who had taken the original concept and modified it to suit their unique talents—an automated puppet show featuring an entire symphony orchestra beautifully timed to lighting and music. We watched mesmerized, none of us able to get over the sheer genius and artistry behind it. Alas, the priceless automaton at Chémery seems to have disappeared sometime after our visit, its fate, and that of its creators, a mystery, at least to me.

At the Château de Chémery

Unfortunately, the fortress-like walls of the château acted as a kind of refrigerator. Sharing the hard floor of the ancient château turned out to be little better if not worse than the tents. There was a lot of restless activity during the night and with us all housed together in one room I got little sleep. All the warmth of a wood fire in the large hearth at the end of the hall, built for cooking, went straight up the chimney.

I wrote a letter to Edi by the firelight with gloves on, my fingers cramped from the cold. George telephoned, sheepishly admitting he'd left the money for our visas in The Pig. Rather than hire a ride to Chémery, he intended to get Tracks to wire him the funds. He was hopeful it wouldn't add much delay. Given the lag, the château seemed a good place for all of us to get to know one-another a little better. A party, of sorts, was planned for the following evening.

There was a cold rain the next morning. I hung around the hearth trying to absorb what little warmth it emitted, kicking myself for not having given more thought to the weather in Europe in late November or the degree to which we would be roughing it. I was so fixated on hauling about an already stuffed and oversized backpack that I'd put aside all thought of carrying extra warm clothing, which, in hindsight, I could easily have discarded once we reached Africa. Now too, I deeply regretted my decision to leave that warm inner liner for my sleeping bag with George and Ninette. So much for my thorough preparations.

Feeling under the weather and in no mood to socialize, I kept my own company by the fire as much as circumstances allowed, second guessing my decision to sign on to this venture. It was my father that talked me into it in the first place, pressing a Tracks brochure on me out of desperation after learning that I intended to cross Africa on my own. "And why not Europe or Asia?" he wanted to know. He worked for a Japanese import-export company with offices in Toronto and was at least familiar with that culture. He probably thought Japan or Southeast Asia safe enough, and yet possibly "exotic" enough, from his perspective, to satisfy whatever itch was behind my seemingly sudden drive to explore the world. On the other hand, Africa, in 1983, seemed to him, and probably many others at the time, a world of darkness and despair, where military coups, famine, disease, and lawlessness were day-to-day realities.

"I don't want to be part of some blundering sightseeing tour across the Serengeti!" I bellowed. "That's not the point." But he was persistent, almost pleading with me to take a closer look at the brochure.

West Africa
Reconnaissance Expedition
18 Weeks £665 Departs 21 Nov
Food Kitty £140

I had to admit the notion of a "reconnaissance expedition" across West Africa intrigued me. Before taking my commission, I trained as a reconnaissance ("recce") soldier with a Canadian Militia regiment, the Governor General's Horse Guards.

Following our successful reconnaissance expedition in November 1979 through Egypt and Sudan to Kenya, we will be undertaking an equally unique journey through remote and rarely explored areas of West Africa. To travel on this expedition will be a tremendously rewarding experience as you will be one of only a handful of fortunate people ever to have had the opportunity to participate on an exploratory project such as this.

"'Remote and rarely explored areas of West Africa' reiterated my father. That's more than you can do on your own if you're intent on this. Plus, there's safety in numbers."

He had a point. I knew from prior experience, backpacking through Britain, that getting off the beaten track without a little help could be problematic. Moreover, there was a suggestion here that this would be a small group of hardy individuals, perhaps with similar interests.

"And look at the price. That's hardly more than a thousand dollars [Canadian] for four and a half months, not including meals. You can't beat that!"

Again, he did make a pretty good point. My meager savings would only stretch so far. In fact, the whole thing sounded almost too good to be true. To my surprise, he was beginning to win me over. Could I achieve my goals as part of a trail-blazing expedition for an adventure travel firm? I had to admit to a certain amount of trepidation about traveling through Africa on my own. What I intended wasn't going to be another backpacking trip through Britain, I was fairly certain of that. Maybe he was right? The destination was Nairobi, Kenya in East Africa, not Durban or Cape Town (my ultimate objective), but I could figure that part out later.

A few members of the group came over to chat with me, despite my standoffish attitude, stirring me from my reverie. Lila was of Polish extraction and apparently fluent in the language. She made a sincere effort to connect (my mother was born in Poland), but my dark mood was apparently all that came off. She would later admit she thought me "haughty."

I thought it best to go for a walk and encountered Kristine, Andy, and Rick on a mission to buy wine for the evening's social event. I forced myself to take an interest and joined them. At Axel's suggestion we went to the home of an old woman who grew and bottled her own vintage. She went to great lengths to explain the whole process and encouraged us to sample several varieties. We wound up purchasing 20 liters, to her great delight.

Dinner consisted of rice and pork, but the portions were small, for some reason, and I was left feeling hungry. Fortunately, someone turned up with a platter of cheese. Paired with the wine, I began to feel more companionable. Jim had brought several small musical instruments with him, including a practice chanter for the bagpipes. The wine and music were enough to inspire an evening of song. Hazel, Mark, and Rick treated us to a Māori haka, the first time I'd ever witnessed such a thing.

George telephoned again with both good news and bad news. He was confident our visas would be issued the following day and would meet the truck in Blois if successful. News that we would be required by a newly implemented Algerian regulation to spend a stipulated amount of money in country as a condition of entry, however, was not well received by most members of the group. A few openly scoffed at the requirement, suggesting that they would find some way to circumvent it. I had my doubts.

To my surprise, I somehow avoided a hangover from the previous evening's festivities. Malcolm offered to drive any that wished to go with him to Blois. Less than half the group, including myself, took him up on it. We scattered in different directions on arrival. Blois, was an old city on the hillside overlooking the Loire. I teamed up with a couple of others to check out the sights.

To our disappointment, the Château Royal, a former palace, was closed for lunch, so we hiked up the hillside to Blois Cathedral, which more than made up for it. I was instantly reminded of Québec City. With the cathedral behind me and the river below, I could easily have been standing in front of the Château Frontenac looking out over the St. Lawrence River. It crystalized for me the extent to which French Canadian settlers (the "habitant" of Nouvelle-France) had fashioned a little bit of their old 'home' in Canada.

We hiked back down to the river and did a bit of window shopping. All through the lower town we were hounded by young French kids begging money from tourists. I was well and truly shocked by this and wondered aloud that if this was going on in the heart of France, what would things be like in Africa? By coincidence, most of our group stumbled on a quaint "Tea Shoppe" by the river all about the same time. Sitting close together, we each ordered something different from a quintessential French pastry cart and very shrewdly divvied up the dainties so that we could sample everything. We rendezvoused with George who had finally succeeded in obtaining our visas for Upper Volta, as well as Algeria. To complete our French culinary experience, our shoppers, to our huge delight, purchased a quantity of baguette and soft cheese. With implements provided by Axel from the château's kitchen, we dined that evening on a classic fondu.

We bid adieu to the Château de Chémery the following morning. George made it clear that we needed to make up for lost time, so we ate on the move and pressed on to the border with Spain with only a break or two along the way. On we drove, southwest down the A63, passing through Tours and Poitiers, and then the truck stalled. Malcolm got out and tinkered under the vehicle. He managed to get it going again, but it stalled several more times before he was able to fully diagnose the problem. It looked as if air was getting into the fuel line at the filter.

We made it to Bordeaux where Malcolm bought a length of plastic fuel line and rigged it to by-pass the filter. That did the trick, but we were now well behind schedule. The decision was made to keep driving through the night. It was well after midnight by the time we reached Bayonne at the tip of Biscayne Bay and still well before daybreak when we reached the north bank of the Bidasoa River and the Spanish border post at the Irún (Spain)–Hendaye (France) crossing.[3] That's when things got "interesting."

We understood from the outset that this was a "reconnaissance expedition," but I think we all assumed this to be a reference to West Africa. We soon realized that few, if any, overland expeditions attempted this crossing at night,

---

[3] The Spanish border station was a kind of sentry post, technically on the French side of the river—an area known as "Biriatou."

less than a half-hour's drive from the heart of Basque Country. Less than ten years had transpired since the end of the Franco regime. The fascist culture that dominated the Spanish military and police had not altered appreciably. Moreover, the Basque separatist organization, Euskadi ta Askatasuna, better known by its acronym, ETA, had committed several notable assassinations, kidnappings, and bank robberies the prior year. Given the circumstances, our arrival in the dead of night in a converted army truck was not well received by the Spanish authorities.

Alison volunteered to act as our interpreter. She patiently translated for our benefit words to the effect that regulations prohibited any more than three individuals to enter Spain in a commercial vehicle. Any more than that had to enter by "motor coach," which our Bedford was not deemed to be, despite our comfortable airplane seats. We did not possess the necessary paperwork for an exemption and there was no one at the post with sufficient authority, let alone reachable by telephone at that hour of the night. There was simply no getting past this technicality.

We sat in the truck for a full hour as George and Alison stood beside the vehicle attempting to negotiate some sort of resolution with a lot of very heavily armed border guards watching intently, but to no avail. I don't think it helped that we had very little sleep. George finally announced that it was useless. We had no choice but to turn around and head back to Bayonne.

Our drivers mounted back up, turned the truck about and headed off. To our surprise, the border guards hopped in their vehicles and cut us off. George got out and quickly stuck his head over the tailgate, just long enough to let us know that he would try this time to see if a bribe would make a difference. He needed Alison's help again to translate. There was no time for us to deliberate or protest.

Alison jumped out and together with George and Malcolm, were ushered away. We waited nervously to see what would come next. Suddenly, the border post was plunged into complete darkness, all the lights inexplicably shut off. For ten full minutes we sat in silence pondering our fate, listening to our hearts beat in the dark. The guards returned with our people and briskly ordered everyone off the truck. "Bring your bags. No talking." They pointed with their guns down the long bridge over the Bidasoa, the end of which was shrouded in obscurity. "That way. Walk."

I had a sudden inkling of how my great grandparents must have felt when the Nazis invaded their town in Poland. Naturally, we hesitated. George, Malcolm, and Alison were apparently not to accompany us and remained standing silently off to one side. Like sheep, we did as we were directed. Clutching our bags, we headed in a frightened column into the night, the river swirling below, guards at our back.

How far down would it be if I had to jump? I thought. It was so dark I couldn't see over the railing lining either side of the bridge and had no idea how high up we were. As we neared the end of the bridge, I could hear the motor from a vehicle following closely behind with its lights off. It was The Pig, I realized, as it idled passed us and pulled to one side.

George leaped out and waved, "Get in! Quickly!" We needed no further encouragement. "They decided to bend the rules for us," he explained as we mounted up, "but didn't want to take the chance that anyone could see and tattle on them. 'Three passengers in a lorry with no merchandise and seventeen travelers on foot.' That's what they'll write in the log. And they won't let us take our planned route through Basque Country. We have to take the long way round through San Sebastián."

Just then, two Cuerpo de Policía Nacional vehicles appeared from the opposite direction. The CPN had no knowledge of what had just transpired, and their suspicions were aroused—a load of scruffy looking foreigners piling with bags in hand into the back of an old military vehicle (pink or otherwise) in the dead of night so close to Basque

Country. Alison was once again called upon to explain the situation. In the end, the police had a good chuckle over the absurdity of the border guards' "old-line" behavior and sent us on our way with a word of caution to keep on driving to San Sebastián and not go wandering off the main road.

We were never, I suppose, in any actual danger during the whole Kafkaesque affair, but I think anyone who isn't accustomed to a police society would be unnerved to find themselves in a situation where you really don't know what is going on, are literally in the dark, and there are a whole lot of guns being waved about. It was a novel experience, at least for me.

By the time the sun came up, we were high up in the Pyrenees mountains and treated to some magnificent vistas. From San Sebastián we took the road to Pamplona and then on to Madrid. It was another long drive with few breaks, but the rugged rolling scenery passing through Soria in the eastern-most part of Castile and León was captivating. We pulled into a campsite on the outskirts of Madrid encountering, thankfully, milder weather for the first time since departing London. George and a couple of others went off with our passports to obtain visas for Morocco, while just about everyone else drove with Malcolm into the city.

Alison led us on a brilliant walking tour of old Madrid. I was impressed by its wide avenues and elegant shops. We then split up and went our separate ways in smaller groups. Near noon, a bunch of us filed into a cantina that opened on one of the many central squares, strings of sausage and pungent garlic hanging from the rafters. We ordered plates of breaded calamari that were fried to crispy perfection and sipped on freshly made sangria.

Mark needed some additional passport photos, so I went with him to the photomat before heading back to camp. Some members of our group cautioned us about riding the Madrid Metro, but either they were pulling our legs or were grossly misinformed because the Metro was wonderfully modern, clean, and efficient. I guess it was the hour of the day, but we were astonished to board the same car as a few other members of our expedition. For a city of over three million people, I don't know what the odds were of that happening.

I was assigned dinner duty that night. Our shopping crew had taken full advantage of the excellent markets in Madrid and so our menu was a cut above the usual. The timing couldn't have been better as it was Inger's 21st birthday. We were able to surprise here with a special celebration. George made it abundantly clear that he'd set his sights on her. She was an adult, of course, and able to make up her own mind. Whether it was appropriate or not didn't seem to be a question. Inger would eventually succumb to his determined attentions.

George managed to obtain our visas for Morocco without a hitch, which meant there was no need to hang about another expensive camping site. The following morning, we moved on to Granada heading due south, passing through the vast semi-arid plains east of Toledo and Ciudad Real where olive producers and wheat farmers miraculously coax life from the rocky soil, and then on to Valdepeñas where we stopped for lunch. Valdepeñas lies in the heart of La Mancha, so I wasn't altogether surprised to find the region littered with windmills (molinos de viento).

The highlight of our dash through Spain, however, was hands-down the beautiful hillsides of Andalucia and the stunning Moorish-influenced architecture. Taking the turn to Jaén, we camped just outside of Granada. The weather, at last, turned warm, the sky clear. Beside the white-washed walls of the camping office draped in fragrant bougainvillea were tables for us to use at our leisure. We savored the evening, enjoying cheap wine, bread and cheese, and thinking the whole experience could never be topped, until Andy and an employee of the campground sat down with us and began to play the Spanish guitar. If I thought romantic images of Spain were a Hollywood fabrication, I now knew better. What a pity, I thought, that Edi was not here to enjoy it with me. None of us really wanted the evening to end.

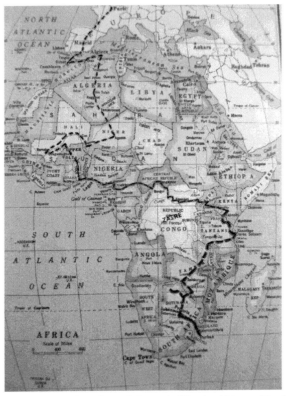

From the Spanish enclave of Ceuta in North Africa to Durban, South Africa—22,925km (14,245 miles). The political map of Africa used to trace the author's route is copied from his daily journal. By 1983, the map was already 12-years out-of-date

We slept in the following morning. It was warm enough for me to cast aside my jacket. We grudgingly packed our bags and drove to Granada where we allowed ourselves an hour to do some souvenir shopping, then on to Málaga. The road was mountainous between Granada and the Mediterranean coast. It wasn't long before The Pig began to stall out on the steep inclined grades. Malcolm speculated that we'd been sold watered-down diesel in Granada. The only thing we could do was persevere, getting out from time to time to push.

From Málaga it was a two-hour drive along the coast to Algeciras. After scouting around, we found a site overlooking the sea where we could set up a bonfire and camp for free. The downside, if any, was that this was the first time we were to camp in an unsecured site. I offered, and the group agreed, for me to establish a picket (camp guard) for the night, mostly to keep the fire going for warmth and to deter any potential mischief-makers. Mark and I took the 03:30 to 05:30 shift, during which I shaved off the moustache I'd borne for several years. I'd been contending with a runny nose since camping in the Bois de Boulogne and the moustache was proving to be both unsightly and unhygienic.

We thought there would be plenty of time the next morning to catch the ferry to North Africa, due to depart at 10:30, but The Pig kept stalling and we made it only by the skin of our teeth. There was plenty of room aboard the big Baleària ferry for our vehicle, but we had to detach the trailer and push it onboard separately. It was a two-hour passage across the Strait of Gibraltar, apparently a longer journey than normal because of dense fog.

Gibraltar raised its iconic head out of the mist and, just as quickly, vanished from sight. Most of us clustered on the forward deck to avoid getting seasick, anxiously awaiting our first glimpse of Africa, at which point we excitedly started clicking away with our cameras. The ferry docked at the Spanish exclave of Ceuta at half-past noon on Thursday, December 1, 1983, eleven days since departing London. "Day One" of my trans-Africa trek and the start of my African adventure, come what may.

While the British Overseas Territory of Gibraltar still garners most of the attention, be it positive or negative, outside the immediate region few are aware of Spain's colonial holdovers, Ceuta and Melilla. Spain, in fact, is the last of all the former colonial empires to maintain a territorial footing in Africa. The territory has a storied past that includes Mount Hacho, one of the legendary Pillars of Hercules, overlooking the Alboran Sea.

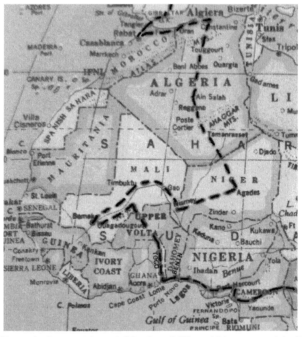

The author's route through North and West Africa as noted in his journal. Dahomey was renamed Benin in 1975. Upper Volta changed its name to Burkina Faso in 1984

We allowed ourselves some time to go exploring. Something like a third of the population of Ceuta were Muslim. The only outward sign that we had entered a different cultural milieu was the obvious lack of public lavatories. We were unaccustomed, and frankly, taken aback by the sight of men in traditional jalaba (or djellaba), the long-flowing full-sleeved robes common in the Maghreb, crouching down to relieve themselves at any convenient spot beside the road. How and where women took care of their own needs, I could not say.

An autonomous freeport, Ceuta was crowded with modern shops brimming with cameras, watches, calculators, and the like, and none of it cheap. If you were the slightest bit interested in making a purchase, you were more or less required to employ an "intermediary." From our perspective, these middlemen were completely unnecessary, annoying parasites. We understood from questioning the shop owners, however, that this method of doing business, although not strictly speaking a legal requirement, was encouraged by the local administration as a way to boost employment and bring in foreign currency. Aside from window shopping, we did the tourist "thing." Mark took photographs overlooking the port until stopped by a policeman who made it abundantly clear that such activity was not permitted, evidently for national security reasons.

It was a short drive to the Moroccan border. The crossing itself was hassle-free, but we did have to sit in a long line of vehicles. We headed southwest to the capital, Rabat, in quest of our next set of visas and were immediately struck by the change. Morocco was an entirely different world. The people were either Arab or Berber. The lush mountainside passes between Ceuta and Tangier even more spectacular, to my thinking, than those we encountered in the Spanish Pyrenees. It was warm and sunny besides.

We were stopped at a police checkpoint on the outskirts of Tangier and our documents carefully scrutinized. This would be the first of countless such encounters. I suppose it offset the rather relaxed interrogation we received at the border, but other than slowing us down, no issues arose. We managed to find ourselves a beautiful campsite in the hills overlooking Tangier. I should have enjoyed it more, but the cold I'd been nursing since Paris began to make itself felt in a more serious and ominous fashion. I could really have gone for a hot shower, but there was none to be had. Moreover, owing to the size of our group, we'd already consumed our supply of clean drinking water. Henceforth, all our water had to be boiled and/or disinfected.

As there were no serious incidents while camping, a decision was made to do away with our over-night picket. I was a little apprehensive about this but was grateful just the same for the opportunity to rest through the night without interruption. Regardless, I spent a sleepless night with a piercing headache. While many of the group went into Tangier the next morning, I slept in until noon, then bathed bird-bath style, washed some clothes, and re-organized my kit. Perhaps I was fortunate. The returning members had little of anything positive to say about their experience in Tangier. Beggars and merchants alike, they remarked bitterly, thought nothing of grabbing a person by the arm until you responded to whatever they were after. Our shoppers came back from market with a large fish head, from which our designated cooks prepared a tasty and nourishing soup.

From Tangier we continued down the Atlantic coast to Rabat. George and Malcolm, perhaps taking pity on me for being so down invited me into the cab for a stretch despite the risk to themselves of catching my cold. We had real trouble finding a campsite near Rabat, finally locating one in a forest. The locals brought us firewood for a very reasonable price.

Having diverted south along the coast all the way to Rabat largely for the purpose of obtaining visas, George, for whatever reason, had no luck obtaining them. Still, the effort afforded us an opportunity to hire a local guide and tour the Mausoleum of King Mohammed V in Yacoub Al Mansour Square. As the Sultan of Morocco, Sīdī Muḥammad Ben Yūsuf, was instrumental in securing Morocco's independence from French colonial rule. Touring the mausoleum, you would be tempted to imagine that it was hundreds of years old. In fact, it was designed by a Vietnamese architect named Eric Vo Toan and opened to the public for the first time in 1971.

With two hours to spare, we walked through the old quarter of the city, or medina, with its maze of narrow streets and tightly packed shops. Throughout our walk, we were routinely approached by young men with drugs to sell. I don't know what level of schooling they had attained, but most of them could speak four or five languages quite fluently. Mark and I ducked into an eatery that seemed slightly less afflicted by the swarms of omnipresent flies. One of the half-dozen patrons present, a lanky chap with a pencil thin moustache, who, I presume, assumed we were Americans targeted us almost immediately.

He spoke English with surprising agility, but what shocked us most was his vernacular—1950s beatnik speak. "I'm a cool cat from way back," he announced with pride, several times over. It turned out that he'd spent a year or more in "Philly" back in 1952 and had absorbed both the club culture and lingo. He turned out to be very agreeable company, wanting nothing more from us than to share a few fond memories from his youth. We chatted pleasantly over a decent meal of steamed chicken in a tangy red sauce with a side of couscous, pretty much a staple for us while in North Africa.

Another thing that struck me about life in Rabat was the number of people, exclusively men as far as I could tell, with apparently little or nothing to occupy themselves. Men, just sitting or standing about, chatting with a friend or neighbor. A great many partially employed individuals occupied the street corners attempting to hawk a couple of trinkets at a time. What made the sight of this seemingly fruitless endeavor even more painful, were the countless thousands of nearly identical items for sale in the small shops scattered everywhere about. To this day, I can hardly fathom how so many eked out an existence in this manner.

The decision was made to press on, but as a consequence of failing to obtain the necessary visas in Morocco, the only other viable option for us was to make for Algiers and try our luck there. This meant a big-time alteration to our planned itinerary. Rather than heading southeast and crossing into Algeria near the oasis town of Figuig, we would undertake a sweeping detour northeast. Our next stop, heading east and inland, was now Meknès.

En route, we made a pit-stop at a roadside market where George purchased a live chicken for 35 dirhams (denoted as د.م., about 4 dollars US). Malcolm dispatched the poor creature moments before we got back on the road. A minute later, we could see clusters of feathers flying past the tailgate as we sped along, George plucking the bird and tossing handfuls of plumage out the window of the cab.

As we drove farther and farther into the countryside, which reminded me a great deal of La Mancha, I was surprised to see the occasional blond blue-eyed child walking together with other obviously Arab or Berber children. I found this especially curious given our rural surroundings. A few discreet inquiries led me to understand that recessive genes could serve as reminders that the French colonial empire once encompassed Morocco, Algeria, and Tunisia. Soldiers, far from home, were inclined to find comfort, if you can call it that, however they might—this apparent blending, the result of either irresponsible or unsavory behavior.

We had budgeted a modest camping fee for this part of Africa. George, with our unreserved support, thought to spend it where it could have the greatest impact, and so, late that afternoon, arbitrarily approached a hardscrabble farmer to enquire if he would permit us to camp on his land. By "hardscrabble," I don't mean to suggest that his lands were arid or sparse. Far from it. The surrounding fields appeared to be quite vast, fertile, and productive, which suggested to us that he was either very poorly compensated for his efforts or only indirectly associated with the adjoining farmland. Perhaps a tenant farmer. We never determined which language he spoke, whether Moorish (Ḥassāniyyah Arabic), Berber (Amazigh), or a blend of both. Communication was achieved through simple intonation and hand gestures. The fellow, by the name of Achmed Behchbe, in any case, appeared happy to oblige.

The ensuing evening was filled with wide-eyed curiosity on both sides. The Behchbe family home was an exceedingly humble affair built of mud brick and corrugated tin, a handful of farm animals scattered about. The Behchbes watched every facet of our setting up camp with unmitigated fascination. The kids were particularly taken with our air mattresses. They were not at all reticent to ask questions about the things they had no experience with. The tiny mostly ordinary things we took so much for granted were a wonderment to them. I caught Bernard's eye at one point. He looked at the children, then at me, and pointed at a star in the night sky. "J'habite la," he said (I live there), which summed up how alien our worlds seemed in comparison to one another.

I have no recollection of how it came to pass, but one of the children questioned how many of us could fit into one of our tents, and so we proceeded to entertain the bewildered Behchbes by piling into a single tent all at once. They must have thought we were all lunatics. The answer, as it happens, was seventeen.

For our part, we had no clear notion of their lives and equally peppered them with questions. Having invited them into our home, in a manner of speaking, the Behchbe family thought it fitting to reciprocate. In small groups, we were invited to step inside their house for a tour. It was a two-bedroom design, one room for the parents and another for their barefoot children, with a central living space. The windows had wooden shutters, no glass. The only other structure of any consideration was a small, dilapidated toolshed.

Although the house was fashioned from mud bricks, the interior reminded me of a Bedouin tent—no furniture to speak of, but blanketed with lavish carpets, many flecked with bright silver spangles, and all lovingly crafted by the lady of the house or, I presume, inherited. These carpets were clearly the basis of the family's wealth and Madame Behchbe was proud as can be to display one of her finest and largest designs for a group photo. George shared with the family the hen he plucked in the cab earlier that day. Jim delighted all with a session on his chanter.

Bidding farewell to the hospitable farmer and his family, we carried on to the ancient city of Meknès. This was our first full-fledged exposure to a traditional North African souk, or open marketplace (there would be countless "firsts" for us along the way). The souk was jammed with hundreds of people, stalls piled high with all manner of clothing, kitchen utensils, carpets, and shoes. Between the countless stalls, were fortune tellers, raconteurs, water vendors (something I'd only seen previously in old movies about the British Raj), Islamic preachers jostling with magicians for attention, not to mention impromptu gambling venues and boxing matches. It was all quite mesmerizing, even thrilling. Almost too much for the senses.

I soon discovered that Tangier was an anomaly. No one in Meknès took any particular notice of our presence or went out of their way to annoy us. We quickly learned, however, that prices were invariably inflated, especially for Europeans and Americans, and that bargaining down to something reasonable was simply the norm, part of the fun, so to speak. Mark quickly cottoned onto this, taking a perverse pleasure in dealing down a merchant as far as he would go, with no intention from the start of making a purchase, which told me a little about his character.

As I was on shopping duty, I went with Malcolm in search of a main course for dinner. We bought three live chickens for 62م.د. (about $8 US), which were dispatched in front of us and efficiently plucked using a make-shift hand-drill with a wire brush attachment. They made for an altogether delicious pumpkin stew later that evening. A city boy, this was the first time I'd ever seen an animal butchered before my eyes, and it made me realize just how much I took for granted. Alison had to turn away at the sight, and I could empathize.

Meknès was only a pit-stop en route to Fez. As we drove along, I pondered the contrast between Morocco and Canada, or at least the Province of Ontario. The land appeared just as fertile. Out of season and depending upon location, obtaining locally grown produce could be a challenge in Canada. On the other hand, Moroccan markets were crammed with a wide variety of locally raised and grown fruits, vegetables, and meat. Yet modern tractors were rarely visible on the Moroccan landscape, except on the wealthiest estates.

Most of the Moroccan farmers I could see active in the fields were tilling with horse or mule teams, sowing their fields by hand. In general, there seemed to be little emphasis on sanitation and hygiene in the countryside. Flush toilets were virtually non-existent. Consequently, I had serious fears about human waste contaminating irrigation canals and shared these concerns with my companions. Even the best-looking fruits and vegetables, to my mind, were suspect.

My fears were largely brushed aside, especially by the large contingent of vegetarians in our group. Fresh salads containing tomato and cucumber remained regular fare and there was precious little I could do about it, save going hungry. Although I had yet to develop "the trots," I was continually letting off gas, which I found both uncomfortable and unpleasant. I could not help feeling there was a connection.

We were able to locate a government sanctioned campsite just outside of Fez. The area was patrolled by the military, which, in retrospect, provided a false sense of security. That night someone snuck into our site and managed to make off with Hazel's shoes and a few minor items of camping gear. A lesson to us to henceforth keep any items of value in our tents.

That evening, December 5, 1983, we were dazzled by a rare sight—a comet in the clear night sky, very tiny to be sure, but unmistakable from its steady course and distinctive tail. I carried with me a handy piece of World War II German military surplus, a palm-sized 6x30 "dienstglas" monocular, manufactured by Zeiss, that we passed around. Not quite a telescope, but better than the naked eye.

With the advent of the internet, I learned many years later that it had to have been Comet 48P/Johnson, named for its discoverer, the South African astronomer, Ernest Leonard Johnson. The number 48 stood for the order in which that particular type of comet ("P" for Periodic) was discovered and that its perihelion (closest approach to the sun) was 2.30 A.U., or Astronomical Units, (A.U. being the average or mean distance between the Earth and the Sun). It was the only time in my life, to the point of writing this memoir, that I have seen a comet so clearly.

We took The Pig to Fez late the following morning and parked outside the city walls. I had thought Rabat an ancient city, but Fez felt like stepping back 2,000 years, a city frozen in time. George allowed us five hours to explore the medina, a virtual maze of crooked alleyways crammed with open-front shops selling brass and glass works, carpets, spices, prepared foods, hardware, and clothing, to mention but a sampling.

High above us, strung between the shop walls, hung sheets of dyed cloth to keep out the harsh desert sun. Where there were gaps, beams of sunlight specked with dust motes pierced the pervading shadow. People and donkeys ladened with goods passed shoulder to shoulder down the tightly packed walkways. There was no escaping the constant ebb and flow of shifting odors that seemed to alternate inexplicably between the divine aroma of sandalwood and the nauseating scent of rotten meat. Like Rabat, the flies were everywhere, a constant irritant. They somehow seemed a necessity.

Mark, me, and three of the women opted to hang together, leaderless. We stubbornly turned down a few immediate offers of a guide, thinking to avoid becoming "tourists," and all that that implied. It took no more than ten minutes to realize that we were utterly lost and might never find our way back to The Pig. Worse, beggars, who seemed to me reasonably healthy and well clothed, accosted us at every turn. It was then, at a point of near despair, that a boy in a well-worn polo shirt, perhaps no more than twelve years of age, approached us offering his services in no less than five languages. A happy-go-lucky kid with an endearing laugh, he introduced himself as "Charlie Brown" and promised us a quality tour, "no tricks." We took him up on his offer and were not disappointed. A quick judge of character he seemed to know just where to direct us, and moreover, safely.

We soon discovered that behind the bleak ashlar walls that faced the alleyways were opulent homes and flourishing businesses centered around sunny courtyards filled with fountains, palms, and dazzling tilework. The highlight of our visit was a tour of a women's carpet co-op, where every facet of production was carefully explained, as well as the local history and tradition. Two of our party committed to purchasing small custom-made carpets that were truly works of art. Arrangements were made to ship them to their homes when completed. I had to admit the prices asked were more than reasonable and I was sorely tempted to buy one, if only to support the co-op. I had fully intended to purchase something of quality during my trip through Africa, but this felt to me a bit too soon, so I passed on the opportunity. In retrospect, a poor decision.

For lunch, Charlie Brown guided us to a restaurant where we feasted (there was no other word for it) on couscous and chicken tajine as only the Moroccans can prepare. Two of our party were on shopping duty and had been tasked to bring back 10 kilos (22 pounds) of dry spaghetti. Not a typical local ingredient, and especially hard to find in that quantity. Even with Charlie's help, it took us ages to accomplish and when we finally did, we were so deep in the medina that we were quite late getting back to The Pig and duly scolded for it. We left Charlie Brown a well-deserved bonus for his services.

One thing I realized upon reflection, is that we gave little or no thought to his personal story. Why wasn't this kid in school on a Tuesday morning? Did he have a "handler" that would take his well-earned bonus away from him? Where was his family while he was out hustling the occasional tourist? What did he do when there were no tourists to be had? It's not like there were many like us visiting Fez.

From what I could discern, most of his classmates dropped out of school to work at about age eleven. I had no reason to disbelieve him. North Africa was teeming with children like Charlie Brown. It was remarkable, on the whole, how quickly one adapted to this new reality. In our ambling, I walked past a shoe shop completely staffed by young children. I have to say, they at least appeared happy and healthy.

Sharing our experience in the medina with the others, we learned that we were fortunate indeed to have stumbled on Charlie Brown. Several of our female companions were physically and verbally accosted, having opted to explore on their own. It was clear that unescorted females were considered fair game for abuse in this part of the world.

Back at the camp, George and Malcolm informed us that the propane tanks we'd been provided for cooking had European standard valves incompatible with any of the dispensing valves available locally. That there was no way, at this point, to do anything about it. We had used up the last of our propane and henceforth a campfire and iron grill would be the only way to cook our meals. The news hit us especially hard since firewood or charcoal would either be very expensive or difficult to obtain as we passed through the Sahara and Sahel. In addition to shopping and cooking duties, we now required a team just to collect firewood each day.

Around the campfire that evening, we met a young couple who were attempting to cross the Sahara on bicycle.

They certainly looked and sounded up to the task, but I've always wondered how they managed.

We woke the next morning to find that the soldiers guarding our camp had used up all our precious firewood to boil their tea and keep warm. A cold breakfast of bread and jam, or Marmite (our Brits cherished their limited private stock of Marmite. Definitely an acquired taste), and we were on our way again.

Breaking camp, Malcolm tossed some empty bottles in the trash. Several Moroccan women who were picking olives nearby saw this and rushed forward to claim our unwanted items. The soldiers who had been watching over our camp were disgusted and angry. They seized the bottles from the women and proceeded to castigate them, declaring that they should be ashamed to pick from the garbage of Europeans. The women, however, proved more defiant than cowed by this rebuke and some very tense words ensued.

As we neared the border with Algeria, the landscape became increasingly arid, no sand dunes, but endless lines of bleak rocky hills. There had evidently been some effort at re-foresting the region, but while this had achieved some success, poachers apparently cut the maturing trees down for firewood.

Our last stop in Morocco was Oujda, a walled city, like Fez, but with a more prominent foot in the twentieth century. George used the opportunity to connect with the Tracks office and bring them up to date on our progress, or lack thereof, while we scattered for a look-about and a bite to eat. I spent my last few Moroccan dirhams on a dish of frozen yogurt. Probably not the smartest thing to do, given the risk to my gut, but it looked so appetizing and refreshing. I couldn't resist.

Crossing the border into Algeria was a challenge, to say the least. First, we had to spend hours waiting for an exit check in an endless queue of vehicles stretched out along a desolate road. The Moroccan authorities, for reasons we couldn't quite comprehend, found something about our transit to be "out of order." It took George, let alone the rest of us, some time to realize they were holding out for a modest bribe without wanting to come right out and say so. The price turned out to be a bottle of Johnnie Walker.

By comparison, the Algerian border police struck us as professional. We endured a thorough individual examination by the Algerian authorities inside the border station. It took us about five hours all told to clear Algerian customs and immigration. We'd been warned about the possibility of a "disbursement requirement" back in Rabat, but the sheer size of the mandate took us all by surprise.

To enter the country, we were each required to exchange a major foreign currency for the equivalent of 1,000 Algerian dinars (or dananir, denoted as, ج.د), about $210 US. This was non-negotiable and non-refundable. On exiting Algeria we were required to produce proof that we'd spent the full 1,000 dinars we'd received. It was a huge financial blow to most of the members of our expedition.

To my mind, it wasn't a particularly unreasonable thing to ask of visitors to Algeria—a practical and progressive way to stimulate the struggling economy at a very local level. That said, I wasn't about to commit to spending so much in Algeria if I could somehow manage to evade the requirement. There was a convenient loophole. Full-time students were not subject to the requirement.

Months prior to this, while still attending university and toying with the idea of going off on my own trek, I thought to make use of student travel discounts. To that end, I requested and received a certified letter from the registrar's office stating that I was "a regularly registered full-time student" for the "1982-'83 session." When it came my turn to be interviewed, I presented this stale dated "evidence" of full-time enrollment and asked to be exempted from the mandatory disbursement.

The agent behind the desk scrutinized the letter carefully, pointing out to me that it was dated "April 21, 1983," more than seven months prior. "Mais regarde," I replied, in my best French. "It is valid through the end of 1983. There are 24 days left to the year." He looked at me with something akin to amusement and decided, for whatever reason, to not to pursue the matter. Lila, Kristine, and Andy were similarly able to produce valid student identification to satisfy the exemption. The remainder of our party were not so fortunate and complained bitterly of the imposition.

It was after 6 p.m. by the time we cleared the border and getting dark fast. George decided to pull off to the side of the road and make camp. Tired and cranky, we settled for a quick meal of porridge and called it a night. The roadside was nothing but barren rock and it took an Olympian effort to peg down our tents. It dipped below freezing that evening and I rued the day I decided not to keep the extra layer to my arctic sleeping bag. Recorded in my journal: Wed. Dec. 7, '83. Algerian border. "Bloody cold!!! Is Africa a myth?"

I awoke the next morning with a dreadful sore throat and an upset stomach. If I were back in Canada, I would have stayed curled up in bed, but this was not Canada, and we had a considerable distance to cover. The drive from the border to the outskirts of Oran was sheer torture, at least for me. It was like flying in an airplane with a full-blown head cold and nowhere or no one to turn to for relief, a pounding headache, blood-red eyes, and sticky green snot running relentlessly from of my battered nose. We had no access to tissues ("Kleenex"), so I went through one washcloth and then two full terrycloth towels using them as surrogate handkerchiefs, then stuffing these appallingly filthy articles into my shoulder bag for washing out and re-use at some future point.

Julie, ordinarily a compassionate and empathetic woman, had the unfortunate luck to seat herself directly opposite me, grimaced in revulsion. "God almighty, Neil," she felt compelled to say, while casting her eyes toward the floor in a vain effort to avoid watching me. "That's disgusting." There was no point in my denying it.

"I'm sorry, but what else can I do?" I replied, struggling for every breath. We stopped for a pee break somewhere along the road. There was an outcropping not too far off. Gasping for breath, I staggered alone to the other side of it and braced myself against it, arms outstretched, knees bent. I was drowning, drowning in the dense mucus that seemed to fill every crevasse of my nose, mouth, and chest. My brain suddenly seized on a word, Pneumonia. You idiot! You've got pneumonia!

Hearing the word was enough, apparently, to encourage a response. Do something quickly, Dukas, or die here and now! I took the two fingers of my right hand and shoved them down my throat, reflexively gagging up clumps of clotted green phlegm. I did this several times over, until I felt I could breathe with reasonable assurance through my mouth. My shirt was soaked in sweat and my heart pounding in my chest.

Exhausted, I held myself bent over and did my darndest to calm down. It seemed like an eternity, but all this must have occurred within just a few minutes. Not to say that this "fixed" anything, but I was amazed, quite frankly, by how quickly my mind seemed to regain some clarity with a renewed ability to breathe. I heard my name called out from the direction of The Pig and guessed my companions were ready to move on, anxious about my whereabouts. I returned to the vehicle, apologized for holding them up, and took my customary seat.

I slept the rest of the way to our next stop, El Malah, wrapped in my sleeping bag. With a bit of rest, I felt well enough to stretch my legs, thinking that it might do me some good so long as I took it easy enough. At some point in its history, El Malah must have been an exceedingly wealthy and powerful colonial hub. We walked endless blocks of palm-lined streets bordered by opulent homes, offices, and shops featuring sumptuous French and Italianate architecture to rival anything you might experience on the Côte d'Azur. Only, in this case, it was all crumbling to dust. The shops were mostly grotty and bare, the littered street-side gutters ripe with open sewage, the ornate facades grizzled, gray, and worn.

Intellectually, I understood that all this shattered opulence was that of an imposed and bitterly resented foreign culture. 'Good riddance to bad memories and interlopers,' I suppose. But I couldn't help feeling depressed by the decay and squalor. Hadn't some middle ground been possible? Something rather incredible had once flourished here and I was hard-pressed to see the current situation as an improvement. It was as if by letting the infrastructure run down Algeria had somehow cut off its nose to spite its face. I was reminded of what befell Britain after the Romans departed. But who was I to judge?

It was just a "feeling" on my part, removed from the experience of an eight-year war for independence and the painful process of de-colonization. My sense of despondency was made the worse by my lagging health and having somehow lost my precious crusher Fedora while walking about town.

That evening, we camped by the seaside at Mers El Kébir overlooking the Baie des Aiguades with a spectacular view down the coast to Oran. The city lights sparkled in the distance. I would have enjoyed sitting by the campfire and reveling in the quiet solitude, but all I could manage was to crawl to my tent and go to sleep.

The coastal highway from Oran to Algiers was magnificent beyond words, the vistas rivalling anything the French Riviera had to offer, perhaps more splendid for its natural undeveloped beauty. Despite the lingering effects of pneumonia, I was entranced by the landscape. We traveled past prosperous farming collectives, generally based on old French estates.

George took pity on me during one of our breaks, inviting me to ride the cab to help fend off the chill. I could see Malcolm struggling with the transmission, The Pig refusing to remain in second gear. Although drivable, there was little doubt this was going to become a major problem for us. That afternoon, we camped in part of the garden behind l'Hôtel du Port in Sidi Fredj, a resort town nestled on a peninsula jutting into the western Mediterranean. The hotel proper was a four-story, white-washed affair with a multitude of alternating rectangular and arched windows situated near the marina. We had the run of the place owing to the season. There were no boats tied up and most everything was closed. The military police came to our camp to introduce themselves. They proved to be both inquisitive and friendly. Their spoken French was faultless.

The next day was spent in bed dosed up on cold medications. Just twenty days into a five or six-month trek, I was reticent to start on antibiotics, fearing that I might need them to counteract something worse down the road. My companions were seriously concerned about my health and pampered me silly. Gail and Lynn brought me chocolate and a bottle of orange Fanta. Others covered for my camp duties. The campsite was a cut-above anything we'd yet encountered in North Africa. The hotel staff, moreover, didn't seem to mind that we used their facilities to wash up.

It was decided, to my relief (it having turned rainy and cold), that we would stay as long as necessary to wait for a change in the weather and allow Malcolm an opportunity to re-build the gear box. Although it was never spoken aloud, it was abundantly clear that if I did not improve by the time the group was ready to move on, they would have little choice but to leave me behind. Malcolm maybe took a little more time than he needed to work on the gear box. At least, I'd like to think so.

I was well enough following a day's rest to accompany everyone for the drive into Algiers. As cities go, I found it rather pleasing. Everywhere I went I encountered the most elegant French. The Women seemed to prefer Western style clothing over hijab and traditional abaya. An immense port, ships were lined up far out to sea waiting to get in. Broad boulevards were lined with smart-looking low-rise apartments albeit showing their age, all painted white and highlighted with Moorish architectural embellishments.

I paid a visit to the central post office to send a letter to Edi and on entering the main hall almost forgot what I'd come for. Designed by Franco-Algerian architect Jules Voinot and French architect Marius Toudoire and opened in 1910, this stunning edifice rivaled some of the great mosques for beauty. It took a real effort to pull my eyes away from the interior of this architectural marvel and refocus on the task at hand.

Unfortunately, the post office was far from typical. You didn't have to scratch too deeply beyond the surface to see the rough underpinnings of the city. The finest hotels looked tired and shabby. Worst of all, the public sanitation system had fallen into utter disrepair, the accessible toilets too horrific for description.

Algeria was an unabashedly socialist country. The cinemas featured mostly Soviet-made revolutionary adventure films. Socialist revolutionary artwork abounded. I expect free healthcare and education was a big upside to the social system, but nearly everything to do with the economy was run as a government co-operative and, I must say, not very efficiently. The shops were mostly bare. The markets had maybe six different vegetables to choose from. The prices were much higher than in Europe, except for bread which was subsidized and could be had for a song. A very simple meal at the Hôtel du Port ran about 60 dinars (about $12.50 US, at a time when a combination McDonald's Big Mac, fries, and a Coke went for about $2.60 US back home).

Here too, I was struck by the large number of people standing about with seemingly nothing to do, or laboring for hours over a drink at a café. And yet, I have to say they all seemed healthy enough and on average better educated than the people we encountered traveling across Morocco. Panhandlers, to my delight, were few and far between.

An interesting aside, I received a 10ج.د coin as pocket change at some point. The design was so attractive and exquisitely executed, that I thought to keep it as a souvenir. Later, I asked an Algerian to translate the lavish interwoven script on the obverse of the coin, thinking that it must surely say something poetic or of great significance. With a wry smile, he informed me that it translated as "Bank of Algeria."

Aside from experiencing the city and doing a bit of shopping, our main purpose for driving all the way to Algiers was to obtain the visas that we failed to obtain in Rabat. To our great relief, the French embassy in Algiers, deputized to issue visas for a handful of African countries, was very obliging and highly efficient. For just 13ج.ﺩ each (about $2.70 US), we were able to swiftly obtain visas for Niger (which I'd obtained on my own hook back in Canada), Togo, and the Central African Republic, plus an extension to the Upper Volta visa that we'd obtained in Paris through to the 10th of January, since we weren't likely, given our detour to Algiers, to meet the expiry.

Back at camp that evening, tempers flared as we hotly debated the route forward. No one argued with George's decision that Tamanrasset, deep in the heart of the Sahara, would be our next major destination, but what route to take to get there? Some voted to take the "scenic" and relatively time-consuming road via Djanet. I lobbied heavily for routing via Timgad, the consummate example of a Roman military colony (founded in the year 100 by the emperor, Trajan), astonishingly well preserved despite the ages. I imagined, quite rightly, that I'd never in my lifetime have another opportunity to visit this remarkable Roman city or any other quite like it.

Others revealed that they had little interest in North African/Sahel culture and wanted us to move as quickly and directly as possible south to what they apparently signed up for, "Afrique Noire," an archaic and scarcely veiled reference to "the Dark Continent."[4] Still others in our group, lobbied

---

[4] A term coined by journalist and explorer Henry Morton Stanley in 1878.

to take the fastest possible route to Nairobi, whichever that might be, and use the days saved as "independent time" away from the truck. Jim tossed in for added measure his disappointment that we didn't stock up on food in Morocco while we had the chance—that George, as the Tracks liaison, should have been aware that Algeria was suffering from a food shortage. George listened patiently to all this, unruffled by the verbal scuffling. "We're behind schedule," he stated without any elaboration. "We'll take the N1 due south to Tamanrasset," and that was an end to the matter. Hazel was fit to be tied.

I think, in retrospect, the heightened level of irritability and impatience was partly the result of spreading head colds and developing tummy problems, a consequence, I felt certain, of not being too particular about what everyone ate while touring the markets. We'd endured several days straight of cold, rainy, weather and yet another storm was brewing. Living out of tents as we were, to say that this was dampening our spirits was an understatement. We all needed a good dose of warmth and sunshine.

Some members of our group discovered a Turkish bathhouse in the city and came back to camp with glowing reports, remarking on its therapeutic value. I'd experienced a Japanese bath, but never a Turkish bath and was game to give it a try. The next day I went with Mark, Barry, and Jim into town by bus, which was a small adventure in its own way, and tried the "bath," which turned out to be a large room sectioned into individual shower stalls each fitted with a chair and a bucket. I had no complaints. The steamy hot water pouring over me, nourished both body and soul. Before heading back to camp, I purchased a can of sardines, some spreadable cheese, candles, and a relatively recent Time Magazine.

As we packed our belongings and prepared to bid Sidi Fredj adieu, l'Hôtel du Port suddenly came to life, preparing to host the country's Fifth National Congress. On our way out of the city, we stopped at the Mali embassy to pick up visas as pre-arranged, but they weren't ready, and we were forced to hang about until noon. Informed that they were finally available, we discovered the price had gone up to 150ج.د each, more than ten times the price we were charged for other countries' visas by the French embassy. There was nothing we could do but grin and bear it and carry on.

It wasn't long after departing Algiers that we encountered the foothills of the Atlas Mountains, and The Pig once again began to exhibit problems with either the transmission or fuel lines. Malcolm couldn't be certain which. No one was keen to return to Algiers, so the decision was made to chance it and press on through the night to Ghardaia (or Ghardaïa). It meant we would miss seeing the mountains except for brief glimpses through the vinyl windows embedded in the vehicle tarp.

We halted midway through the night at an all-night "mule stop" and treated ourselves to hot coffee and savory crepes. By this time, we'd entered the Great Western Erg, a vast arid plain fringing the Sahara. No more rain or cloud-filled skies. It was about this point that I took to wearing a Palestinian pattern shemagh and agal, a traditional middle eastern Arab headdress, to keep the sun off my pre-maturely balding pate, as I'd lost my cherished crusher Fedora some ways back. My parents had given the shemagh to me as a gift after a trip to Israel many years before. I'd tossed it in my bag before leaving for London just in case. My purpose was entirely practical, but I now found myself receiving frequent salutes in brotherhood with the Palestinian cause. I became accustomed to this, even saluting back, and continued wearing the headscarf, so long as it proved useful. It was indeed very effective at filtering the clouds of dust kicked up by The Pig and preventing the sun from frying the top of my head.

As we gathered to re-board the truck for the final leg to Ghardaia, a bright blue meteor shot across the velvet black sky, much to our delight. It was still dark by the time we reached the outskirts of the town. Malcolm parked The Pig on the side of a hill, and we slept in our seats.

After sunrise, we breakfasted and then drove into the city in search of a campsite. Finding nothing suitable, we camped, fortuitously, at the Oasis de Ghardaia, about 7 kilometers out of town. The oasis was a magnificent bowl-shaped valley filled with luxurious date palms, hemmed in on all sides by a ridge of broken limestone (the "Shebka"). There were numerous homes within the oasis, simple flat-roofed affairs fashioned from solid stone or heavy brick, each with a garden profuse with figs, dates, flowering pomegranates, orange, and lemon trees, that in combination, amazed and overawed the senses.

Waist-high walls fashioned from ochre-colored bricks edged the winding roadways. Clear water flowed from community taps. There were few cars to spoil the effect. Everywhere you turned there seemed to be a donkey or house cat eyeing you as you passed by under the progressively remorseless sun. I looked forward to hearing the hauntingly passionate calls to prayer (adhaan) sung by gifted muezzin from nearby minarets at prescribed times of the day. If we stopped for even a moment to admire a particular garden, the owner ("propriétaire") would step out to make a present of his dates or vegetables.

The Oasis de Ghardaia was an earthly paradise, but for one unsettling aspect. This was the M'zab region, after its namesake river that flows perhaps once in a dozen years, and home to the Mozabite people (ethnic Berbers, mostly Ibadi Muslims), a region settled a thousand years earlier by Hybadites, a persecuted sect of Islam. Mozabite men tended to wear a rounded brimless cap, and plain white shirt tucked into a traditional pair of saroual, a baggy trouser held tight at the ankles, distinctive for its extraordinarily low-hanging crotch. Married Mozabite women of the oasis wore a capacious white shroud in public, draping every part of their body from head to toe and allowing just a small diamond-shaped hole for one eye to peer through.

The women walked past us in uncomfortable silence, like ghostly apparitions. I found myself unaccountably drawn to that singular chink in their soft armor, looking to catch a glimpse of the human being concealed within. Behind the high walls of their secluded gardens Mozabite women lived their lives relatively unencumbered, or so I gathered.

I should mention that the women in our expedition were reluctant to modify their own attire to accommodate the puritanical sensibilities of the Mozabite. They tended to dress in a very summery fashion, freely displaying bare legs and arms. There was no law to force our folks to do otherwise and I guess they felt no duty to volunteer. Lila took to wearing a light shawl about her shoulders, and one or two of the others, a kind of make-shift sarong, but that was about the extent of it.

Malcolm needed to take The Pig into town for servicing and volunteered to take along anyone that wanted to join him but made it clear that we would need to find our own way back to camp. I tagged along with Mark and Lila. Ghardaia was an architectural jewel, perhaps an archetype for cubist painters like Picasso—a jumble of ochre-colored squares and rectangles arranged in circular terraces ascending the hillside, topped by a mosque and obelisk-shaped minaret pointed toward the sky like an accusing finger.

There are five such cities in the M'zab, and Ghardaia was the capital. Between the 15th and 18th centuries, salt, slaves, gold, ivory, and ostrich plumes flowed through these towns. The city was a labyrinth if ever there was one. For a city, everyone we encountered seemed unusually relaxed and friendly. There was a barely concealed and thriving black market. Lila sold an old jacket that she had no further use for in the souk for 250ج.د ($52 US). Mark didn't have anything he wanted to sell but enjoyed the exercise of literally offering the clothes off his back or a hypothetical bottle of Johnnie Walker just for the fun of seeing how much he could get for them. Not that the idea of selling a bottle of whiskey just for the experience didn't appeal to me. I happened to have one with me but was holding off for the right opportunity.

There didn't seem to be any bus or taxi to be had to get us back to camp, so we tried our hand at hitch-hiking for the first time. In North Africa, you don't "thumb a ride" as you do in the West. Pointing your thumb like that could be construed as offensive. No, what you did instead was wave an extended arm up and down with your palm horizontal and flat to the ground, much the way traffic cops in the West will do to flag you down for speeding. Mark struggled to get his head around the concept, but we did eventually succeed. To my amazement (who, after all, would pick up three "European" strangers on an isolated road?), we were rescued by a man in a large black sedan who apparently thought it was the hospitable thing to do.

We didn't learn until the very next morning that it was Mawlid (or Mawlūd), marking the birthday of the Prophet Muhammad. A number of celebratory parties were planned and some of the group were fortunate enough to receive invitations. Daoud Babaouamer, a civil engineer, invited four or five of us, including myself, to afternoon tea at his new summer home, still under construction. The house was framed in concrete, the inset walls fashioned from large sun-dried bricks. From Daoud, we learned that a great many of the homes in the oasis were summer retreats for professionals from Algiers or Ghardaia, when the summer sun could reach fifty degrees Celsius. Some owned two, three, or more homes, relocating as the seasons and temperature change.

Three young brothers invited us to join them for a Mawlid "fête" at the home of an accountant whose name I never quite caught. We feasted on a communal plate of couscous, danced, and made music by drumming on instruments improvised from empty water jugs and olive oil tins.

A hashish pipe was casually passed about. My determination not to experiment with such temptations made me even more of an outsider than I already was. I shrugged apologetically whenever my turn came around, and usually got a friendly 'no big deal' look in return. The party didn't break up until 3:30 in the morning. It goes without saying that Mozabite women were not present at this celebration, never participating in any form of entertainment that might involve strangers, including the simple act of stepping into a café.

The Mozabite men were a puzzle to me. Obviously, extremely well educated. They weren't the slightest bit reticent to socialize with the women from our expedition or to engage with them in conversation on more or less equal terms that could easily be construed as controversial. Never once did I hear them offer our women the slightest disrespect. That's more than I can say of our experience in other parts of North Africa. Yet, what the Mozabite women in turn thought of their men socializing so freely and uninhibitedly with European women, I will never know. Perhaps, afterwards, in the privacy of their own homes, the men shared the gist of the conversation with their wives. That, or they had it out.

We got back to camp so late, or should I say so early, that I opted to stay up and watch the sunrise with Lila from atop the rocky crest overlooking the oasis. The braying of donkeys greeting their owners and the morning call to prayers echoed across the landscape below us. We spent the better part of the day just lazing in the sun and soaking up the beauty of the oasis. I guess we'd made a positive impression, enough that Daoud and some of his friends sought us out again. Lila had done so well selling her old jacket that she went back into town and sold a cheap bottle of Spanish brandy for 300ج.د ($62 US).

All good things must come to an end. It was time for us to move on. Our next objective was In Salah (or Aïn Salah), about 675 kilometers due south, in the heart of the Algerian Sahara. It was not long before we got our first fleeting glimpse of what television and the movies portray as the

Sahara, undulating sand dunes and camels. Still, to my eye the landscape was mostly "Martian" in character, dry jagged valleys and alternating plateaus rimmed by bare hillsides of broken limestone.

We camped at El Goléa (since renamed El Menia) for the night in an isolated patch of desert on property that once belonged to the Catholic church. A handful of palms offered some respite from the sun. El Goléa, which I understood to mean 'impregnable castle,' was captured by the French in 1891. The high brown walls of the ancient "château," as the local inhabitants were wont to call the crumbling 10th century fortress, were plainly visible atop the treeless escarpment overlooking the oasis.

The abandoned fortress at El Goléa

Both the land and the culture had changed so dramatically and precipitously since departing Ghardaia that the group with unusual unanimity agreed to take some time to further explore the area. Although the population was predominantly Zenete (or Zanata) Berber, this was the first time we'd seen Africans, as distinct from Arabs or Berbers, in any significant numbers, and women, so abruptly after our time in Ghardaia, who thought nothing of walking about bare-armed and heads uncovered.

I walked with Lila to visit l'église Saint Joseph (Saint Joseph Church) and the grave of père (Father) de Foucauld. Charles Eugène vicomte de Foucauld, served with the French army in North Africa and participated in the suppression of a revolt in South Oran during the 1880s where he developed a fascination for the land and its people. He is often described as a sort of "French Lawrence of Arabia." Resigning from the army, he set about exploring the Moroccan desert in the company of a rabbi and later wrote a book about his experiences, titled Reconnaissance au Maroc, which earned him a degree of notoriety. Ordained in 1901, he returned to North Africa with the intention of establishing a monastic community with ecumenical overtones. Then in 1904 he moved to live amongst the Tuareg of the southern Sahara, learning their language and way of life, translating the Gospels into Tuareg and compiling a Tuareg-French dictionary. He eventually adopted the life of an ascetic, living alone high up in the Hoggar (Ahaggar) Mountains above Tamanrasset.

World War I provided an opening for rebellion against French rule in Algeria. Foucauld was killed in 1916, caught in a crossfire between French forces and Algerian insurgents. The twin-steepled church beside the old French graveyard where Foucauld lies at rest is an imposing sight, rising unexpectedly from the barren plain, surrounded by a copse of Royal Palms in defiance of the searing sun.

In exchange for a small donation to the church, we were gifted two exquisite "desert roses," naturally occurring rose-colored Saharan gypsum with "petals" formed from flattened sand crystals. There is something rather magical about these natural wonders given their desolate environment. We then made the climb to the striking ruins of the château. The climb was not very steep or demanding, but without a guide there wasn't much for us to take away from the experience. The sweeping vistas, however, were well worth the effort, and the fortress itself, a photographer's dream.

View of the Grand Erg Occidental at El Goléa

In the early afternoon, I walked with Mark to check out the endless sea of rolling sand dunes that began a half kilometer or so from our camp, past an area bordered by small semi-marshy salt ponds, the locals called Los lacs. This was the eastern tip of the Grand Erg Occidental "where Mother Nature showcases her ruthlessness"—a vast track of shifting dunes devoid of life, at least on the face of it, yet offering a kind of stark incomparable beauty. Walking the undulating dunes with nary a sign of civilization on the horizon was a surreal experience. Two young boys on mopeds, initially specs on the horizon, spotted us and sped over to check us out. We spent a few minutes entertaining one another with gestures and a few shared words of French before heading back.

As we skirted a small house near one of the salt ponds a woman emerged and came over to greet us, soon joined by her young children. I was surprised by how unconcerned she was about welcoming two complete strangers. More so, when she invited us into her home, a humble dwelling. We obliged, curious and delighted at any opportunity to engage with someone from the local community. She wore an abaya of simple design and a hijab placed indifferently over her hair, chatting away without a word of French and beaming proudly as she introduced her children to us one by one, all boys except the youngest.

I don't know where her husband was, but that did not seem to be an issue. We were directed to sit down and proceeded to stare at one another in awkward silence. Our host courageously attempted to break the ice, but neither Mark nor I had any clue as to what was being asked or said. Of course, the same was true in reverse. The children were no help, so we mumbled something about Canada and New Zealand, as if that somehow explained our presence. Eventually, she went over to a ceramic jar and fished out a handful of dates which she then displayed on a plate for our enjoyment. I gazed at these offered delicacies in horror, as they were positively crawling with small white maggots. "Mark?," I stammered, pleading for a way out. He hesitated just long enough to gauge the situation.

"You've got no choice," he replied. "Just look at her." Mark was right. It would be the height of insult. The woman seemed to be holding her breath while we dithered. Reaching over, he plucked a date from the plate and popped the whole thing in his mouth. Eyes narrowed, he chewed and swallowed, extracting the cleaned over pit between his thumb and index finger. "Very nice," he said, patting his tummy for good measure. "Your turn," he grinned, with a sadistic smile.

I resisted with all my will the urge to gag and followed suit. "Bon," I said, running my tongue around the inside of my mouth and over my teeth to ensure no unwanted visitors were left behind. "Très bon. Merci madame."

She prompted us to keep eating, but I tapped my wristwatch indicating we needed to move on and departed rather hurriedly. She seemed happy, in any case, that we'd paid her this visit. I never could quite get my head around why, or if she was expecting something from us in return. I honestly never got the sense that she had any expectation other than the pleasure of a chance meeting; a spur of the moment decision to seize upon something out of the ordinary. It was a rare privilege to enter someone's home at any point during my trek across Africa. I thank her for it, whatever her motivation.

We were treated that night to a fresh lamb dinner, courtesy of two French contractors working on a nearby hospital. As it happens, I was destined for yet one more adventure at El Goléa. A waxing gibbous moon was visible throughout the afternoon portending a clear star-filled night. As the sun began to set, Lila pointed to a hill in the distance and suggested that we might enjoy an unobstructed view of the night sky from the top, away from the intruding lights from our camp. The idea certainly appealed to me. I've always been a bit of a star gazer, so off we went.

We soon realized that distances in the desert can be deceiving. The hill was much farther away than we imagined, but still in a clear line of sight back to camp. We had already invested some effort to get there, and so, decided to press on. The hill, once we reached it, was much like every other promontory in the region, an accumulation of shattered limestone rising above the desert sands, coated with a reddish-yellow-brown layer of iron-manganese. You had to watch your footing on the loose shards, but the slope was gentle enough that we were able to make it to the top in less than ten or fifteen minutes.

It was already quite dark by the time we reached the summit, where we were surprised to discover that it wasn't so much a hill, after all, as a ridge, like the rim of a crater. "There'll be even less interfering light from down there," suggested Lila. The descent seemed to me no more difficult, and she had a point. So down we went.

I don't think I've ever experienced anything before or since to equal the sensation of standing on the floor of that geological bowl. There were no stars edging the upper rim, just an impervious ribbon of purple-black void, but beyond that ribbon of darkness, directly above our heads, spread the Milky Way in all its majesty. No planetarium I'd ever visited came remotely close to conveying the reality of a flawless night sky or the overwhelming sense of eternity.

The light cast from the firmament was so bright and clear that it illuminated the rocks directly beneath our feet like a spotlight, and yet the walls of the crater around us were shrouded in relative shadow. Lila reached out to hold my hand and we stood together in silence, our heads bent back, jaws agape, taking in the wonder and beauty of it all. The minutes ticked slowly by and Lila gave my arm a gentle tug. I looked down and could see in her eyes exactly what was going through her mind—an instinctive urge to preserve this extraordinary moment in time. We sealed it then, with a kiss, in the Sahara, under the Milky Way.

This was not, however, the beginning of some budding romance. I'd grown close to Lila, as one does a very good friend, but I felt no spark, as it were, at our embrace. I knew Lila well enough by this point to know that this was more of a "sharing," for want of any better expression. People have different standards. If she was thirsting for a more intimate relationship, she never let on, and I certainly didn't intend to deceive her with any false vibes. So, I don't think it would be cruel or unfair to admit that my feelings for Edi, if anything, were crystalized at that very instant. Given the choice, I knew whom I would have preferred, in all honesty, to have shared that special moment.

But the reality was that I was with Lila, then and there, and the combination of circumstances would never be repeated. We smiled at one another, continued to hold hands, and started back up the rim of the crater. When we reached the top, we fully expected to see the lights from our camp, but there was nothing, only the desert below. "We must have got turned around," said Lila, with a hint of apprehension. I nodded and we traveled back down the rim to the bottom and up the opposite side, but again, there was no sign of our camp. "It's not that late. They can't have all gone to bed."

"Let's try that direction," I suggested. So down the slope we went, once again. At the bottom I paused to look around. The thing about rocks, especially in the dark of night, is that they leave no trail. Not a hint. "It all looks the same," I admitted. "I can't tell which way we came." It didn't help that we couldn't see much farther than five feet in front of our noses.

"Up this way," said Lila. By that point, one way was as good as another to me. When we reached the top there were still no lights of any kind in any direction. I can safely say we were both very much aware at that point of having made a very serious mistake. When we left camp our plan seemed straight forward, not in the least bit complicated. But there we were without jackets, water, or even a flashlight between us. And the temperature was dropping, quickly. Moreover, we hadn't bothered to tell a soul where we were going. "We can't keep doing this. I think we should head that way."

I went along with her suggestion, having no better idea. Down we went, leaving the hill behind us and started out across the desert. Lila started to tremble from the cold, so I draped one arm around her shoulders where the uneven ground allowed for it. We walked for hours in this awkward fashion, up, over, and around countless obstacles. The moon seemed to keep moving on us, sometimes lighting our path, other times leaving us in darkness. We both knew without uttering the words that we might very well be walking deeper into the desert but kept plodding on. I was so tired and cold by this point that I was scarcely aware that we'd crested another rise. Near the bottom, something caught my ankle and I stumbled forward and landed on the ground with a thump. Lila let out a cry, "Are you all right?"

Looking back, I saw that it was thick rope, in fact, a guy wire to a large black tent. Surprised, I scrambled to my feet, but apparently wasn't half as startled as the occupant of the tent, a Bedouin, who burst forth, obviously frightened from his sleep. He shouted something incomprehensible into the dark before spotting the two of us. In his wildest dreams, I don't suppose he ever expected the likes of us, standing before him like silent apparitions.

He blinked uncomprehendingly for a moment, then launched at us in Arabic, plainly both angry and confused by our presence.

Lila had the sense to ask, "l'église?" (the church). It was inspired thinking. If he could direct us toward Saint Joseph's, we could easily navigate our way back to camp. He shook his head in disbelief but beckoned for us to follow. It was no more than ten minutes to the point where he stopped and pointed out the silhouette of the twin steeples. We realized immediately that we'd been walking in circles.

We thanked the fellow profusely for his assistance. He waved his hand dismissively and disappeared back into the night. It was perhaps another fifteen-minute walk from the church to the point where we could see our campfire. We arrived to find that no one had taken the slightest notice of our absence. I kissed Lila affectionately on the cheek and said goodnight. Mark commented upon my return that he wondered what had become of me.

The highway was in decent repair for about 200 kilometers south of El Goléa. After studying the map closely, I noticed something that totally intrigued me, the name "Fort Miribel" a relatively short distance off the main highway, but utterly remote from almost anything else in the world. I pleaded with George to allow for this small detour, and I guess I was persuasive, because he merely announced to the group that we were taking the Chebaba (or Shababa) detour and, once again, that was that.

The road to Fort Miribel was little more than a track over rocks and sand. Still, there was something rather exhilarating about exploring a road to nowhere. If you've read the novel Beau Geste by P.C. Wren or watched the 1939 movie with Gary Cooper, you'll have some inkling of what I'm talking about—a French Foreign Legion outpost in one of the most isolated and inhospitable regions on Earth.

As a boy growing up in Ontario, I often wondered what it must have been like for British soldiers sent to defend the Canadian wilderness during the 18th and 19th centuries, far from home, besieged by hordes of blackflies in the summer and exposed to sub-zero temperatures in the winter. This part of the Sahara was the polar opposite, parched, desolate, lifeless. From the little bit I've managed to glean about the fort, it was built in 1894 to shore up the conquest of El Goléa and to prepare for the annexation of regions farther to the west. It was occupied by troops up until the Algerian War of Independence, and in its final days used primarily as a base for mineral exploration.

Off the beaten track, Fort Miribel

I can only think the poor sods sent to defend the place must really have had few options in life to agree to live and fight in such unimaginably harsh conditions. The fort was surreal, like a Hollywood movie set, situated on the barren rock-strewn high ground overlooking every approach.

The wood and iron gates to the fort were long-since scavenged, the materials a precious commodity in the Sahara. There was a peculiar quality to being the only ones there to explore its abandoned quarters and workshops fitted with vertical embrasures for firing rifles.

We walked the ramparts and peered over the rounded battlements overlooking the endless desert, imagining what it must have been like for those trapped inside. Our footsteps echoed across the empty parade square. There was a well at one end. I dropped a stone down it and could not hear it hit bottom. Some distance outside the walls of the fort was a plinth and column which I suppose was once served as a monument to those who gave their lives defending the fort, but the names and dates had been erased and their place in history forgotten.

We made good time back on the main highway to In Salah with more and more breathtaking views of rolling sand dunes and contrasting black hills. The inhabitants of In Salah, it seemed to me, possessed a good deal more civic pride than I'd encountered elsewhere in Algeria. I was impressed by the combination of Islamic design and desert influenced architecture applied to brand new buildings, giving them a very "modern" feel, but respectful of local traditions. There was a pleasant coherency and sense of progress about the place.

We camped in a palm grove for the night, a pretty location, but swarming with mosquitoes. I was reminded of military exercises in northern Ontario. Beautiful places too, but teeming with merciless blood sucking flying insects. Nights in the desert, if I haven't made it clear enough, can be brutally cold. It's surprising just how quickly the rock radiates away the heat it has stored up during the day. I wished I'd the foresight to bring a folding cot along. My pathetically thin air mattress, although easily packed, provided no real insulation against the cold ground, even combined with a quality sleeping bag. I spent many an agonizing night in the Sahara, literally shaking from cold that pierced through to the bone until my body succumbed to exhaustion. It was a hard-earned lesson in preparedness.

After In Salah, the road south rapidly deteriorated into little more than a direction. There was a roughly maintained corrugated track to follow, but this was so covered in "pistes" (washboard-like rippling that caused the whole vehicle to shake violently) that traffic, which was now few and far between, had little choice but to forge a parallel path of its own off to either side. But even the improvised track came to a sudden and unexpected end about 45 kilometers north of Arak. The road was blocked, orange signs with black lettering pointing to an informal detour.

It was slow going and severely challenging terrain. We quit early, if only to give Malcolm a well-deserved rest. I couldn't say exactly where we were. Somewhere in the desert southwest of Arak, amid small patches of struggling scrub-grass and stubborn acacia trees. There was a small mountain or large hill, depending on your point of view, within walking distance of our camp. With plenty of time still left in the day, Mark and I decided that climbing the highest prominence might be an enjoyable thing to do. Never a fool twice, I thought this time to let others know and brought along plenty of water.

The hillside was rugged and steep. You could fairly describe the effort to surmount the enormous boulders that formed this peak as "just shy" of mountain climbing. It was a good hour and a half before we even came close to the summit. At that point, the route up became too narrow for us to continue side-by-side as a team. Rather than following behind me, Mark announced that he was going to skirt around to my right and look for his own path up. He'd meet me at the top. I forged on and made the summit about a half-hour or so later. The sky was bright blue, nearly cloudless, and the view over the desert and down to our camp stupendous. But Mark was nowhere to be seen. I thought, well, I'll just relax and enjoy the view until he shows up. He can't be much longer.

A half hour later there was still no sign of him. I began to worry that maybe he'd injured himself, so I skirted around the summit, peering over the edge in places and calling out his name. No response. You're overreacting, I thought. He's just delayed and will be here soon. Go back to where you were and wait for him. So, I waited another twenty minutes, half-hour, until the sun showed signs of going down. By then it was clear that Mark had turned back for some unfortunate reason, or worse, had taken a tumble and needed help. It was past time I headed back down and alerted the others.

I'd waited too long, however. The sun set like a stone over the horizon, and I was immediately plunged into darkness. I had a small flashlight, but there was no way for me to hold it and use both hands to navigate the mountain. I had little option but to inch my way down, probing each step with the tip of my boot for a foothold.

More times than I care to remember, I found myself clinging to a boulder with both hands, while reaching with one foot into the darkness only to find there was nothing below but empty air and oblivion. Obviously, I survived this ordeal, but it took hours for me to make my way down safely. I got back to camp to find Barry and Jim in the process of organizing a search party. Mark was not among them. Some of the group were a bit angry with me, and I don't blame them, but most, notably Lila, were clearly much relieved to see me. "Have you seen Mark?" I asked.

"He's been back for hours."

"What?"

"Yeah. I think he's in your tent."

I found him there, writing a letter as I recall. "What happened?" I demanded.

"Nothing 'happened,'" he replied. "Where were you?"

"Where was I? Waiting for you, asshole! I sat up there for a good hour and you never showed."

"I guess I got to the top before you. I waited and then came back down."

"How long did you wait?"

"Oh, I don't know, five, ten minutes."

"Five or ten minutes? You said you'd meet me at the top, dip shit. I looked all over for you. It never occurred to me you'd come back down on your own."

"Sorry. I thought you'd changed your mind."

"You're an F-ing jerk, Mark."

I'm not one to hold a grudge, generally, but it took me a VERY long time to cool down, which made life in our little two-person tent a bit tense. Lila and Ronnie, as it happens, were not getting along all that well. Ronnie moved out and Mark, at Lila's invitation, took advantage of the vacancy. It was the best arrangement for all concerned. I was happy for the privacy and the space.

We were up the next morning at 5:30 and on the road by 7:00. The detour around Arak brought us back to the main road below In Amguel (or Aïn Amguel) beside a line of hills worn smooth over the eons, known as the Adrar Tesno. In the shadow of the highest peak, Anou Tesno, a few kilometers west of the main route, is a marabout—the tomb of a Muslim holy man, Moulay Lahcène (alternatively, Lahsene or Sidi Hassen, to use the honorific), who is said to have died on a pilgrimage to Mecca sometime around 1835. You couldn't easily find it on a map.

The building was a simple single-story, white-washed affair painted with sky blue trim and topped with a handful of colorful banners, evidently a refuge or place for religious study from time to time. There was little else of any note about the building. The windows were shuttered, doors locked, a slot for alms giving, a few surrounding graves identifiable only by an assemblage of rough undressed stone. Yet it was a "Mecca" in its own very unique and special way.

You see, to cross the Sahara from north to south, or vice versa, was a difficult undertaking, fraught with hazards. Only the most prepared managed it successfully and those, at least at the time we visited, were relatively few. Transport trucks, shifting goods between Nigeria and the Maghreb, constituted the vast majority of trans-Saharan traffic. These were fantastic vehicles, mostly "souped up" Mercedes-Benz freightliners that would have been right at home in a Mad Max movie, moreover, jammed so full and so high with goods beyond the natural limit of the trailer's ribs, they seemed always about to burst.

The drivers of these awe-inspiring vehicles pushed them to their limits, kicking up dust for miles, engines screaming either in protest or delight. Hard to tell. As if this were not enough, the drivers had a ritual. The tomb of Sidi Lahcène was not along their direct route, but they habitually made it a point of pilgrimage. At the tomb, they gave alms, then either for luck or as a sign of gratitude, got in their rigs and hit the gas, circling the tomb three to seven times as fast as they possibly could. There were rarely more than one or two drivers doing this at any given time, but sometimes from opposite directions, circling the marabout at full throttle and then continuing on without stopping again. It was a thrill to behold. I walked with Andy up the closest promontory to catch a bird's-eye view of this unforgettable spectacle.

From In Amguel to Tamanrasset was a distance of just over 320 kilometers. It was all rough track covered in pistes until about 50 kilometers outside of Tamanrasset, where it was evident from all the heavy equipment that the government was preparing to push the paved road north to bridge the gap. Tamanrasset was an entrepôt for goods traveling north and south across the Sahara and a region dominated by a branch of Berber peoples—the Tuareg—themselves, a loose confederation of many clans scattered across a great swath of the Sahara and Sahel.

Tamanrasset was a fair-sized city, sheltered at the back of a deep reentrant of the Hoggar Mountains. Our campsite, this time, was along the banks of a dry riverbed, the Oued Tamanghasset, a short walk through a literal camel park to the Hôtel Tahat, a reasonably posh establishment.

Eleven of us willing to spend a few of our precious dinars, pooled our resources to hire a couple of guides to take us to Mount Assekrem, the hermitage of the unfortunate Charles Foucauld, the missionary killed in 1916 and buried at El Goléa. The guides were equipped with surprisingly new and well-maintained white GMC Suburbans with roof-racks. Our guide, Bella Achmed, was a strikingly handsome soft-spoken African who dressed in a white grand boubou (or gandora) and a pale green headscarf (tagelmust) worn like a turban with an accompanying veil, nearly concealing his face in the Tuareg fashion. His name, Bella, suggests he was descended from Tuareg slaves. Like many other men of the Sahara, he wore a pair of battered dress shoes without laces, easily slipped on and off.

Our guide, Bella Achmed, at Assekrem

Assekrem was a two-and-a-half-hour drive north of Tamanrasset across a rugged volcanic landscape of stark Martian-like beauty. The hermitage still attracted ascetics, mystics, and students of the desert who must surely have possessed iron constitutions, as there were no comforts or amenities of any kind. Herds of quasi-wild donkeys roamed the base of the mountain, not in the least hesitant about pressing visitors for treats.

Reaching the hermitage, at 2,700 meters, was a bit of a climb, but the weather was just shy of hot and rather pleasant. The Touring Club de France installed, at some point, a straight-angle panoramic map of the landscape, with the names of far-off peaks and their elevations. The view was so riveting that conversation at the summit was naturally subdued, as if we were in a house of worship.

When we got back to camp, Ronnie let it be known that she'd rented a room at the hotel, and if we were discreet about it, we might all make use of the shower. It was genuinely thoughtful of her. We'd just clocked a month on the road and, for the most part, only had access to sponge and basin facilities for our ablutions. We rarely had time or opportunity to properly wash our clothes. So, no surprise, we stank. It didn't help that getting to the hotel necessitated our passage through the immense camel park below the hotel. In short, we were not the sort of patrons the hotel welcomed having about.

Sneaking nineteen of us through the hotel lobby, even two at a time, was too much to hope for and it wasn't long before the hotel security got wise to us and put an end to it. Fortunately, I was one of the few to manage a quick wash and scrub.

The following day, Christmas Eve, most of our group spent the day lazing about Tamanrasset. I stopped at the central post office to check the poste restante and was excited to find a letter from Edi waiting for me, only to find that it was, for whatever reason, pretty dispassionate and thin on specifics. Not what I was hoping for. It put me in a funk.

Seven of us met up at a local restaurant for lunch where we sat together at an outdoor table adjoining the sidewalk. Everyone was in the holiday spirit, made all the better by generous plates of well-prepared roast chicken and chips (fries) and that helped to lighten my mood.

Christmas Day, we packed up early and hit the road, destination Assamakka, Niger, about 370 kilometers due south. I don't know if it was because it was Christmas or for some other reason, but we were just about the only vehicle on the road. Twenty-five kilometers or so out of Tamanrasset, just where the foothills of the Hoggar Range peter out, the paved road slipped beneath the desert, and was gone. Ahead, lay a barren expanse of shifting sand dunes and sunbaked earth as far as the eye could see.

We all piled out of The Pig to scan the horizon, one hand hovering above our brow to fend off the sun's reflected glare. I was unsure where my feelings lay, somewhere between awe and wariness. It was not the desert that gave me or my companions pause so much as the sight of ruined and half-buried vehicles scattered in all directions. The iron bones of those who dared the Sahara and did not make it.

It became necessary to keep the tarp completely buttoned down to keep the dust out, making it gloomy and stifling hot in the back. Adding an increasingly bumpy ride to the miserable mix was all that was needed to bring on motion sickness. I fought to resist it, but in the end had to tap on the glass with a plea for Malcolm to stop and let me take a breather.

Mounting back up, he surprised me with an invitation to drive for a time. I'd plenty of experience driving an army truck before, which George and Malcolm were aware of, so the size of the vehicle was not an issue, nor was the amount of traffic on the road (there was none, and no "road" besides), but a left-hand stick was something entirely new and unnatural to me. I can't say that I ever quite got the knack of it, but it was loads of fun and I soon forgot my queasiness. Once the others saw that I'd been granted this privilege, several demanded equal opportunity. It was a pleasant diversion for all of us and helped to overcome the tedium of sitting helplessly in the back of the truck for endless hours.

We quit the road early, to prepare a special Christmas dinner with extra helpings of couscous and raisins. Someone, I'm not sure who, came prepared with party hats for all. Not exactly traditional, but festive. George and Malcolm produced a Christmas pudding from their secret larder, which was a great treat, washed down, of course, with Christmas carols and a tot of whisky.

Jim and Julie thought to finish the evening with a romantic walk under the stars. Lila, always looking to capitalize on especially memorable moments, asked if she could join them on their promenade through the desert, and prompted me rather forcefully to keep her company. Frankly, I was happy to oblige. Of all my fellow travelers, Lila, I think, was the only one who cared to share thoughts and impressions about our experiences each day. In fact, I'd taken to making quick notes and sketches, often inspired by her comments, in my Lonely Planet guidebook.[5]

The Sahara—a wrecked sedan in the distance

We were some distance from camp when Jim and Julie begged off and went their own way. Lila and I continued on, holding hands and deep in conversation, paying more attention to the stars than to where we were headed. Eventually, the light came on. Lost! "We've done it again!" exclaimed Lila, in dismay. "You'd think we'd know better." There was absolutely nothing in the way of a landmark to suggest or remind us of which way we had come. The danger, of course, was that we would now head deeper into the desert.

"Ach," was all I could think of saying. "Let's just turn around and hope we're headed in the right direction." It was

---

[5] Africa on the Cheap written by Geoff Crowther.

really our only option. That familiar sinking feeling returned to ruin an otherwise wonderful evening. It was sheer dumb luck that after more than an hour of wandering the desert we stumbled on Jim's unmistakable footprints in the sand and were able to retrace his steps back to camp. It felt as if a greater power had been watching over us. After having done something so incredibly stupid once before, we hardly deserved to get away with it a second time.

The Algerian border post with Niger was at In Guezzam (or Aïn Guezzam). The closer we got, the more sand we encountered. It was like traversing a vast tract of cream of wheat. Time and time again, all nineteen of us had to get out and push. As the dunes worsened, so did the number of visible wrecks and abandoned vehicles, each with its own unimaginable tale of human suffering. The thing that truly amazed me, were the ridiculous number of wrecked sedans. I had to shake my head. What kind of person would attempt this crossing in a family car?

In Guezzam was as desolate and inhospitable place as one could ever imagine, little more than a tin-covered shack, a couple of gas pumps and a vehicle compound surrounded by barbed wire shimmering on the parched horizon. The young soldiers sent to garrison this God forsaken place could only have been sent there as some form of punishment. Yet the challenges they faced on a daily basis were formidable, including traffic in goods and visitors of nearly every possible description. Where regulations were not entirely clear, the border agents made up the rules for themselves and punished violators with a chilling degree of imagination. Their way, I suppose, of fending off the heat and tedium, or a kind of perverse quid pro quo for having been sent to this hell hole in the first place.

There is a special kind of camaraderie that exists among people crossing the Sahara, but this cordiality, frankly speaking, only goes so far. There were two young dejected and frustrated Germans with a camper van being held in limbo at In Guezzam. The customs officer would not accept their generic student cards, stating that such things could easily be forged, which was true. He insisted upon a certified letter such as I had from Queen's (phew!) or an unexpired student card issued by a genuine university. In the absence thereof, the Germans, as we'd been forewarned, had to prove they'd spent 1,000 dinars in Algeria to be allowed to exit the country.

Unhappily for them, they'd only expended 250ج.د. They were free to proceed only if they gave up the outstanding 750, but in doing so would be short money to buy the diesel fuel they needed to go either forward or back, a kind of Catch 22.

The two young men were disgruntled, but philosophical, pointing out for us an isolated vehicle a hundred or so meters beyond, frying in the desert sun. "It could always be worse," they intoned. "There's a fellow out there. He tried to skirt the border post in the night and either broke down or hit something he didn't expect. He's been out there all alone for days. The border guards say he's in a military zone and won't let him come in or anyone to go out there. His goose is as good as cooked."

This was the first time I'd any real sense of the potential dangers which could befall a traveler in Africa. The night before I was to leave, my closest comrades from the Toronto Militia Garrison treated me to a meal at a downtown eatery. Wine and beer flowed freely. One or two of my fellow officers had done a bit of homework and proceeded to interrogate me. Did I know about the growing drought in West Africa and fears of widespread famine? What about the Marxist coup in Upper Volta and South Africa's war against the ANC? Was I concerned about recent political violence in Nigeria? The conflict between Chad and Libya? The civil war in Sudan following the imposition of sharia law? And so forth.

I assured them that I was aware of all these doings, well, most of them, but believed, or at least hoped, that there was little risk stemming from any of this to a passing "tourist."

Besides, I thought to myself, there was certainly more to Africa than these events plucked at random from the headlines to elicit my reaction. If it weren't so, why would Tracks even contemplate a trans-Africa overland expedition? No, I asserted, I was far more concerned about the mundane perils of diarrhea and malaria.

A hardy-looking Welsh woman named Sara Hughes, with cropped red hair, bleach white skin, and amber eyes, three years my senior, had managed somehow to hitch rides all the way to In Guezzam from Morocco and was looking for someone with whom she could continue on. Sara confided that she'd spent a night in jail at In Salah for some offense or other and how the border guards at In Guezzam considered her a "Christmas present," whatever that implied, and was only spared that particular humiliation by the two stranded Germans who threatened to report the guards to their superiors. According to Sara they were now "behaving themselves." I admired Sara's gumption but couldn't help wondering if the risk to a woman traveling alone in this part of the world was worth the reward.

Since we were all paying customers, my Tracks companions were not inclined to take on a hitchhiker, no matter his or her predicament. George was adamant that it was also against company policy. I argued that we ought to make an exception in her case, if only on humanitarian grounds, but the majority just wanted to get over the border quickly. So much for Sara and the two unlucky Germans. They would have to manage for themselves. We, on the other hand, having adhered to the regulations and carrying supporting documentation, were processed quickly once we reached the front of the queue and carried on, never looking back.

The scuttlebutt at In Guezzam was that the corresponding border post at Assamakka in Niger was even less predictable. It was a short 20-kilometer drive to Assamakka, indeed a sort of mirror image of In Guezzam, but with more goats and camels. We couldn't help but notice too, that the border guards were ethnic Africans, rather than Arabs. The fellow that inspected my passport was unable to pronounce "Neil," the "eil" combination apparently just too far removed from his experience to get his tongue around. He spotted, however, that my middle name is "Bernard" and therefore addressed me as such, but in the French fashion with the last letter silent (it being a consonant). From that point forward, I was "Bernard" rather than "Neil" in the countries where French was the lingua franca.

The post at Assamakka at first seemed focused on checking documents and inspecting our baggage for illicit items. Then the shoe dropped. As a group, we were required to pay an "entry fee" of 3,000 French francs (about $365 US). George, moreover, had to purchase a carnet (temporary import permit) for The Pig for about $21 US. We were then informed that we were required to take the road to Agadez for a second customs check at Arlit, some 200 kilometers south-east. None of us were keen on that, not just because it was a detour from our intended route due south, but because we had no idea what new entry fees might materialize at Arlit.

The customs agents at Assamakka had us remove and open all our stores and baggage for a detailed examination. It took hours to accomplish, but they were, I have to say, professional in their dealings with us. Four French adventurers at the border were not quite so fortunate.

Like us, they were completely caught off guard by the entry and carnet fees, naively assuming their bought and paid for Niger visas would be sufficient. Looking back on it, the 13 dinars the group paid for visas at the French embassy in Algiers (myself excepted) was, indeed, too good to be true. While we were able to muster the financial resources to move on, these poor wretches, having exited Algeria, now had no valid visa to re-enter it or even the foreign currency necessary to purchase the mandatory 1,000 dinars even if they'd wanted to. There was no possible way for us to cover their fees, even if we'd felt inclined. We did, however, take sufficient pity on them to leave the four French nationals with two-days' worth of food. This really was a desolate and lonely spot. I couldn't imagine a worse place to be stranded.

Departing, George prodded Malcolm to veer off and take the road south from Assamakka, hoping to sidestep customs at Arlit, but the border police were not so easily hoodwinked, dispatching a vehicle to intercept and turn us back. George feigned ignorance and they took ample care to ensure that we set off down the "correct road." Frankly, I was surprised by how well the Nigerien police took our little attempt at evasion.

While all this was going on, our eyes were drawn to a passing caravan, at least two dozen camels being shepherded along by a group of Tuareg on foot. The scene resembled something you might see in a painting by a 19th century French master. As we watched this majestic and impressive procession, one of the more independently minded camels at the very back of the column decided it had enough of the whole procession, turned, and made a break for it in the opposite direction.

Those of us aboard The Pig, watching from the sidelines, cried out in astonishment and alarm, but well out of earshot of the Tuareg. Eventually, the beast's absence was noticed. There was a fair distance between it and the rest of the caravan by this point. A member of the column was dispatched to fetch it, running with arms flapping above his head, and, one supposes, uttering a string of expletives. Unfortunately, the Nigerien border police were still shadowing and urging us along, so we were unable to watch this delightful drama play out to the end.

Niger was a whole new world for us. The frontier was flat as a pancake, nothing but sand as far as the eye could see, not even a hint of the hardened patches of gravelly soil and broken rock that interrupt the dunes on the Algerian side of the border. A light wind was enough to obscure the tracks of any vehicle that may have preceded us. Vehicular traffic along this route dropped to a trickle.

Without a road or track to follow the only way for anyone to navigate this part of the Sahara was to follow a line of widely dispersed oil drums. To accomplish this, you first had to locate one and pull up beside it. One of our company would then climb atop the roof of the cab and using a pair of binoculars find the next drum. Thus armed, we would drive until we hit the barrel, figuratively speaking, repeating the process over and over, often needing to get out and push whenever The Pig bogged down in the sand.

Taking a break at one point, someone spied a couple of dots on the horizon. Through the shimmering heat, we could see that someone or something was headed our way. Was it a "mirage"? Slowly, the object began to take shape. Out of the desert rode two Tuareg, a man and a young boy, on camels heading who knows where. They dismounted upon reaching us and led their camels, one a black and white paint, the other a bay, to settle majestically on the sand behind them with legs tucked cat-like beneath their great frames.

They squatted on the ground before us and rested a while, using the opportunity to enjoy a bite of plain bread and a drink of water. The boy did not wear a head covering despite the sweltering sun, a great shock of roughly shorn hair swept back from his face. They spoke to us in quiet composed tones, and although we plainly did not understand, it did not seem to trouble them in the least. Having conducted the customary proprieties, they proceeded on their way.

A semi-nomadic people of Berber descent, the Tuareg were severely affected by a drought in the Sahel during the 1970s and thousands took refuge in cities, notably Agadez. I believe they were contending with yet another drought throughout our time in the Sahara and Sahel. Although not a hard and fast rule (it varies according to clan), Tuareg men are often distinguished by gandora, a kaftan-like garment, and tagelmust (combination veil and turban) dyed a rich indigo blue. The blue dye has a habit of rubbing off and staining their skin. Our visitors, in this case, were no exception.

Tuareg men commonly wear amulets around their necks and decorative pouches made of blackened leather and brass. You will often see a Tuareg male with a rifle over one shoulder or a sword that closely resembles a Roman gladius at his hip. Interestingly, Tuareg women, as far as I could tell, were not overly concerned with headscarves, donning them according to personal preference, or even doing without.

We pressed on and eventually made it to the secondary customs post on the outskirts of Arlit where the agents did indeed extract an additional sum from George—£100 for "insurance" (or about $145 US), thankfully sparing the rest of us. We had nothing to complain about, looking back, not in the scheme of things.

Arlit was a bustling, dusty, and ramshackle sort of city, with a 'Wild West' feel to it, owing largely to the mostly negative influences of the nearby uranium mine. I was happy to leave the place behind, all the more so because of the beautifully paved highway that had been built for the ore trucks all the way from Arlit to Agadez, over 200 kilometers distant. Except for the occasional mining truck, we seemed to have the road all to ourselves. On the downside, we were subjected to police checks coming in and out of every major town we passed through, and our passports stamped by the local authorities.

With all this stamping of passports, I was going to run out of available pages before the end, as no authority would place a stamp on top of an existing stamp. I decided to call at the next Canadian embassy along our route to see if they could add a few extra pages. The smallest oversight can trip you up in such circumstances. Our passenger manifest prepared by Tracks in London, for example, was just that, a "passenger" manifest, leaving off George and Malcolm (technically our "drivers"). The police, however, invariably expected a comprehensive list of everyone aboard the vehicle and sorting out this technical oversight each time we were stopped resulted in confusion and delays.

Agadez was a well-ordered city of sparsely treed adobe compounds and streets of matching hue paved with tightly compacted earth. You could easily encounter a camel parked next to an expensive black Mercedes. Tuareg dominated the city, particularly the Kel Aïr. It's a generalization, of course, but I found them a hard people, the opposite of hospitable and not the least bit curious about visitors, even less so, upon discovering that English was my first language. Not that I had cause to judge them, but it was, nevertheless, a bit jarring after the especially warm reception we received throughout Algeria.

To take photographs, it was necessary to obtain a "license" from the relevant authorities, which set me back 500 "CFA" francs (CFAF), or about $1.20 US.[6] A trip to the bank to cash a travelers check was necessary. I'd need a quantity of CFA francs to get by in Niger. The food kitty was also getting low, but Jim was right on top of it, twisting arms and threatening to break legs, if need be, to top it up.

I intended from the start to purchase a few things that sort of exemplified art in Africa, at least for my taste and interests. There were two objects in Agadez that especially caught my eye. I resolved to purchase some version of them. One, was an Agadez Cross. The other was a Tuareg short sword.

The Agadez Cross is one of over twenty beautiful "cross" designs (for want of a better description) created using lost-wax casting and worn as distinctive pendants by the Tuareg to indicate their clan or regional affiliation. Each design is different, but always incorporates four "arms," one of which is topped by a loop so that it can be worn on a chain or

---

[6] CFA stands for Communauté Financière Africaine,—two separate monetary zones formed by several West African and Central African nations. At the time, the CFA franc was heavily regulated by the French treasury.

string. These were sold in shops all over Agadez, so I focused my effort on the sword.

One street of shops appeared to specialize in them, so I walked up and down poking my head into each of them searching for one sword that seemed to speak to me, and, moreover, a shop owner inclined to treat me with some degree of civility. I eventually found one to my liking (a sword that is)—bronze pommel and cross-guard, with an elaborately embossed black leather scabbard—and informed the owner that I was "sérieuse," which elicited an appreciative smile.

The negotiations began at $100 "américaine." It took about ten minutes to bargain him down to $40, but I got him to throw in an Agadez Cross. He was very satisfied with the deal, calling it a "prix d'honneur" (in this context, a fair price). Like the ancient Roman gladius it resembled, the sword was only about 60 centimeters in length, so it fit nicely in my bag. Nevertheless, taking it across multiple borders, I felt, might be problematic. I'd have to give that some thought.

My successful purchase put me in a good mood. Moreover, it was warm each night and I felt, for the first time in a very long while, that I'd at last shaken off the cold that had dogged me all the way from the Bois de Boulogne. I celebrated with an orange Fanta. Mark teamed up with me to have our combined laundry cleaned.

Heartened by my experience that morning, I went window shopping with him while waiting for our laundry. We were peppered all along by adults and children alike, "Ça va, comarade? Cadeau?" (How's it going, comrade? A present? i.e., gift for me) Or even more forcefully, "Donnez-moi un BIC." (That is, Give me a BIC [pen]). You do your best to tune out this sort of thing under the circumstances, because it seems to never let off.

The silversmiths of Agadez were extremely skilled, producing some exquisite filigree work, often in the shape of animals. It is my understanding that they were blacksmiths in former days, employed at making objects like swords, spears, muskets, and the inner frames for camel saddles. This was a highly respected trade, passed down father to son.

The prices for their filigree artworks were, understandably, way out of my league, but they were evidently manufactured locally, and I was curious about the process. I asked a shop owner about this, and he said his son would be pleased to show us how it was done. I made it clear that I was not looking to buy anything. I just wanted to see how these objects were made. "Pas de problème, camarade," 'no problem, comrade,' he replied, gesturing for us to follow his son, so Mark and I eagerly went along.

We followed the fellow down several back streets to a gated compound where a small column of smoke rose from behind the wall. Inside the compound were three men, squatting in an open semicircle around a small but efficient clay furnace. Another man was busy hammering out silver on an anvil.

I was blown away to see that next to the furnace was a basket containing a sizable cache of one of the most exquisite coins ever produced, silver Maria Theresa thalers each dated 1780. Of course, these were reproductions—what are called "trade dollars," respected for their uniform standard and quality and consequently restruck, bought, and traded around the globe as a kind of universal currency. Nevertheless, it was a surprise to find them in use here, apparently the main source of silver for those fine filigree creations.

Excited by this discovery, I was anxious and ready to learn about the rest of the manufacturing process, when the shop owner's son appeared with a basket of finished filigree animals, demanding to know which one I was going to buy. "No!" I blurted. "I'm not interested. I told you." He responded by thrusting one particularly beautiful and expensive piece in my hand and quoting a price. "No. I'm not interested," I repeated, standing up and tossing the precious filigree back into his basket.

"Ah, les anglais!" he sighed, with loud, melodramatic emphasis. His companions murmured in agreement.

"I'm not English. I'm Canadian!" I hollered in anger and made to leave. Mark was all for that. By the time we reached the gate a considerable crowd had gathered. Apparently, word had gone round that a couple of "Englishmen" had arrived and stirred up expectations. Their disappointment on learning the truth was palpable, and it was abundantly clear that we'd made a serious mistake coming to see the silver works. In the street outside the gate the crowd swiftly transformed into an angry mob. We booted it and they gave chase close on our heels until we were well out of the neighborhood.

I was more than happy to put some distance between myself and Agadez, notwithstanding my purchases. The road to the capital, Niamey, was in good repair and the landscape recasting itself in new and interesting ways. The desert was receding, allowing for many more forms of life to thrive on the vast open spaces. From the truck, we could see small herds of healthy looking "Red Fulani," longhorn cattle. "Longhorn" was no exaggeration. These beasts could give a Texas longhorn an inferiority complex. Sheep were plentiful too. A breed known as "Uda" they had long legs and a face like a goat, a kind of half-goat, half-sheep. We called them "geeps" to be on the safe side.

A wild desert melon that closely resembles a plump round watermelon grew in abundance beside the roads we traveled, and just to look at them made your mouth water on an oppressively hot day. But it was the ultimate tease. Known locally as "egusi," its scientific name is Citrullus colocynthis. I gather the seeds can be made into a useful flour, with a good deal of preparation. Though the fruit may possess some medicinal value as well, the local fauna knew better than to even nibble on the curséd things.

As we got closer to Niamey, we could see vast fields of millet, which I was only familiar with as a staple food for the colorful parakeets ("budgies") we kept as pets when I was a child. Here, it was ground into flour and used as an iron-rich staple to feed millions of human beings. In the fields we could see raised huts everywhere for keeping millet dry and away from nuisance critters. Huge clay pots outside homes were used for storing rice. There were bananas on the store shelves too, and peanuts. Throughout the Sahel we dined primarily on rice, millet, cracked corn, and fish, when available.

Permit me to interject here with a story about peanuts (scientific name, Arachis hypogaea) and the next to stupidest thing I've ever done—Friday, December 30, 1983, the day we pulled into a roadside shop for a 10-minute break. I looked around, decided against any of the dusty, slightly rusty tins of dry goods on the shelves, or anything wrapped in brittle faded parchment, until my eyes settled on something "local" that might just do for a traveling snack.

On a tray by the till were golf ball sized orbs that clearly smelled of peanuts. With a little creative sign language, I was able to determine from the nice lady behind the counter that these rock-hard spheres were intended to be melted down and used as a base for a stew. Edible, I thought to myself, and, moreover, not an uncooked veggie. Therefore, safe, I rationalized. I could suck on one of these puppies to pass the time until we reached Niamey, like the "Jawbreaker" candies I enjoyed as a kid. "I'll take two."

Back on The Pig, I sucked contentedly on one of these great concentrated peanut balls, complimenting myself on my culinary ingenuity, while counting geeps and longhorns to pass the time. We parked that evening near Tahoua, just about halfway to Niamey from Agadez, but don't ask me what the camp was like. I was far too busy spewing vomit and diarrhea from every orifice.

In a nutshell, I'd sucked my way through a giant ball of undiluted botulism. Ronnie drew from her medical kit a dose of sodium bicarbonate, mixing it with water to draw out the poison. As if this weren't torture enough, she followed that with a course of Pepto Bismol and some kind of muscle relaxant. I spent the rest of the night and well into the next morning bent over in a farmer's field with my guts turned inside out. It was a day, and night, I won't easily forget. It would be at least ten years before I could even come close to a peanut in any form, let alone smell one without gagging.

The thing about traveling with a group in an isolated part of Africa is that one has very little choice but to "buck up" and carry on. We were on the road again by 7 in the morning. I wedged myself into my seat on The Pig, curled up, and slept, too weak to do anything else. Inexplicably, the police all but waved us through the various checkpoints as we neared Niamey, reaching the outskirts of the capital just about the same time that news arrived that a coup d'état had taken place in Nigeria! Of course, it was an awful turn of events for the people of Nigeria with potentially horrific consequences. Selfishly, all we could think of was how this might upset our travel plans.

We made camp for the night, warned from the outset to beware of thieves armed with knives operating in the area. Everyone we encountered seemed quite friendly and easygoing, but that could possibly have been attributable to the fact that it was New Year's Eve.

Alcohol was difficult to come by in North Africa, but Niamey, for some reason, was exceptionally well-stocked. A quick supply run into the city and all was ready for an evening of festivities. Alas, it was too much too soon for me. On Ronnie's orders, it was bread and water and bed rest. I crashed listening to the sound of revelry outside my tent, but slept like a baby, due, in part, to a change for the better in the temperature. It was the first evening since landing in Africa warm enough for me to put aside my insulated sleeping bag. I could manage, henceforth, with just a folded-over fleece sheet tucked inside a thin water-resistant bivvy (bivouac) bag.

The combination of warm weather and improved roads enabled us to roll up the tarp on either side of The Pig and enjoy the vistas unencumbered. Though there seemed to be no holding back the Sahara in the long-term, the countryside appeared much greener by degree as we got closer to the Niger River.

This part of the Sahel differed from the Maghreb in several significant ways: there were sizable herds of cattle on the grasslands, traditional homes were circular and fashioned from mud or rough clay with pointed thatched roofs, and the men tended to dress in bits of well-worn Western clothing while women donned handsome garments decorated with colorful prints.

A far cry from Ghardaia where the women were all but hidden from sight, in Niger it was not unusual to see a woman walking topless, something we couldn't help but notice the first time we encountered it. Habitually carrying heavy loads balanced atop their heads required exquisite posture. Between their proud outfits and their exceptional carriage, there was a certain dignity and presence about the adult women of Niger that seemed to me lacking, in general, amongst the men.

One thing I found especially off-putting was the widespread, and, moreover, relentless scale of begging conducted by young children and adolescents. We were endlessly badgered with "Cadeau! Cadeau!" while on or off the truck. I didn't mind it quite so much if the youngsters we encountered offered something, even the smallest trifle, in exchange, but that was rare indeed.

At one village we briefly stopped at, I gave out candies to a group of demanding children that were hovering about The Pig and they just about tore my arm off. There was nothing about their appearance to indicate desperation. I certainly would never have doled out candies to hungry children. We were inclined to be generous, but the often-frenzied responses were enough to put us off giving out handouts. Once the adults joined in, the lesson was well and truly learned.

We made the outskirts of Niamey in good time and made camp at a location used by other overland expeditions. There was Sara, the Welsh woman who we'd abandoned to her fate in In Guezzam! She'd managed to beat us to Niamey by hitching rides and clearly took some pleasure in the accomplishment.

Malcolm drove us into town the next morning to check on visas. The Nigerian embassy, given the recent coup, was closed. I had a couple of hours free time to wander about the market. Niamey was a city of great and sometimes unsettling contrasts. It was nice to see fruits of all kinds for sale. Peanut butter was a popular staple (yeech!). Businesses practiced taking a 'siesta' of a kind from 12 to 3 p.m. each afternoon. The throngs of young sponges were present, as usual, and persistent, but inclined, at least, to shrug off my equally persistent rebuffs with a warm-hearted smile. That was a pleasant surprise.

'Shocked and astonished,' however, are the only words I can think of to describe my reaction to the number of people in the city suffering from Hanson's Disease (better known then as leprosy) and polio. I'd imagined these diseases had been eradicated. Extreme poverty, parasites, occasional virus-related outbreaks, water-borne diseases, even rabies, I kind of expected to see in the poorest African countries, but nothing in my studies at university prepared me for Hanson's and polio—young people with gray nubs where fingers and toes used to be or bodies twisted from the ravages of these frightful ailments.

Some agency, God bless them, was churning out low-rise tricycles for a select number of those affected, granting them a high degree of mobility and, consequently, a shot at a better life. Some of these bikes were a fair size, even motorized, remarkably fast and LOUD, having been fitted with their version of a Hollywood "Noise Maker" muffler. Their young owners careened down the main streets of Niamey the same as any witless biker I'd ever seen back home, pushing their machine to the max and largely heedless of their surroundings.

After lunch in camp, Mark and I headed down to the river where we encountered a group of boys kicking around a soccer ball. We joined in and were having a great time until Mark cut his toe pretty badly. A serious thing, under the circumstances. It was just like him to play barefoot in the dirt. Anyway, it was unfortunate and worrisome. Ronnie helped fix him up.

Barry told us how he'd also gone down to explore the riverbank and stopped at a little variety shop within the Rio Bravo Hotel. The proprietor tried to sell him an excursion on the river. He even pointed to a "letter of recommendation" tacked to a pillar. Barry had to bite his lip so as not to bust a gut. The letter was written in English some six months prior by a traveler off one of the Guerba Expeditions trucks, which this fellow to his detriment could not read.

Malcolm went to explore the village very near our camp. Rather than being beset by young mendicants seeking a cadeau, he was dismayed to find them pleading for basic medical care. He retrieved the medical kit from The Pig and a few of us went with him to help clean the gaping pus-filled fly-infected sores of a handful of children.

Health conditions in the village were, on the whole, quite dire. Villagers would pull back the sleeve of their shirt or blouse as we walked past them to reveal a pustulant wound, regarding us with silent pleading eyes. Or they might ask us timidly for an aspirin, anti-malarial, disinfectant, or a bandage. Nor was it unusual to see children with distended bellies shaking with chills in the sizzling mid-day sun.

What vexed us the most was the fact that there wasn't so much as a tube or bottle of antiseptic available in the entire village—this, no more than twenty kilometers from the capital, although there seemed to be no shortage of cigarettes and bubble gum in the shops. How and why, this was the case, I couldn't rightly say. Just that the complete dearth of very basic medicines so near a major urban center, moreover the nation's capital, struck us as inherently wrong.

In sharp contrast, my body had received all manner of medical precaution before traveling to Africa. This was sometime before the World-Wide Web or Internet. For up-to-date advice on how to protect myself from the array of harmful bugs I could potentially encounter I visited the Queen's University Department of Community Health and Epidemiology. It was evident that I had no clear idea before heading out of what I might be in for, especially in more isolated locations.

My primary concerns, "aside from malaria, hepatitis, bilharzia, cholera, and typhoid," they proposed, were the dangers of dysentery and infection in places where there might not be ready access to medical care. At the doctor's suggestion, I carried a quantity of Imodium, an anti-diarrheal, and Novo-Trimel, an antibiotic, "just in case." These he prescribed along with strict and detailed instructions on when and how to self-medicate, but only in extreme circumstances.

Five years earlier, I had applied to the military for a peacekeeping mission to the Middle East (I was ultimately rejected for the posting because of religious bias, but that's another story) and received as part of my processing a series of less than common-place inoculations courtesy of the Department of National Defence, including a polio and diphtheria cocktail.

The Travel and Inoculation Clinic at Toronto General Hospital supplemented this with a typhoid fever booster as well as jabs against yellow fever and tetanus. Smallpox, I was advised, was "no longer done" and I was provided, in that case, with a "certificate of exemption."

For a cholera vaccination, I was referred to yet somewhere else, St. Michael's Hospital Department of Infectious Diseases. The cumulative effect of all these pokes hit me like a ton of bricks. It took a good week to recover, and I pondered if the deterrent wasn't worse than the disease, but looking out at these pitiable villagers, I couldn't help contemplating just how fortunate (and privileged) I was.

That night Ronnie shaved her head, declaring that she was "done" with trying to keep the dirt, grime, and insects from her hair. It seemed to me, and I think to most of the others, that this was taking a rather extreme approach to the problem. I wondered if other members of our expedition would follow suit, but no one else ever did.

Happily, we had no problems obtaining visas for Benin (having obtained our visas for Togo back in Algiers), but the Nigerian embassy remained shut. We decided that if we couldn't get into Nigeria when the time came, we'd look at taking passage by boat from Cotonou in Benin to Cameroon (there were still reports of fighting in Chad, which pretty much ruled out that option). Before coming back to camp, we purchased three guinea fowl for 2,500CFAF ($6.00 US). For the carnivores in our company, they provided welcome variety from our usual diet.

I walked to the river with Mark and Lila, passing termite nests along the way that stood like towering pinnacles, some taller than Mark or Inger, both six foot-three. We were continually badgered by people trying to sell us excursions on the Niger, but I had to smile at this because it reminded me so much of the cab drivers flogging rides outside of LaGuardia Airport in New York. We stopped at the Rio Bravo Hotel, actually, little more than a shack, and saw tacked to the pillar the very warning that Barry had mentioned: "To Whom It May Concern, this is to introduce Ahmed—a classic rip-off artist of the first order . . . ."

The poor shop owner, as I mentioned, had no idea what the letter said, and no one that read it seemed inclined to let on. Although we declined his offer of an excursion, he did manage to get one over on us. It was a hot humid day and he had in his cooler a stock of 10-ounce bottles of Coca-Cola. We knew from experience that these typically went for 70CFAF (about 17 cents US) and helped ourselves to drinks with that in mind. Our mistake. Our canny friend was quick to grasp the fact that we hadn't clarified the price first. "220 francs. . . each," he informed us, after we'd guzzled our drinks. Live and learn. It was, after all, a cheap lesson, barely 50 cents per bottle.

He smiled with grim satisfaction as we exited the shop. How is it, I wondered, that Coca-Cola can retail in Niger at an average 17 cents a bottle? I hadn't seen those kinds of prices in Canada since the early 70s.

Our final day in Niamey, I walked with Lila and Alison to Boubon, a village untouched by time, along a bank of the Niger River. Wednesdays were market days and if I did nothing else in Africa, my brief visit to Boubon satisfied every itch to see this part of the world before it was irreparably changed.

A haze seemed to always settle over the river. Goods and people were brought in by dozens of dugout canoes (pirogues) which were pulled up to the bank, side by side. A line of reed and tin-roofed shelters were erected four or five meters from the shoreline for the vendors to lay out their goods. Every facet of the market was run by women in their colorful attire. Despite whatever hardships they faced in life, these women exuded strength and confidence. It was impossible not to be impressed.

Lila and Alison took their purchases back to camp and I went off to explore the riverbank on my own. I'd picked up a few things at the market for a picnic lunch, including a small tin of mackerel packed in tomato sauce, fresh baked bread, and an onion. The tin of mackerel, coincidentally, was manufactured by Mitsui, the same import-export company my father worked for.

Having found a suitably quiet place near the river where I could watch the pirogues, I set myself down for lunch, slicing up the onion and folding it between two halves of bread together with the mackerel in tomato sauce. I was maybe halfway through my sandwich when the children discovered me. In no time at all perhaps a dozen had gathered, separated from me by only two or three meters. They stood or sat, watching me in silence as I ate my modest meal. I couldn't finish it under the circumstances, and yet there wasn't enough to equitably share in a way that would satisfy any of them. I knew, besides, that the attempt might well lead to mayhem, and I was here alone.

When I got up to leave, one of the older boys pointed to my empty tin of mackerel and gestured for me to toss it to him. There was no good reason not to, so I obliged. He and a few others tussled over the can for the small amount of sweet tomato sauce still clinging to the inside. I departed, too sickened and distraught to look on. I wished with all my heart that I could have done more for these kids. As heartless as it sounds, that was not my purpose. I'd come to Africa to observe and nothing more.

If I'd even hinted at buying them a few cans of mackerel for their own, I knew with certainty the word would have spread in a heartbeat. I'd have started a riot only to move on, accomplishing worse than nothing. It was hard not to think about the abundance of the market I'd been to that very morning. Niamey was, indeed, a city of great and sometimes unsettling contrasts.

Although the road was no longer paved, it was a swift journey up the north bank of the Niger to the border with Mali and a return to the southern limits of the Sahara. The closer we came to the border, the closer the desert ran to the banks of the river. Tuareg also began to make a reappearance. The Mali border guards at Labbezanga made it obvious without being explicit that they would welcome tokens of good-will. Crossing the border, consequently, came at the very modest price of a ballpoint pen and a BIC razor, which George donated on our behalf.

Mali and Niger differed in other significant ways. For one thing, the sheep had wool, unlike the "geeps" we encountered in Niger. The degree and intensity of begging was much reduced, too, to a level more akin to what you might encounter in any Western city. Moreover, the children had a much different approach to gaining our attention. They would often chase our passing truck, shouting and excitedly waiving their arms, hoping I suppose, that we would have something special to share. The daring ones would leap atop our trailer and ride along with us for a bit, until they realized there was nothing to be gained and had to get off. Inevitably, they would do a nose-dive into the dirt at a fair clip. It was frightening to watch.

The last notable difference had to do with vernacular. In Niger we were habitually addressed as "comarade," while in Mali, it was "patron" (boss). I don't know how many Maliennes gave much thought to the expression or what the impetus for it was. A hold-over from colonial times, I suspect, deliberately or inadvertently reinforced by Whites, society, or individual Maliennes, but there was a considerable difference in the subsurface message to my way of thinking. Calling every White man or White woman you encounter "boss," was an unhealthy practice as far as I was concerned and I openly discouraged it, undermining, thereby, my personal "Prime Directive" or pledge only to observe.

We camped for the night just outside of Labbezanga and pressed on to Gao the following day. Just my luck, I awoke with yet another head cold, and a real doozer. My body hadn't fully recovered from the previous bouts and that unfortunate run-in with the peanut ball. This was a heavy blow to me, both physically and mentally.

The road to Gao was in reasonable repair, but there were numerous police checks along the way to slow us down. George and Malcolm, for some reason I can't now recall, stopped briefly at a small village about halfway to Gao. Those of us in the back remained onboard The Pig. We were immediately surrounded by a large group of boisterous children and adolescents. There are several major groups of people in Mali. These kids, as best as I could determine, were Songhai (or as they pronounced it, "Sonrai"), all terribly handsome and fit.

Thinking we would be moving on at any moment, Lila made the now unforgivable mistake of handing out a few toffees. If you've ever seen a clip of piranha in a sudden feeding frenzy, you can imagine what happened next. Several children quickly had hold of her arm with a notion that if they pulled her from the truck the toffees would follow suit. She hollered out in fear and pain and several of us jumped forward to free her.

Undeterred if not emboldened, several of the older children climbed up the side of the truck and joined us in our seats. A girl, or should I say, a young woman, perhaps sixteen years of age, plunked herself down next to me eyes ablaze, breathless both from excitement and the exertion from the climb. I understand that beauty is in the eye of the beholder and that it comes in many guises, but aside from being taken completely by surprise, I was rendered speechless by her overwhelming presence. She was next to me only a few moments, but the memory of her is forever etched in my mind. Responsible adults showed up and chased the kids off the truck. The girl, whoever she was, succeeded in obtaining a couple of toffees for her efforts.

We camped a little way outside of Gao. Short on water, the decision was made to draw a supply from the Niger River. Giardia, as in many parts of the world, was a very real risk with particularly nasty consequences if contracted. It was proposed that we could add some iodine to the water and boil it before use. I had some doubts about the efficacy of this, but there seemed to be no alternative.

We drove into town the next morning and to my great amazement, were never once annoyed by anyone seeking or demanding a cadeau. The very suddenness of this transformation took me aback, in an agreeable way, of course, but I found it quite inexplicable. Even the solemn and usually distant Tuareg seemed cordial. I plucked up the courage to point out the difference in temperament to a Tuareg I was negotiating with in the market, and he seemed not in the least surprised, attributing it to a difference between the clans of Mali and Niger.

I needed Mali francs for my own use (then, 820MF to the US dollar).[7] My visit to the bank was an experience in its own right. The branch was only open three hours each day, from 8 to 11. The tellers were mostly adolescent boys (this was, by the way, Mali's second largest bank). That was surprising, but even more astonishing was the fact that my teller was legally blind. Somehow, incredibly, he was able to perform his duties and, moreover, seemed both competent and confident. He had no ability, however, to make exact change. I stared at the young man in front of me in disbelief when he handed me a large denomination note and instructed me to go to the market to break it and come back with the change to finalize our transaction.

I forked out for a beefsteak lunch at a local dive, which, in retrospect, proved ill-fated, as my stomach began to cramp shortly after. Mark teased that I should have joined him for a meal at l'Hôtel Atlantide which was apparently first rate and had left no aftereffects.

It was a long drive the next day, 200 plus kilometers northwest to the town of Bamba. Except for occasional glimpses of the river, the countryside was a monotonous expanse of thorny brush and arid landscape inhabited by donkeys, goats, and camels. Cattle were few and far between in this part of the country owing to the extended drought.

The road was rough and interspersed with gaps of sand, but passable for a truck such as ours. We encountered fewer vehicles than you can count on one hand along the way. At one point, we made to pass what we thought to be an abandoned car. A young boy suddenly appeared next to it and appealed to us for food and water. It turned out that the car had broken down the previous day. The boy's father left him to guard it while he went off to find help, but the man, for whatever reason, never returned. We gave the lad a ride to the nearest town.

---

[7] Mali readopted the West African CFA franc only months later.

Making camp at Bamba I crawled straight into my tent, my head pounding, a nagging head cold and my stomach turning revolutions. Mark and Lila, concerned that I was undernourished, brought me boiled eggs and some cooked whitefish to bolster my strength.

There was no good opportunity for me to rest, however. The next day we were up early and pressed on to Timbuktu (alternatively, Timbuctoo, or in the Malienne vernacular, Tombouctou). Reaching the city took a Herculean effort. I wondered that anyone in their right mind would ever attempt this stretch of desert. We literally pushed our truck across miles and miles of sand under a broiling sun, getting out of The Pig every fifteen to twenty meters to lay down the perforated steel Marston mats.

In a shallow ravine where a few scraggly shrubs had taken root we stumbled on a gutted Soviet BTR-40. I'd trained to go to war with the Eastern Bloc for the better part of eight years and recognized the vehicle immediately, a 4-wheeled armored personnel carrier, but had never seen one in the flesh, so to speak. It was clear evidence of the kind of proxy war being waged between the West and the Soviets in Africa.

We were exhausted by the time we'd reached the outskirts of Timbuktu and quickly settled down for the night with the city lights shining tantalizingly in the distance. My sinuses, by this point, were burned out from a month and a half of persistent head colds and my nose filled with clotted blood.

For anyone planning a similar overland trek, it took us precisely fifty days from London to reach the fabled city of Timbuktu. This was the beating heart of a thriving trans-Saharan caravan route from the 13th to 16th centuries, trade in salt its mainstay. With prosperity, the city grew as a center for education, arts, and science. It was home to a large and influential university and several renowned madrasahs (schools for Islamic instruction). Much of the romance associated with the name dates to this golden age. Through the many tombs of Muslim holy men, libraries, and distinctive clay-covered mosques one could glimpse a bit of that ancient glory.

London to Timbuktu, the "Pearl of the Desert," overland in 50 days

There was an enduring sense of "story" about the place, made all the more wonderous by the city's extreme isolation and the ever-encroaching sands. The inhabitants seemed quite aware and extremely proud of their history. The effect, unfortunately, was slightly undercut by hordes of children shouting "Donnez-moi un BIC" and the presence of a modern "Superette" (supermarket) sustained by a military airport serving government officials and well-heeled tourists keen on avoiding the worst the desert had to offer.

We couldn't make a move from this point on in Mali, certainly Timbuktu, without registering at the local office of the Société malienne d'Exploitation des Resources touristiques (SMERT). SMERT and the police worked hand-in-hand to exploit, as the name suggests, the few tourists about—a mix of high-end adventure travel aficionados, diplomats and their families, and overland expeditions like ours. Our passports were collected and held by the police for the duration of our visit and not returned until the SMERT fee was paid, and this was relatively substantial—16,000 Mali francs per person or about $390 US for the lot of us, demanded separately, moreover, in every major town in Eastern Mali.

The irksome imposition of SMERT aside, I was very disturbed and disheartened, to put it mildly, to find several vendors in the market at Timbuktu openly selling tins of herring clearly marked as gifts of food aid from the Federal Republic of Germany. The image of those kids on the outskirts of Niamey tussling over a bit of leftover tomato sauce still haunted me. Galling is the only word that comes to mind. The authorities cannot have been unaware of the practice and were evidently indifferent to it.

Our next destination was Mopti, the center of a fertile watershed stretching some ways north of the Niger River from Korienzé to Djenne. The trip out of Timbuktu was no more comfortable for the first several kilometers—Mark and Barry were thrown from their seats and badly knocked about going over patch of road that caught Malcolm off guard.

About fifty kilometers outside of Timbuktu we passed the city of Goundam and I have to say that Timbuktu, or Fez, for that matter, were poor imitations by comparison. You had to use your imagination and apply your knowledge of history to fully appreciate Timbuktu, but Goundam was something else entirely. "Magical" is the best word I could use to describe it, as if the sultana, Scheherazade, had borrowed something of its essence to compose her tales for One Thousand and One Nights. I wondered openly at all the fuss made over Timbuktu when almost nothing was said about this imposing neighbor.

The road was much improved southwest of Goundam. I assumed, in retrospect, that most people made the overland trek to Timbuktu from this direction, rather than endure the hardships we encountered, but then again, we met virtually the opposite complication—seasonal flooding.

We intended to travel to Mopti from Timbuktu, but the police at Niafunke (or Niafounké) prevented us from continuing because the December flooding had not yet receded and the road to Mopti, consequently, impassable.

There was no question of turning back and apparently no way to go forward anytime soon.

We made camp, poured over our maps, and debated what to do next. A decision was reached to detour more or less cross-country heading toward the Mauritanian border, skirting around the watershed (technically, the Inner Niger Delta or "Macina" region), then cutting south to Ségou and on to the capital, Bamako. From Bamako we would travel back up the opposite bank of the Niger to reach Mopti.

At this point, we were tantalizingly close, just over 200 kilometers from Mopti, as the crow flies. The proposed route meant a detour of about 980 kilometers, much of it through country with no clearly defined roads. There was never any guarantee that we could obtain the visas we still needed in Mopti, so I had to agree that it made some sense to first make for Bamako where our chances were greater, but a detour of this length was kind of a double-edged sword. It meant that our existing Upper Volta visa would likely expire before we got there. Of necessity, our revised plan was to obtain extensions on the Upper Volta visas in Bamako and to try, yet again, for that elusive Nigerian visa, before moving on to Mopti.

Our maps had very little to say about the road toward the Mauritanian border connecting a few scattered towns and villages, but it turned out none too bad owing to the firmness of the terrain. We stopped at the village of Léré where we were very cordially met and enquired about obtaining potable water. The well was in the center of the village and accessed by heavy buckets lowered down a very great distance by ropes and pulleys. It took a communal effort to haul the loaded buckets back up and we had a fabulous time working with the villagers to accomplish the task.

Léré was too far off the beaten track to have a formal SMERT office, but a local official did charge us 2,000MF for permits to take photographs. That was par for the course by this point, so we brushed this irksome necessity aside and didn't allow it to ruin the experience. A few of the village women, in their ubiquitous colorful print dresses and head scarves, asked us to help top up their own water containers and we happily obliged.

We made camp at Nampala, just 25 kilometers or so south of the Mauritanian border. It was tempting to pay the country a brief visit. Aside from the fact that we had no visa, there were too many other unknowns involved. We were, moreover, too far behind schedule to indulge our curiosity.

I was struck by how often and how dramatically the landscape changed throughout our detour, alternating between hills and plateaus, scrub and palm groves, arid plains, and vast grasslands. We intended to cut due south and follow the Niger down to Ségou, but the annual flood waters blocked the main road south, as it had at Niafunke. We had no option but to head still farther west before edging down, adding another 230 kilometers to our detour.

After endless miles of less developed tract, we were startled by the sight of verdant and orderly rice fields. The World Bank had helped to establish a sprawling "Rice Research Station" at Kogoni where they were experimenting with various ways of rehabilitating Mali's irrigation infrastructure. We were maybe twenty kilometers outside of Kogoni when we spotted our first African wildlife—a troop of monkeys, something we had long been anticipating. I'm guessing they were Erythrocebus patas, or "patas."

I can't recall and my journals don't record why, but we made the decision to motor on from Kogoni to Ségou rather than head directly to Bamako. My guess would be that we were blocked from reaching the capital, yet again, by seasonal flooding and that the calculation was made that we might be able to cross the river at Ségou and backtrack west to Bamako over dry land.

As we came closer to Ségou and reconnected with the main road, the countryside once again featured structured fields of millet and, closer to the river, paddy fields of flood-fed rice. But there were, to my eye, far too many goats and cows present on the surrounding grasslands to be sustainable. It was plain to see that the vast herds of ruminants were rapidly denuding and compacting soil that might otherwise have remained fertile, opening fresh paths for the expanding desert to exploit.

We took a double-pontoon ferry that was on the small side across the river to Ségou, a tight fit for The Pig. It rode very low in the water, which caused us some unease. But the vessel was more than equal to the task and our apprehension unwarranted.

Ségou, much like El Malah in Algeria, was a beautiful, if crumbling, former colonial outpost of the French empire. Many of the government buildings were a wonderful blend of Mali Empire and Islamic architectural styles. I would have loved to take a few photographs, but the local SMERT demanded 5,000MF each for the privilege. Not so very much, but all these fees, you may have noted, added up over time and I was always short on local currency, the average wait to exchange money at a bank in Mali being about an hour and a half.

The road from Ségou to Bamako, offset some distance from the river, was first rate. It was a tremendous pleasure, besides, to look upon a consistently green landscape once again. Bamako was a vibrant bustling city that reminded me of the frenzied shopping that used to take place in Toronto on Boxing Day before the advent of the Internet and online Black Friday deals. I had a quick look about the city and by rights should have been enjoying myself, but I was cursed with bad luck. Yet another head cold and a serious case of the runs to boot!

Truth be told, this wasn't "another" head cold, but one long lingering persistent germ that had got hold of me in the Bois de Boulogne and had been doing its best to kill me off ever since, and only occasionally receded just to taunt me and give me false hope. I'd lost count of how many bouts I'd endured. Added together with my unfortunate encounter with the peanut ball I was on my last legs, pallid and looking like death warmed over. Fortunately, it was going to take George a day or two to see about our visas. At Lila's encouragement, I checked into a hotel on the spur of the moment, hoping that I could regain my strength with a little bed rest and the use of proper toilet facilities.

I should emphasize that l'Hôtel Majestique at $8 US per night prepaid was a value hotel with a capital 'V.' I was assigned a second-floor room that was small, dark, and dingy. A simple lattice work door separated the room from the courtyard, so there was no real privacy or security to speak of.

There were mosquito coils freely available in the room, but the lattice door made their use an exercise in futility. A hard mattress atop a steel tube frame rested only an inch or two above the floor, which was nothing in itself, except that enormous roaches wandered freely about, and this positioned them a little too close for comfort. The room boasted an unconcealed toilet with no seat and a bidet. A cold shower could be had down the hall, if one were brave enough to attempt it. The one true concession to comfort was a slow-moving ceiling fan that made a deep "whomping" sound with each revolution.

I managed to survive the night, although there were a few very touch and go moments. Nevertheless, I felt somewhat improved the following morning, possibly the result of having downed a quantity of Imodium. George, Malcolm, Lila, and Mark came to pay me a welcome visit. They were genuinely concerned for my health, but I don't think there was any doubt in their minds or mine that I would be left behind if I couldn't get it together quickly. Just in case, they'd brought my bags along, "assuming I'd want them," if that didn't make matters clear enough. I was happy for one thing. I could make use of the mosquito netting that I kept in my bag.

This time around, the French embassy required our individual presence to process our visas. If I planned to continue with the group, I needed to report to the embassy at 8:30 the following morning. The better part of that day was spent in my room, reading, writing letters, and dozing, but I felt well enough by late afternoon to go out for a short walk. I discovered that if I walked briskly enough and looked ahead with an air of confidence, I could avoid much of the incessant panhandling, but this had the unfortunate downside of messing up my ability to take in the sights.

Passing a respectable looking diner, I decided that I might benefit from what I fatuously deemed to be a nutritious dinner. A well-cooked meal, I presumed, would help me regain my strength and, hopefully, slip quietly past my stomach without issue. I ordered a plate of steak and chips for 1,800MF, which was something like $2.20 US. I was surprised to run into Mark, Lila, and Alison after dinner and invited them back to my room to help chase roaches, which they did to humor me.

The steak and chips, no surprise, proved to be a dismal mistake. The next morning, I awoke with a worsening case of diarrhea. I braved the shower and made my way on wobbly legs to the embassy.

The government of Upper Volta had been seized in a coup just five months prior by Thomas Sankara, a charismatic idealist and Che Guevara inspired revolutionary. Sankara swiftly established a Marxist regime. Mali and Upper Volta, consequently, were "no longer on amicable terms." In some convoluted way, this translated for us into a rejection of our request to obtain an extension on our existing Upper Volta visas. However, we could apply, we were told, for "new visas" for 6,000MF each. This would take another day to arrange.

I hadn't come to Africa to lie in a hotel room, so I accompanied Mark and Lila on their exploration of the city and capitalized on the opportunity to do some banking. We checked out an upscale supermarket where I was impressed by the variety and quality of the fresh produce. On our way to the Hôtel L'Amitié for afternoon tea, some thug tried to pickpocket Mark, of all people. Mark, however, was more alert and much quicker than the fellow expected. The evildoer cried in terror as the towering Kiwi held him firmly by the wrist with one hand and by the shirt collar with the other, all the while publicly berating the man with some choice New Zealand invective. Not surprisingly, this drew a good deal of attention, but no one made the slightest effort to intercede. I presume what had occurred was obvious to all. Feeling sufficiently avenged, Mark released the fellow, and he ran off, presumably glad for his life.

I spent another awful night, including vomiting and diarrhea, which overwhelmed the limited capacity of the ancient toilet and septic system. There was another toilet down the hall, but my sessions were so frequent that I couldn't make it that far and resorted to filling up the bidet, for which purpose the device was never intended. By morning there was nothing left to drain out of me. I was horrified and disgusted by both the stench and the mess I'd made of the toilet and bidet, never mind the bed. I used the contents of my water bottle in a vain attempt to free up the commode and bidet, but that just made matters worse.

Mark and Lila showed up at my door in the middle of all this with word that our Upper Volta visas had been processed and the group was moving on to Ségou after lunch. I thanked them without letting them into the room and assured them that I'd be ready by noon and would rendezvous with the group outside the main post office.

I packed in a hurry, downed a double dose of Imodium, scribbled an apology note for the condition of the room and left it together with a $20 bill in an envelope. Dropping my key at the front desk, I skedaddled as fast and as far away from l'Hôtel Majestique as my unsteady legs could take me.

With time to spare, I searched the chemist shops for an over-the-counter alternative to Imodium on the assumption that the Imodium was too precious to waste unless I was really on death's doorstep. I wound up with a box of Intétrix capsules, an intestinal antiseptic, and crossed my fingers that this would do the trick.

Lila greeted me at the post office and although pleased to see me, was clearly in a funk. When I asked why, she explained that they had camped at a forestry station outside of town, known locally as "the Plantation." Next to it was a walled enclosure. During the night a group of people had cornered a dog inside the compound intending to beat it to death, but the dog apparently put up a good fight and the people involved were just afraid enough of the animal to poke and hit it with sticks from a safe distance, which meant a slow and painful death for the poor beast. This went on for quite a long time, the dog alternating between angry snarls and painful whimpers until it was all over. "Why would they do such a thing?" I asked. "For sport?"

"No," said Lila. "I think they ate it." Brits are notoriously fond of animals, particularly dogs. Lila could not shake off her memories of that night for a good many days.

Standard throughout Mali, we faced a police check exiting the city, but as this was the capital, we were confronted with a more thorough interrogation than usual. The police were apparently concerned about our stated destination and diverted us to the SMERT office for additional questioning. George had no reason to cover up our intentions, we were passing through Mopti and then over the border to Upper Volta. "The fee for visiting Mopti is 16,000 Mali francs per person," replied the agent, matter-of-factly (again, about $390 US in total). George was momentarily speechless. It was one of those situations where you didn't appreciate the significance of your words and now that you've gone and stepped in it realize the full implication and must do your best to tap-dance your way out.

"We're not actually visiting Mopti," he corrected. "We're a new company testing out the route. We're going straight to Upper Volta and just taking the road from Mopti to Ouagadougou."

The agent regarded him suspiciously. "No stopping in Mopti?"

"No," confirmed George. "Straight to Upper Volta. See, we have new visas."

The agent considered this for a moment before making up his mind. "Okay, go," he replied with a dismissive wave.

George was quick to get us back on the road and on our way before the man had time to reconsider. It was a warm and kind of hazy day. The road was in excellent repair. We buzzed past Ségou and on, while I stared lazily at the passing landscape, which quickly reverted to arid scrub dotted with bloated baobab trees, home to troops of monkeys, and towering termite nests. We were stopped coming in and out of every village and town, sometimes by police, other times by adolescents performing some ill-defined "survey." By the time we reached the town of San and made camp, we'd logged more than 400 kilometers.

My diarrhea continued to worsen, taking on a distinctly green and unsettling hue, even without eating anything of much substance. I was becoming more and more lethargic and knew enough that if I didn't take more serious preventative measures, and soon, I could die from the combination of malnutrition and dehydration. The Intétrix seemed to be having no effect, nor did upping my intake of salt and water. When I mentioned this to George, he gave me his bottle of Lomotil, with a promise from me to replace it at the next opportunity. At a shop in San I made a purchase that I can say with heartfelt conviction, saved my life—a quantity of vanilla flavored baby food by the brand name of Blédilac. It was smooth going down, filling, and actually rather tasty. For the next couple of weeks, Blédilac would be my go-to meal, with the exception of toasted bread.

At San, we encountered a young French Canadian hitchhiker from Montréal named Alain. I was blindsided by the group's decision to give him a lift to Mopti, remembering quite clearly how they'd left the Welsh woman, Sara, to fend for herself at In Guezzam, a thoroughly dangerous place, "on principle" and how George had insisted that picking up hitchhikers was against company policy. I had little empathy for the guy and struggled to understand how Alain's egocentric personality had won over so many of my fellow travelers so very quickly. But there he was, the argument in favor of "bending policy" on the new excuse that taking on an occasional hitchhiker could provide "useful intelligence."

A little more than midway between San and Mopti lay the city of Djenne. Getting there meant a 40-kilometer round-trip diversion, and that was not the only hurdle. The road to the city traversed the Bani River and we would not know until we reached the banks if the way forward was flooded out. The Grand Mosque at Djenne, however, was famous enough and close enough at hand that the group voted to give it a try.

On reaching the near bank of the Bani, we could see the great mosque rising in the distance, like a clay-covered version of Westminster Palace on the River Thames. I could understand, now, the allure. In another month, perhaps, the river would dry to a trickle, but for the present, the murky brown water flowed deep and wide enough to be crossed by pirogues and rafts pushed using long staves. There was no ferry large enough to hold The Pig. Malcolm, paced back and forth along the bank, intently observing each crossing. "Watch the poles," he directed, shielding the hard sun from his eyes with one hand.

We did as he directed and soon caught his gist. The poles used by the pirogue pilots were dipping no more than a meter below the surface. "I can do it," he proclaimed. "I can ford the river."

We appreciated his self-confidence but pointed out that we had no way of knowing with any degree of certainty how firm the riverbed might be and that it was a good half-kilometer to the far bank. Where would we be if The Pig got stuck in the middle? But Malcolm was determined. Ambushing a wizened-looking old boater, Malcolm interrogated the fellow using a combination of hand gestures and 'international speak.' "He says that if I enter where the road disappears under the water and continue straight, it won't be a problem. The road will support us." His excitement was palpable, but our skepticism shone brighter. "This is a Bedford," he persisted, as if that was all that needed saying. He looked to George for support.

George shrugged noncommittally.

"All right," he beamed. "Everyone up!" We did as we were told, taking our seats and readying ourselves for any eventuality, including jumping ship. Malcolm edged The Pig over to the water's edge and shoved it into low gear. We held our breaths as he slowly nudged his way forward and the water surged around us. For a moment we seemed to stand motionless, and I wondered if the Bedford might stall, but just as the thought occurred to me, Malcolm pressed on the gas and The Pig ploughed forward pushing water up and over the Marston mats, creating a large wake behind us. The sight of our big pink Bedford motoring through the water must have been quite a sight. People stopped what they were doing to watch and cheer us on. It felt to me like a boat ride on the Severn River.

We made the far bank and congratulated both The Pig and Malcolm on a job well done.

A spectacular open market sprawled within the shadow cast by the fantastic walls of the Great Mosque, which were made new each year as a community undertaking, a demonstration of both faith and civic pride. There were endless rows of woven baskets and plastic bins filled with nuts, grains, herbs, spices, and all manner of fresh produce, including pineapple and mango. Photos would have been nice, but here too SMERT was on our case, so we went without. Hundreds of people wandered the market, searching for deals, bargaining loudly.

The great diversity of colors and patterns worn by the women intrigued me and I took comfort in this overt adherence to African-grounded fashion. I was disappointed, however, to discover that much of this magnificent cloth was imported from Europe, particularly the Netherlands.

Apparently, this hadn't always been the case. Cotton was an important cash crop in East Africa and there was a spirited domestic manufacturing capability up until about 1965. The factories shut down post-independence partly due to political turmoil and government nationalizations, but also from a virtual deluge of cheap second-hand clothing.

The issue of second-hand clothing is a complicated one. I read somewhere that something like 70 percent of all donated clothing items in the West eventually wind up in Africa. I don't know how true that is, but it is certainly a large percentage. The trade in second-hand clothing has become a multi-million-dollar industry in Africa employing many thousands, and, as such, is not likely to disappear soon.

To my mind, there are good reasons to find this a regrettable development, but I understand why it occurred. The most obvious reason is the cost. A couple of dollars, perhaps, for a used shirt or used jeans. The small investment required for a startup business in used clothing is another reason. A third, is a perception that even used, these items are of a better quality than newly manufactured garments imported from Asia. Lastly, a youthful aesthetic that goes in for prominent American or European brand names, especially those worn by revered athletes and celebrities. In 1984, however, most of the used clothing I saw in circulation was of the lowest imaginable quality, not what you might find today in a "gently used" thrift shop.

The retail market for shoes was dominated in 1984 by a single firm, Bata. "Pas un pas sans Bata," went the slogan (Not a step without Bata). Bata at one time maintained several production facilities in the more populous and economically developed regions of Africa employing thousands, some of these factories dating back as far as the 1930s. Like the textile industry, the firm struggled to keep its plants in operation, especially in the face of increasing low-cost imports from China.[8]

Mega projects costing millions upon millions created through "tied aid" were common enough in Africa—roads, railways, hydro-electric dams, and the like, but employing relatively few in the long-term and adding significantly to the national debt. Industries like textile and shoe manufacturing that had the potential to employ large numbers in Africa and could feed straight into local economies were wanting, so far as I could see.[9] Given a sizable population and a wealth of available resources, I found this dependence on imports, at least for ordinary household goods, unsettling. When I stumbled on an artisan selling handcrafted batiks with a powerful African theme, you can appreciate why I jumped at the chance to buy one. I still have it, a recurring scene of children playing soccer with a spotted leopard lurking ominously between the village huts.

Our visit to Djenne was short, but memorable. Moreover, George's Lomotil, or the combination of Lomotil and Imodium, was having an impact and I was able to enjoy my time there. On our way out, a young boy whose name none of us could pronounce (we took to calling him "Bill") approached us and asked for a ride to Mopti. It was setting yet another precedent, but he managed, somehow, to ingratiate himself, and joined Alain on the truck.

With two additional passengers The Pig was becoming a tad crowded. Mark proposed, and it was accepted, that he and I should ride perched atop the bulkhead separating the cab from the bed with a clear view over the roof. It was quite safe for two or even three people to stand up there, although

---

[8] At the time, Bata was headquartered in Toronto. Bata's global headquarters was transferred to Lausanne in 2004. The firm continues to make significant investments in Africa, making good on brand loyalty and a focus on higher-end and specialty merchandise.

[9] Unfortunately, that ship has sailed. Automation creates good paying jobs, but relatively few.

the Bedford was never designed for this. The weather was perfect for it, and we had a glorious view of the Mali countryside from high up above the cab.

I don't think you'll be surprised to find that given all the hype we were determined to have a peek at Mopti, no matter George's pledge to the contrary. The Mopti police were fine with this but insisted that we turn all our passports over to them and then report to SMERT to pay the mandatory fee. Instead, we explored the city, which seemed overrated to me, at least in comparison to Djenne, then went back to the police station with fingers crossed to collect our passports, never having reported to SMERT On the assumption, I suppose, that we'd been "cleared," they returned our passports and we hightailed it out of town using the back roads, leaving both Alain and Bill behind.

Needless to say, we were more than a bit weary of SMERT by this point. George discovered that the agency's reach was not limitless. If we took the lesser used road to Bankass and avoided passing through Bandiagara, we might avoid their offices altogether.

The Bankass route turned out to be an especially fortuitous choice. We camped that night outside the village of Somadougou precisely two months after departing London. Mark asked me to join him for a walk into the countryside, a mix of scrub and rocky outcrops. We noticed, for the first time, scorpions in jet black body armor scurrying about and made a mental note to check our boots before slipping them on.

A short distance from our campsite, we stumbled on an isolated Dogon village perched high on a cliff face. I remembered seeing Dogon artifacts at the Royal Ontario Museum as a child. If you'd asked me then if I ever expected to come face to face with Dogon people in the flesh, I would have replied, "in your dreams." Yet here I was. If you have a picture in your mind of what African art looks like, chances are it is Dogon influenced.

We were spotted, of course, the moment we looked upon the village and very cordially greeted by a man named Moussa Karambe, who spoke French with reasonable skill. He invited us, then and there, on a tour of "Gamba," a village too small or off the beaten track to appear on our maps, which was probably for the best.

Gamba, as it turned out, was comprised of twin communities nestled high up on either side of a reentrant pointing back toward a towering cliff face. A narrow chasm separated the two halves, a clear spring running down the middle. The homes, with a secure view of the approaches, were clustered along cliff top terraces for growing millet. The terrace walls were surmounted with decorative clay caps modeled, no doubt, on the mushroom-shaped termite mounds pervasive throughout the Sahel. The Dogon, it was quick to see, were justly renowned for their ornately carved doors. Each, unique, almost mesmerizing to behold.

There was no avoiding a comparison between Gamba and the Hopi cliff dwellings of Mesa Verde, an example, perhaps, of convergent evolution. Not precisely the same, but remarkably similar. All the villagers were quite insistent upon coming out to shake our hands, including the children, who greeted us without a stitch of clothing. Having shown up uninvited, this was all very humbling. Moussa was adamant that we return for another visit, and that we should, this time, bring everyone along.

Mark and I recounted, as best we could, our serendipitous encounter and as a group we traipsed over to Gamba the following morning, as bidden. Once again, all the villagers turned out, shaking hands with each and every one of us. The children danced and sang joyfully, as if a special holiday had just been declared. Questions were asked and answered in both directions, though never fully understood.

We were shown about and welcomed to take as many photographs as we liked, a rare privilege in Mali. In fact, encouraged to do so. It was not unusual in this part of the country to find women working topless. The men, in a curious reversal of cultures, NEVER SO, by the way. We tried our best to be discreet about it when taking photos. There was no quid pro quo, no expectation of anything in return. Just the same, I asked Moussa if there was anything I could do for him. He gave it a little thought and pointed to the leather wineskin (Spanish bota) I used as a canteen for water. I would have happily given him my own, but I had a long journey ahead of me still and was not ready to part with it. I took his mailing address and promised to send him one when I returned to Canada. He seemed content with that.

It's hard to put into words the sense of privilege, let alone awe, that you feel after a visit such as this. You could have heard a pin drop in the back of The Pig for hours after taking our leave, so extraordinary was the experience.

The scenery along the road from Somadougou to Bankass was exquisite, unspoiled grassland dotted with broad baobab. We camped near the village of Koro, about 35 kilometers from the border, clearing customs and immigration the following morning without the slightest difficulty. Only a small outpost marked the border with Upper Volta. The border guards gave us a very cursory examination and sent us on our way with instructions to clear customs at Thiou, another 25 kilometers to the southeast, and on the main road to the capital, Ouagadougou.

The Upper Volta countryside was mostly thorny brush. The villages consisted of small walled-in family compounds that looked to me like something you might find in a movie about serfs living in medieval times.

We had no problem with customs or immigration at Thiou either, but it was a different story when we reached the town of Ouahigouya where we were required to "register" with the police. Our documents were reviewed, stamped, and then reviewed again, our vehicle carefully examined for contraband. The whole process took hours with nothing for us to do but stand about, but hey, we had reached Upper Volta!

"MY TRIP" – JOURNAL No. 2

IN CONTRAST TO THE ARDUOUS EXAMINATION we were forced to undergo at Ouahigouya, the brief police stops coming in and out of the smaller towns were nothing to complain about. Not knowing what to call a person from Upper Volta, I just up and asked. "Voltaics," I learned was the proper demonym, which just seemed plain weird to me. After the country was renamed Burkina Faso, they became Burkinabé, which I find so much more palatable.

In the districts we drove through, a typical Voltaic mud-brick compound with a few goats and chickens included two or three circular buildings with thatched roofs and a tinned-over shed. You would often see women working together in rhythm to pound millet beneath what little shade a baobab tree had to offer, while a buzzard or two picked at the kitchen midden in search of gastronomical treasures, all but oblivious to the humans working nearby.

The road to the capital was in good repair. Ouagadougou (or "Ouaga," for short), was an exciting, bustling metropolis, a giant marketplace where mopeds and bicycles fill the gaps between cars. There were soldiers posted at every major intersection and anti-aircraft gun emplacements protecting the government buildings. In the shallow culverts that edged the broad unpaved avenues, it was quite common to see flocks of vultures and rooting pigs.

The National Revolutionary Council of the recently installed head of state, Captain Thomas Sankara, was just beginning to stretch its wings. We were back to being called "comarade" again, which I heartily approved of, but found the widespread propaganda troubling. If I passed anyone with a transistor radio pressed to their ear, they were invariably tuned to the show trials of the former regime up on charges of corruption.

I decided that I should exploit any opportunity to rest and booked myself into the Hotel Kadiogo for 3,000CFAF ($7 US) per night. Owing to all the police checks, visas, visa extensions, and SMERT registrations, there was almost no more space left in my passport, and it was an augmented business size. So, I dashed over to the Canadian embassy where a staff member, named Lebel, much to my relief, glued an accordion-style eight-page extension into my passport.

That evening most of the group gathered at Chez Tantie, a popular eatery (which, I understand, is still in business) where we chowed down on hearty plates of "riz gras"—tomato rice topped with a generous portion of grilled fish steak and boiled greens. The wait staff had the most endearing habit of shaking each customer's hand before taking their order. I discovered too, that, at least in Ouagadougou, people spoke a smattering of English.

Then it was over to the club Rendezvous Chez Ami next to l'Hôtel Tropicale where we danced to disco beats and drank colas until sometime before curfew. The club was jammed with young people intent on having a good time. Dancing was foremost on their minds and none of the locals seemed particularly surprised to see us. If this was one of the poorest countries in the world (based on GDP per capita), Voltaics seemed utterly unaware of it. Even in Bamako, the capital of Mali, horse carts and donkeys comprised a major mode of transportation. But in Ouagadougou, horses and donkeys were few and far between, the streets jammed with motorcycles, mopeds, and bicycles. In Mali it was hard to find a soft drink, but in Upper Volta even the smallest village was well stocked with soda pop and beer. You could get a Coca-Cola in Ouagadougou for the equivalent of 24 cents US.

Plainly, I had pressed my luck trying out the local fare. Too far this time. My diarrhea returned with a vengeance in the middle of the night. I could hardly stand up the next morning, my legs quaking beneath me with each step. Yet again, I'd fooled myself into believing that feeling better was a license to live like a normal healthy person. This was serious and no amount of Lomatil, Imodium, or Intétrix was going to improve the situation. I needed to see a doctor. But not until I'd gone with the others to the Nigerian embassy to apply for visas (priorities, eh). Unhappily, the embassy staff turned us away for unexplained reasons, suggesting that we might fare better inquiring at the embassy in Togo.

I made my way back to the Canadian embassy and, explaining my situation, asked Monsieur Lebel if he could suggest a local doctor. He made a quick call on my behalf and told me that the doctor favored by embassy staff, a Togolese, came highly recommended and would expect me that afternoon.

Dr. Ayessou's office was near the Hotel Michael and, as I recall, a sort of annex off of a very fine home, not his actual clinic.[10] Although a practicing gynecologist and obstetrician (not exactly what I needed), he was certified in internal medicine. He spoke very little English, and my French was not quite up to snuff when it came to my ability to describe my symptoms. Nevertheless, he questioned me patiently and methodically from behind an elegantly appointed desk, then came around to check my vitals.

The doctor pulled no punches describing for me the dangers of dehydration. Naturally, he wanted to do a thorough exam and send off samples to a lab, but there just wasn't time. I pleaded my case and was prescribed Sacolène for treating acute diarrhea, Hordenol (concentrated caffeine) to rouse me from my lethargy, and Bactrim Forte, an antibiotic. He also provided me with a quantity of UNICEF

---

[10] Clinique Koumda Gnonre.

rehydration sachets, for free, of course. I thought to myself, if this doesn't do the trick, what chance do I have?

Before I left, Dr. Ayessou asked me a few obvious questions about my travels through Africa thus far. I got the distinct impression he thought our expedition amounted to little more than a bit of frivolous self-indulgence but was far too polite to say so. It can't have been easy for a doctor working in one of the poorest nations in the world. When I asked him about himself, he told me that he took in a small number of foreign (meaning White) patients and charged them well for his service, but only to help pay for the clinic and to supplement his research and work amongst the less advantaged. I was truly grateful for the time and attention he paid to me. He charged me the princely sum of 2,500CFAF (about $6 US) for the consultation. I thought there'd been a mistake, but he apparently did not place me in the same category as his usual embassy referrals.

I'm pretty certain the Blédilac would not have been enough on its own to see me through the remainder of my journey. I wasted no time filling the prescriptions and taking my medicine (the pharmacy shelves were chock-full of supplies compared to Mali), crossing my fingers and hoping for the best before going to sleep that night. The combination of meds turned out to be quite effective and I was back to a semblance of normal within a few days. Of course, "normal" was a relative term because no one's stomach is ever quite right traveling and living as I was.

A strict curfew ran from 11 p.m. to 5 in the morning. I never thought to test it. I was up early the next day, feeling pretty good on the whole and rather astonished by how quickly the medicine had taken effect. I walked straight to the main post office and was bummed to find, once again, no letter from Edi.

There was a row of old-style telephone booths to one side. I decided to give one a try. Working through the international operator I placed a call to her. I heard Edi answer the phone, but the connection was terrible, all static.

To make matters worse, she apparently thought it was a call from someone in her family, either from Spain or Uruguay, and kept repeating "¿Quien habla?" (Who's calling?). I don't suppose Edi ever imagined I would try to phone her from Africa. I shouted, "Edi, it's Neil! It's Neil!" But to no avail. The operator actually apologized to me for failing to make the connection and did not charge for the call. Anyway, it was nice to hear her voice.

A pit stop in northern Togo

After checking out of the hotel, I re-joined the group and we set off for Togo, a tiny sliver of a country that extends down the "hump" of Africa to the Atlantic Ocean. About 100 kilometers shy of the border, we stopped to camp near the village of Tenkodogo, a desolate sort of place, but there was a neat little shop selling crafts made by students at a school for people with disabilities. A small three-sectioned change purse made from soft pig skin caught my eye. It was an original design and brilliantly crafted. The little wallet is still functional and attractive after nearly forty years. It's not unusual for people to comment on it when they see it.

Crossing the border was smooth sailing, no surprise fees, interrogations, or inordinate bureaucracy. I never understood why, but the Togo authorities told me that Canadians did not require a visa, something the French embassy in Algiers, apparently, was unaware of. We could tell right off that Togo was considerably more developed than Upper Volta. I would have expected the differences along the border to have been more gradual. Heading south, the landscape varied between savanna, cotton fields, and great swaths of farmland being cleared with fire. Our heads swiveled in all directions, cameras at the ready, when we passed a road sign that read "Danger éléphant," but no elephants ever made an appearance.

That night, we pitched our tents atop a dense bed of dead leaves on what I would consider classic African savanna, near the village of Dapaong—a lightly forested area, interspersed with brush and grass. It was a beautiful clear night and Barry helped me to identify Betelgeuse within the constellation Orion. As we parted for the evening and were heading to our tents a hush fell suddenly over the camp. We stood frozen mid-step, ears tuned to an unexpected sound. There were drums in the night.

I crawled into my bivvy bag and fought the need to sleep, unwilling to let the electrifying rhythm of the nearby drums go, but exhaustion soon won out and I drifted off into a deep, deep sleep. I was awakened in the early morning darkness, however, not by the sound of drums, but something even more unexpected and closer to home—the sound of millions of chewing insects.

They were underneath my rubberized groundsheet, they were outside the walls of my tent, they were in the bush that surrounded us. Termites. Countless millions of them. Our campsite was alive with them, chewing on anything that was vaguely organic and we were camped right in the middle of ground zero. It takes time for the mind to focus coming out of a deep sleep. The sound must have built up slowly, enough that our brains couldn't quite make sense of it. We were all of us awakened about the same time by the gnawing crescendo and scrambled panic-like from our tents. George and Malcolm shouted for everyone to clear out quickly and not to trouble ourselves with carcful packing.

About two hours down the road we entered the boundary of the Parc Nationale de la Keran where we strained our eyes and necks hoping to catch a glimpse of big game. Our quarry, I suppose, were smart enough to stay clear of the main road. Our one and only treat was the sight of a large primate in a tree. I don't know if it was intentional or not, but a great stretch of the country south of the park appeared to have been ravaged by fire not long before our passage. I wondered if Togolese farmers in the northern half of the country engaged in wholesale slash-and-burn agriculture and to what extent this encroached on the great forests to the south.

Traveling down the road we passed groups of playful children on their way to school all sporting trim school uniforms. Every village of moderate size seemed to have its own small but well-built schoolhouse. The country also seemed to have a prosperous, if small-scale, manufacturing capability, including cement, roofing, plastics, even textiles.

The farther south we went, the more mountainous and noticeably tropical grew the scenery. We reached Lama-Kara (or "Kara") by mid-afternoon, owing to our early start. Kara boasted a thriving open market that included a dizzying array of Voodoo ("Vodun") amulets, fetishes, and reliquaries. There were animal skulls and bones of every imaginable variety, powders, feathers, pelts, polished stones, seashells and small lustrous carved figures bound with wire. You could make your selection based on intuition or seek the guidance of a fetish priest on hand in the market. There was no doubt in my mind that this was all rather routine fare to the Togolese going about their shopping, but an unsettling, if fascinating novelty, for those exposed to Voodoo practices for the first time.

The most astonishing thing happened as we were boarding The Pig and about to depart Kara. A young man came up alongside the truck to stand right below where I was seated. He took stock for a moment as if weighing out whether to ask me something and finally bucked up the courage, "Where are you from?"

"Canada" I replied, to which he responded, "Where in Canada?"

"Toronto."

He hesitated once again, then asked, "Have you ever heard of Queen's University?"

My jaw dropped in bewilderment. 'Queen's University'?! My alma mater? Now Queen's has always had a pretty solid reputation, but the student population of Queen's at the time was probably fewer than ten thousand. I've never been very good at math, but the chances of this young man or anyone else encountering a Queen's student during our very arbitrary pit-stop at Lama-Kara could not have been less than one in a hundred million.

"Hold up!" I yelled to Malcolm. The few companions sitting nearest to me and close enough to pick up on this extraordinary exchange moved in to hear how it would play out.

"My name is Flavien. Clive Thomson, an assistant professor from the Queen's University French Department, was here to do research. I was a student, and he was very kind to me. Would you pass Clive a message from me?"

"Sure. If I can find him when I return home. How long ago was he here?" I asked.

"Maybe two years," replied Flavien. "We have been writing to one another ever since." I took out my journal to note down Flavien's message in point form:

'I had to drop out of school because I am ill. I start to cry if I stare at a paper for more than a minute and occasionally see double. I know what I want to write down but can no longer draw the letters. I have pain in the left side of my chest when I lower my head to the left. The doctors do not know what is wrong with me.'

He looked up at me with pleading eyes. "Will you tell Clive, please. He could not know why I suddenly stopped writing to him. He will want to help if he can."

I showed Flavien my journal to prove to him that I'd written down his message, then handed it to him and asked him to write his own address on the opposite page. He did so with the help of a friend. "It might take months to get him the message," I emphasized, "and that is only if I can find him."

Flavien was happy enough with that assurance. "Thank you. God speed."

Rather than keep you in suspense, I'll tell you now that when I returned to Kingston, I was indeed able to track down Clive. He remembered Flavien fondly and recounted for me how this young Togolese had accompanied him during his research and had been an eager pupil and helpmate. Like anyone who has heard this story, Clive marveled at the odds of my encounter. We both openly wondered just how many passing globetrotters Flavien, in his determination, had approached before he'd finally encountered someone from Queen's who could pass along his message. Clive promised, in any case, that he would write to Flavien and I left it at that. Whether he was able to help restore Flavien to health, I cannot say, but I do know for a fact that 23 years later (2007), Flavien, or someone who closely matches his description, was instrumental in helping rebuild an abandoned schoolhouse for the village of Kpézindé.

George was intent on making up time while the roads were good and the traffic was light, so we ended up doing about 350 kilometers in a single day all the way from Kara to Kpimé, traversing about a third of this tiny country, the very central part.

The road snaked through forested mountains, offering sweeping vistas off to the horizon. We noted, with some alarm, the number of breaches in the guard rails where drivers had failed to navigate a turn and tumbled, perhaps to their doom. Since we witnessed no such event during the day, we could only suppose this was one of the hazards of nighttime driving in Togo. Still, Malcolm needed to be attentive. School children with their books and women carrying great loads of produce or firewood balanced atop their heads walked along the edge of the road, trusting drivers to keep an eye out for them.

It is hard to imagine, but Togo was Germany's prized possession in Africa until 1914, a by-product of the murderous competition for empire. August 1914, French and German forces skirmished at the first town we passed, Bafilo. The colony fell to a combined French and British force shortly after. All these years later, Togo was still a popular destination for German tourists. It was not unusual to see signs posted in German as well as French, or to hear German spoken in a restaurant.

Bafilo was a Muslim enclave. The men and women we encountered dressed in traditional North African garments, much like those we'd seen in Morocco. Past Bafilo, the women we saw walking along the side of the road or in the markets generally wore the same elaborately patterned skirts we'd seen in Niger and Upper Volta. The difference seemed to be that Togolese women, more often than not, preferred simple Western-style tops. Skirt lengths were shorter too, anywhere from the ankle to below the knee.

There were plenty of magnificent waterfalls in central Togo. We paid a quick visit to the cascade de Ayomé and rested at Notre Dame d'Ayomé, an unpretentious whitewashed open air church of contemporary design nestled into the hillside. For a country where traditional African religions account for the beliefs of about one third of the population, Togo must have claimed bragging rights to more churches per capita than any other country in Africa. Every small town we passed through seemed to have a dozen houses of worship.

I'd been lounging about Notre Dame d'Ayomé for several minutes before I realized there was a bloody great lizard, a meter or more in length, sunning itself atop a low wall almost within arm's reach. From what I learned later, the creature was not native to the country. Probably a Nile

Monitor brought to central Togo as part of the fetish trade, but obviously feeling quite at home.

We camped that night on the grounds of a fruit plantation within walking distance of the cascade (or "barrage") de Kpimé and the hydro-electric station. I felt, for the first time, that I'd reached the tropics. It was hot and humid and the forest, albeit largely tamed, surrounded us. It was an idyllic setting, the waterfall framed with tropical crawlers and lacy ferns, elusive monkeys chattering away on the cliff face.

I walked with Mark and Lila into town where our boots echoed off the boardwalk. There was no power after dark, but people were out enjoying themselves and the shops were open, kerosene lamps on outdoor tables casting a soft yellow glow and long flickering shadows. It was easy to make acquaintances in this relaxed and pleasant atmosphere.

We were asked if we had sampled Togolese food, something the inhabitants were evidently proud of. We couldn't say we had as yet, and that was quickly remedied. I was feeling well for a change and tempting fate decided there was just no way I was going to miss out on sampling the local fare. I was supplied with a generous bowl of "Akume," a savory porridge made from corn ("maize") flour and fermented cassava, the same plant used to produce tapioca. This was washed down with a tall glass of "Tchakpallo," a beer made from fermented millet (the fellow that supplied me with my drink called it "Tokutu"). Both the beer and the porridge were as good as advertised, particularly the beer.

Seventy-one days out of London, we reached Togo's capital, Lomé. Having successfully crossed the "hump" of Africa, we celebrated by driving right up to the Atlantic shore of the Gulf of Guinea and sticking our feet into the water. After so many days traveling the interior, it was a thrill to breathe the salt air and to cast our eyes over the endless expanse of ocean. The Sûreté Nationale, a division of the Interior Ministry, was able to extend our Togo visas for less than a dollar, long enough that we didn't have to rush off, and an added opportunity to do a little more exploring.

Finding a reasonably priced campsite was no easy task, however. A couple of lucky inquiries led us to the village chief of Davikami. Chief Yassou Koffi invited us to camp within his personal compound on a handshake and an agreement to provide him with "reasonable compensation."

You won't find Davikami on any map that I'm familiar with. Don't quote me on this, but I "believe" it lay within Baguida, a canton of Lomé, about 10 or 11 kilometers east of the capital. We were given to understand the village was divided into six divisions and boasted a population of about 300.

The author, with children of Chief Yassou Koffi at Davikami

The chief's stave-enclosed compound was postcard perfect—cool palm-frond huts with thatched roofs sitting on a thick bed of warm sand amongst a random planting of coconut palms, ficus, and cocoa trees. There were children everywhere, not surprising, given that the chief had four wives and "about" 20 children.

We were more or less adopted by his "second wife," Josephine, as sweet and generous as anyone could be. Josephine's kitchen was a simple firepit near the entrance to one of the huts. She was frightfully superstitious. Every time

I saw her add salt to a meal, a pinch went over her shoulder. She worked tirelessly from sunup to sundown and looked to be about 60 or 70, although her actual age was 45.

The young women of West Africa were generally some of the most handsome I've met in all my travels over the years, but it seemed to me that they aged very rapidly after reaching 25 or so, due in part to the many hardships they endure. The men, on the other hand, rode donkeys or sat in the front of the canoe while the women paddled or walked ahead with gargantuan loads of wood or water carried on top their heads. I don't know about today, but at that time, equity, let alone fairness, did not seem part of the West African gender equation.

A bunch of us went out in the morning to help the villagers place their nets or to help haul them in. We were paid for our services in either fish or cash. I made good friends with one of the chief's young sons, Bogart, named after the actor, believe it or not. I went for a swim in the Atlantic, awestruck by all that water after weeks traversing the Sahara and the Sahel. The children shared their homework with me, and it seemed to me they were receiving a good education. As the chief's offspring, their experience may not have been typical.

Our second day in Davikami, I went with most of the others into Lomé. I was intent on picking up a few tiny but distinctive gifts to take back home to Canada and was reasonably pleased with what I found. As a novelty, I picked up a hippopotamus tooth from a vendor of Voodoo charms.

The Musée national was open, and I opted to take in the history of slavery exposition. It was eye-opening, of course, but standing in the historical vortex, so to speak, somehow made it all that more poignant. Although a worthwhile and important experience, it was disturbing, and I felt better for a trip to the beach afterward. I swam in the ocean, watched zillions of tiny crabs go about their lives, then napped on the sand until Malcolm showed up with The Pig and drove us back to camp.

Another day in Davikami, the mosquitoes were oppressive. I opted to converse with the chief's children, repairing the worn-out soles of my boots, and mending the holes in my tent left from the termites outside of Dapaong. That evening, I went with Mark and a few others to watch traditional Togolese dancers at l'Hôtel Sarakawa. After the show, a "fire eater" performing with the troop shared his homemade palm whisky with us. It didn't take me long to realize that the term "fire eater" was a play on words. I knew better than to try the stuff but turning down a drink freely given was easily misconstrued.

Mark was approached by a fellow offering Nigerian currency (naira) on the black market at an exceptionally good rate. His pitch was that we would never do as well if we waited to exchange currency in Nigeria. A couple of discreet inquiries confirmed this. I intended on spending a little more in Nigeria, in any case, and the "official" bank rate at the time was anywhere from .67 to .73 naira (₦) to the US dollar. Word was I could get as much as 2.1₦ to the dollar on the black market, so that was the bar I set for myself.

This is where a talent for foreign currency gymnastics comes in handy because I would be trading CFA francs for naira, not dollars for naira. See if you can follow this: The black marketeer was offering one naira at the "unofficial" rate of 140CFAF. If a dollar was going for 412CFAF in Lomé, that came, by my reckoning, to about 2.94₦ to the dollar. Good deal. The black marketeer, however, would only deal with Mark. Too many cooks, apparently, spoil the broth, but I was permitted to observe the transaction.

Retaining just enough CFA francs by my calculation to see me through, I handed the balance, 14,000CFAF, to Mark and consented to make the exchange. Now, black market deals are not generally conducted in the open. They are done clandestinely in a quiet corner where no prying eyes can witness the interaction and the chances of being collared by the police minimized. All this is meant to say, the transaction, once agreed upon, is quickly completed and the parties concerned go their separate ways without delay or fanfare. Mark handed the gentleman my 14,000. In return, the fellow counted off and placed in Mark's hand 100 naira (theoretically, equal to about $34 US) in small denomination bills, which amounted to a fair-sized wad. The man then thanked us for doing business and disappeared in the blink of an eye.

Mark fingered the pile of naira and began to turn them over to me, one at a time, counting off ". . . 55, 60, 65 . . . ." He paused mid-count, the realization dawning on his face. "70, 71, 72, 73, 74, 75" he continued. And the final note in the bunch, "76. Seventy-six naira," repeated Mark, dejectedly. Our black marketeer was evidently also a sleight of hand artist! Somehow, he'd managed to palm twenty-four naira in front of our very eyes. My actual rate, given the loss of 24₦, was closer to 184CFAF to the naira, rather than the promised 140. I still made out on the deal as compared to the official bank rate of .67₦, just not as well as I'd expected. Caveat emptor.

It was time to move on. I would have liked to have spent a day or two in Ghana, as the border was within spitting distance, but that would have taken us in the wrong direction and would have taken too much time to obtain the necessary visa. We bid Chief Koffi, Josephine, and the chief's children an emotional farewell. Chief Koffi was content with a token payment for our stay plus 5,000CFAF ($12 US) to help repair the road in front of his compound. I gave Josephine a handsome necklace and ankle bracelet that I'd picked up in Lomé. It was small compensation indeed for their genuine hospitality. I hoped they'd enjoyed our visit as much as we'd enjoyed the welcome of their home.

Owing to the very peculiar political map of Togo and Benin, it was a journey of less than 40 kilometers to the border. We encountered no difficulties leaving Togo or entering Benin, but it did take a good three hours to process us through.

Before the French seized the territory in 1904, Benin had been, for several centuries, the Kingdom of Dahomey, famous for the courage and skill of its Mino warriors (so-called "Amazons"). It is a bit confusing, but the historical Kingdom of Bénin was situated in eastern Nigeria, not Dahomey. A simple explanation for the modern-day republic's name is that it was derived from its geographical location on the "Bight of Benin."

Every village we passed in Benin, no matter the size, maintained a Voodoo shrine within sight of the main road. These were generally fashioned from concrete in the shape of a large skull and bedecked with the sort of offerings we'd seen for sale in the Togolese markets. At the same time, churches were plentiful. The Béninois had no apparent trouble operating the two belief systems side-by-side.

We decided to "free camp" well outside of Cotonou, the largest city and financial hub of the country, setting ourselves up in the disused section of a schoolyard in the village of Houeke-Honou, near to Akassato on the road north to Abomey. In the wee hours of the night, we were awakened by the sound of drums and rapturous shrieks from the next field over, evidently part of a Voodoo ritual. The sounds, and my imagination, kept me awake well into the early morning hours.

Our camp was just north of Lake Nokoué and the village of Ganvié. Every guidebook we possessed suggested a day trip to Ganvié was worth the effort. All the homes and shops sit atop piles driven into the estuary of the Sô River. We arranged a group tour of the town by motorboat. It was fascinating, I had to admit, to see people living and conducting business all on the water. Instead of palatial homes and gondolas, Venice fashion, there were thatched huts and pirogues. I have only one or two photographs of my visit because a cadeau was demanded on each occasion. I could understand that. Tourism, otherwise, had no value to them.

I did find the human impact on the lake distressing. Lake Nokoué was the prime food-source for the better part of the country, but everything, I mean everything waste-related was dumped into that poor lake. Intellectually, I understood this was a desperately poor nation and day-to-day survival took precedence over anything else, but that didn't make the unconstrained pollution and its impact on people and the environment any easier to accept.

Our trip to Ganvié also furnished my first close encounter with a monkey. A young boy kept a tantalus monkey (Chlorocebus tantalus) on a leash on a patch of dry ground beneath one of the shops. I didn't know this monkey's story and wasn't in a position to judge how well it was cared for. To me, primates are not "pets" in the way we think of cats or dogs, so I had mixed feelings about the experience. Still, it was a fabulous encounter. The experience made it clear to me just how closely related our species are to one another.

The next day, we drove into the capital city of Benin, Porto-Novo, on the Yewa River. Greeting visitors entering the capital was a large red and white banner stretched high above the busy interchange with a simple message: "MORT AUX TRAÎTRES" (DEATH TO TRAITORS). Which pretty much set the tone. At the time, Benin was run by a Marxist-Leninist regime led by Mathieu Kérékou. I was fascinated by the fact that the country's national assembly was organized by profession rather than geographical divisions. The largest number of seats in the assembly were reserved for peasant farmers and craftsmen. There was even a certain number of seats reserved just for retirees. Imagine that! A bold, but ultimately doomed political experiment.

For the gift of a pineapple, we were able to get our exit stamp for Benin at the Foreign Residents' Registry Office. Our group then went off to explore the city while George, for the last possible opportunity, went to obtain visas for Nigeria. My stomach was in turmoil, so I opted to sit tight and "guard" The Pig. Mark came back to check on me after a couple of hours. By that time, I was doubled over in pain. "Mark," I pleaded. "You've got to find me somewhere to take a dump, and soon, or I may explode. I'm not joking."

He looked over the sea of humanity swirling around the truck. "I'll see what I can find," he replied, and disappeared into the crowd. I contemplated what the reaction would be if I dropped my drawers and let go right next to the vehicle. My guess was that it would not be well received. Every minute that ticked by was sheer agony, the gases within distending my belly and exerting so much pressure I could hardly breathe. Mark returned, thankfully, having found a place for me to relieve myself.

"It isn't far," he said, reassuringly. He helped me down from the tailgate and walked with me propped under one arm. Miraculously, a short block away, there was a smart-looking board and batten evangelical church atop a knoll, like an island oasis amidst the urban desert. As fate would have it, this was a Sunday (the 5th of February 1984). The church was filled to capacity, the congregation singing hymns in beautiful and passionate harmony.

Along the exterior wall of the church, affixed to it like a series of flying-buttresses, was a row of outdoor privies. Mark helped me into one and waited outside the door. The second I dropped my drawers, I exploded. This is no exaggeration, the gas and excrement shot out of me with an audible "bang," as if someone had fired off a cannon. The force of my evacuation, moreover, was so strong, it actually shook the outhouse walls, and as these were attached to the exterior of the church, it apparently reverberated through the adjoining wall.

To my everlasting shame and embarrassment, the congregation cut short their singing mid-hymn, several members rushing out in great alarm to investigate. Mark, very demurely, reassured them that no attack was in progress. It wasn't until I emerged and they could see from the vacated latrine that nothing was especially amiss, that they felt safe enough to return to their ministry, one or two of the parishioners shaking their heads in bewilderment. It was, otherwise, a pleasant sunny afternoon, and I was able to enjoy the ride the rest of the way, much relieved for having purged myself of the vexing contents of my stomach. George, to our great relief, had finally managed to secure the visas we needed for Nigeria.

We camped that evening off the coastal road, very close to the border. The Benin authorities charged us a token amount to exit the country the next day. There was a certain amount of excitement and anxiety associated with our crossing into Nigeria. We wondered at the impact of the recent coup d'état, and what effect it might have. Nigeria we knew to be a large, diverse, and dynamic country, an economic powerhouse in Africa. For me, it conjured up childhood memories of horrific starvation witnessed on television and the pages of magazines, the scene of a ruthless civil war over Biafran independence during the late 1960s.

For an "optional" 40₦ ($20 US at black market rates), we were able to avoid a detailed customs inspection. Malcolm had to personally fork out an additional 20₦ because his visa was stapled rather than glued into his passport. None of us had spoken much English except amongst ourselves since departing Dover and it was a strange feeling indeed to hear it once again on a day-to-day basis.

It was a 50-kilometer drive to the outskirts of Lagos, the capital at the time. A new capital, Abuja, was under development in the interior of the country, but would not be completed for another six years. Entering Lagos via the coastal road was a shock to the system. The four-lane highway was chockablock with transport trucks hauling all manner of goods under canvas, nose to bumper with small diesel spewing German-made cars and mini-buses.

A wide median divided traffic in either direction. This was filled with broken down vehicles, burning trash, empty diesel drums, and travelers pulled over to prepare meals over open campfires. At one point we passed the scene of an accident between two trucks. One had been hauling a load of longhorn cows, their bloated and rotted carcasses left in the center of the road until those responsible could muster the resources to clean up the mess, however long that might take.

A layer of red ochre-colored dust clung to everything that remained stationary for more than a minute and a gloomy haze hovered over the entire city. Along the unpaved side streets, homes, and shops with irregular corrugated tin roofs ran in nearly unbroken lines with nary a tree, bush, or blade of grass in sight. An open culvert filled with waste trailed down one side of each street, pedestrians, of necessity, forced to cross it on rough planks reclaimed from any number of sources. The city boasted a gazillion yellow cabs, adding to the general gridlock. The cab drivers felt a perverse need to lean on their horns at the slightest provocation. Hawkers weaved in and out of the stalled traffic selling everything from windshield wipers to fresh-baked samosas.

Outskirts of Lagos, Nigeria

I had no idea where we might find a campsite amidst all this urban sprawl. George, with one exception (more on that later), never let us down. On this occasion he somehow managed to convince the manager of the EKO Holiday Inn Hotel, just off the beachfront from Kuramo Waters, to allow us to camp free of charge in an adjoining compound where a Korean firm was constructing the new cafeteria.

The next morning, I accompanied Hazel, Bernard, Lila, and Alison to the main office of Union Bank, a Barclays subsidiary, to cash travelers checks. I had obtained my naira by other methods, as you may recall. The bank would only entertain Lila's request, as she had an account with Barclays, but even there she was stymied because they would only exchange travelers checks denominated in British sterling for pound notes, not naira. I don't recall how they managed after that. I suppose they used their ingenuity.

Owing to the differences in our nationalities, we each had to fend for ourselves to obtain Cameroon (or Cameroun) visas. Cameroon would not join the Commonwealth for another eleven years and thus maintained an embassy rather than a "high commission" in Nigeria. Lila and Alison buddied up with me on a cab to the embassy. The visa was cheap enough, 4.40₦ (just over $2 US), but required twenty-four hours to process. In a mood for more adventure, they opted to join me on a trip to the Mitsui office in the business district of Lagos. I was concerned about the silence from home and hoped the Mitsui staff would help me to send a Telex message to my father. The letter of introduction that my father had prepared in advance would now either prove or disprove its worth.

Mitsui, an international trading firm, did big business in Nigeria, buying and selling everything from canned fish and Toyotas to freighter loads of raw minerals. A staff member read my father's letter, which suitably impressed him. Enough for the man to usher us over to the executive director's office. I had my trepidations about how we would be received, because after 79 days living out of the back of a truck, we were all of us looking a bit ragged.

Mr. Uwhubetine was the Nigerian face for an otherwise very Japanese operation. He greeted us very cordially, politely enquiring about our travels before handing us over to his managing director, Mr. Kawachi, a Japanese national, who offered me the opportunity to use the telephone to call my father. Much better than an impersonal Telex. Unfortunately, it was too early in the day owing to the time difference. Much to my delight, however, he agreed to ship the sword I'd purchased in Agadez to Canada, relieving me of that particular burden.

He was clearly fascinated by the whole idea of traveling in a group from London to Kenya, so much so that he surprised all three of us with a dinner invitation at his home that very evening so that we might continue the conversation. Moreover, Mr. Kawachi offered to let me call my father on the phone from his house.

We traveled back to camp, washed our hair, cleaned under our fingernails, and rummaged about for some decent attire. Lila and Alison conjured up a couple of becoming outfits and applied a hint of makeup. I'd brought along a white permanent-press sports jacket, which I fished out from the bottom of my kit and donned for the first time out of respect for our hosts, while the rest of our companions looked on in amusement. We caught a cab to the official Mitsui residence on Victoria Island. To my chagrin, I somehow mangled the "plot number" on Akin-Olugbade Street. The cabbie was at least able to get us to the correct street. After that, we were on our own.

It was a gated community of elegant mansions and small landscaped gardens, a far cry, indeed, from the dirt and hub-hub of the suburbs (I understand the area has since been redeveloped and is almost unrecognizable). But which house? We puzzled out the address as best we could and girded up the courage to knock on the door. We were greeted by the mistress of the house, a very elegant and well-spoken woman by the name of "Mrs. Rowe." Evidently not the right address.

Mrs. Rowe was the epitome of charm and hospitality. She invited us to wait in her living room and served us refreshments, while she researched the address to the Mitsui residence in the phone book. Her home was like a movie-set from the 1930s or '40s, filled with precious artifacts from all over Africa, even a few pet monkeys. It turned out that the Mitsui residence was just two doors down. We were soon knocking on the correct door, somehow still on-time for supper.

Mr. Kawachi had a good laugh at our story about showing up at the wrong house, then introduced us to his wife and children. There was another guest present, a Japanese mendicant monk traveling the world. This took some education on our part. We learned about Zen monks undertaking takuhatsu—a rite in which the monk, free from ego and possessions, offers Dharma (spiritual teachings) or a chanted sutra (scripture), in exchange for food or money.

In Zen Buddhism this form of almsgiving (dana) is a virtuous act that lifts and ennobles. In Japan, takuhatsu may be the only means of supporting members of an entire temple. In more recent years, monks, like Mr. Kawachi's guest, had expanded on the rite to travel the world as part of a personal journey of limited duration, or as a step toward higher aptitude, expanding their horizons while bringing spiritual comfort to the adherents of Zen Buddhism. It can't have been an easy life. Certainly not without risk. The young man in question impressed me in terms of both his knowledge and fortitude. Mr. Kawachi was plainly honored to have him as a guest.

The conversation was otherwise wide-ranging. We were, I thought, probed with thoughtful questions about what we hoped to achieve by our experience in Africa and about our impressions thus far. There seemed to be a particular curiosity about the difference between West and North African cultures, at least from our perspective.

It was hands-down a thoroughly enjoyable evening and a memorable one, especially given the unexpectedness of it. I gave my father quite a shock when I called him at his office. We thanked the Kawachi family profusely for their hospitality and I gave Mrs. Kawachi a small malachite lion that I'd picked up in Lomé as a token of our appreciation.

Her husband, after all, had sprung our invitation to dinner on her that very afternoon. She seemed not the least perturbed by it, so I hope she enjoyed the evening as much as we did.

The next couple of days in Lagos were uneventful, but no less memorable. I hung out with Mark at the hotel coffee shop, the Kuramo Café. The hotel was still under construction, so there was little traffic and little for the wait staff to do but chat up the few customers on hand. Several waiters were plainly fascinated by our expedition. One in particular, Sylvester Edien, was a kind-hearted dreamer with an endless stream of questions. He may have thought his interrogation of us an imposition that warranted a favor in return, because our bill was always discounted, which only encouraged us to keep coming back. The further we traveled, the more people it seemed were astounded by our accomplishment. Mark, I have to add, suffered a true identity crisis. Very few people we encountered had ever heard of New Zealand and the realization cut him to the core.

The Number 84 Racecourse Bus into town was just 10 kobo, the equivalent of five cents. I picked up my Central African Republic visa for 15₦ and paid a quick visit to the National Museum to see their display of magnificent Benin bronzes. These artworks, plundered during colonial times, were especially cherished by Western museums and collectors, and are now the subject of repatriation efforts. It was also an education on the major linguistic and cultural groups that inhabit Nigeria. Lagos, for example, was primarily Yoruba. Heading east, we would mostly encounter Edo in Benin City and Igbo in Enugu. Far to the north, where we would not be venturing, there were Hausa and Fulani. These are among the largest of Nigeria's tribal groups, which have been estimated to total anywhere from 250 to 400.

Tangentially (I don't know how it is today), it was impossible in 1984 not to be struck by the inordinate number of Nigerians suffering from Albinism, a genetic disorder that impacts the amount of melanin pigment in the skin, hair, and eyes, imparting a starkly white or bleached appearance to their features. These unfortunate individuals suffered from higher rates of cancer and poor eyesight as well as the unwanted attention their condition garnered, much of it, apparently, based on superstition.

Incidentally, the practice or habit of calling Whites "Boss" (patron) in Mali bothered me, but that was nothing in comparison to being called "Master"(!) in Lagos, no matter how innocently. At first, I thought I was mishearing, that they were saying "Mister." I corrected, or rather chastised, the individuals concerned without hesitation, often to their astonishment. "It's not appropriate," I would tell them, "Stop doing it," but this just seemed to compound the problem.

During the time we camped in Lagos, I made the trip into town four or five times which meant that I passed the same stretch of beach several times over in both directions. That short walk remains one of the most powerful and poignant memories of my entire time in Africa. A small colony of raggedly dressed children, apparently homeless and/or orphaned, camped by the water living in a rabbit warren fashioned from cardboard, wire, and empty oil drums, relying on one another for the necessities of life. They played at running down the beach rolling iron hoops on the point of a stick, always greeting us with laughter and song, joyous grins painted across their playful faces. I was sort of reminded of the "Lost Boys" of Barrie's Peter Pan.

We rarely walked in groups larger than three or four, but with twenty in our expedition I suppose there was no avoiding our constant presence during the few days we camped beside Kuramo Waters as there were few, if any, other White tourists promenading along that stretch of beach so soon after the coup. The older children, if only for the novelty of it, took to competing with one another for the chance to help us carrying our shopping as far as the hotel compound, the littlest ones delighting in our willingness to hold their tiny hands as we walked along together.

I could be wrong, but I think the children were generally regarded locally as a nuisance and the little attention we paid to them welcomed and received in kind. It goes without saying that we offered these incredible kids modest rewards for their courtesy and the pleasure of their company, but this they steadfastly refused making it abundantly clear that the pleasure was all theirs!

On parting, they would wave to us gleefully and return to their desperately difficult lives. Try as I may to remember their ability to find joy in the smallest of things, their irrepressible spirit, and hope-filled eyes, I struggle with the thought that their disposition would inevitably succumb to the harsh realities of their world. I don't doubt for a moment that they were quite aware of their predicament. Somehow, they knew instinctively to capture every ounce of happiness within their grasp while the grasping was good. The world is a cruel place, I think, to routinely stifle such genuine innocence, but I'm blessed for having witnessed it. The memory reminds me that such places and people exist somewhere on earth, and it fuels hope in me during times of personal despair.

The other great memory I have of Kuramo Waters was of the street vendor who kept a food stand just outside the compound gate. He made a spicey Spanish omelet to order that was habit-forming. I was able to bundle it for a discount together with a half-loaf of fresh-baked bread and a cup of hot Ovaltine.

The bread sold by street vendors throughout West Africa deserves special mention. It was baked fresh in the middle of the night in traditional brick or clay ovens and sold for next to nothing. Because of health regulations in the West, we rarely experience the flavor of bread baked "the old-fashioned way," employing ingredients and techniques that many parts of Africa still enjoyed. Even so-called "artisan" breads, sold at a premium, would be hard pressed to compete with a fresh baguette purchased at a food stand in Lagos for the equivalent of 27 cents. "Progress" isn't everything it's made out to be.

Although I was intimidated by Lagos at first, the city and the people quickly grew on me. I suppose that had something to do with being able to speak English pretty much everywhere. That said, there were certain formalities that had to be learned and observed. Being too direct could raise a disapproving brow. If, for example, you needed to use the toilet, the polite expression was to ask, "where do I pay my water rates?" ("loo" and "w.c.," let alone "toilet" were considered vulgar). Notwithstanding these minor differences, it was easy to strike up a conversation and there was still so much about the city to discover.

Unavoidably, it came time to move on. Our next objective was Benin City (Nigeria), about 300 kilometers to the east. Formerly known as Edo, Benin City was once the capital of the Bénin Kingdom and still home to its titular heir, the Oba of Benin. It was a long drive, so we made plenty of rest stops. I was struck by several changes as we headed farther east. The first noticeable change was the disappearance of mosquitos. I have no idea how or why this occurred, but I was hugely grateful for the reprieve, no matter how fleeting.

From what I could discern, the Nigerian states of Bendel and Anambra combined to form the evangelical Christian heartland of Nigeria. The region was flush with trim white churches and roadside billboards proclaiming the Gospel. It was not unusual to see men sporting blazers and starched white shirts, carrying themselves like Witnesses on God's mission. Panhandlers were non-existent. Weirdly, only ten days earlier, very nearly every village in Benin that we passed through boasted a Voodoo shrine. The contrast was surreal.

We camped in a town just on the outskirts of Benin City, a sort of miniature version of Lagos. The markets sold bush meat—wild animals harvested from the hinterland. I did my best to avoid those stalls. Unavoidable, however, because it was sold so pervasively, was the giant cane rat (Thryonomys swinderianus), cooked up fried, grilled, or stewed, no part of the body wasted. Cane rats resemble, in many ways, our muskrat and may even taste alike. I wouldn't actually know because I've never deliberately tasted muskrat. Street vendors sold various kinds of suya (kabobs) spiced with peanut, salt, and oil and eaten together with akamu (or "pap"), a fermented corn prepared and served much like Hawaiian poi. One of my favorite dishes were fritters made from beans mixed with red chili peppers. Plantains were cooked up and served the way North Americans enjoy potatoes.

We drove into Benin City proper on Sunday morning to stock up on a few last-minute supplies before continuing east. Just as we were gathering back at The Pig, a beautiful blue carriage pulled by two handsome grays passed right next to where we were parked. The carriage belonged to the Oba of Benin. King Erediauwa, the hereditary ruler of the Edo people, was one of a great many rulers of traditional African states whose titles and moral authority are still recognized by the modern nation-states that have eclipsed and absorbed their predecessors. We were told that the Oba enjoyed meeting visitors from abroad at his palace, which would have been an amazing experience. Our bad luck, it was Sunday, his day for personal reflection. Erediauwa died in 2016 and the title passed to his son, Ewuare II. The Oba of Benin remains one of the most influential and renowned traditional rulers in Africa.

Mark and I took another turn at riding up above the cab at our first rest stop after Benin City. We were up there enjoying the unobstructed view for perhaps ten minutes when we were spotted by a Nigeria Police Force (NPF) patrol. Two vehicles revved into high gear and came storming after us, sirens blaring. When Malcolm pulled over, one constable ran to watch our tailgate while two others raced to the front of the cab, gesticulating and shouting angrily, their ire very obviously directed at Mark and myself.

The senior officer present, wearing a crisp set of khakis and a natty forge cap, the very epitome of British military fashion, stood silently and discreetly to one side.

"Come down! Come down!" his subordinates shouted. We meekly obeyed and were soundly berated for our "stunt."

The police apparently considered people riding atop the cab a threat to public safety. We were, of course, curious why and politely asked them to explain. "Bandits," they replied curtly and somewhat enigmatically.

We apologized for any misunderstanding and promised not to do it again. Even so, a small cash "fine" payable on the hop was apparently required. I watched as George handed the money over to one of the constables. The senior officer overseeing this pathetic shakedown took the opportunity to go for a short stroll, one hand folded within the other in the crook of his back, but not far enough away that I couldn't see the S.O.B. turn his palm open to receive our payout and then quickly slip it into his own pocket. I wanted very badly to run over and dress him down in front of his subordinates as a disgrace to his country and his uniform, but of course I did nothing of the sort. I had no misgivings about what these men were capable of.

Mark and I rejoined our fellow passengers in the back of The Pig, staring morosely out the window at the passing scenery. A few kilometers shy of the Niger River, the words of the NPF came into dramatic focus—lying next to the road in the hot afternoon sun was the hideously bloated remains of a human being! Malcolm, very wisely, kept on driving. For the second time, we each gave real thought to our own safety (the first time, if you recall, was at In Guezzam).

An impressive truss bridge spanned the Niger, rebuilt after the civil war of 1967 to '70, connecting the states of

Bendel and Anambra.[11] The bridge was one of the first casualties in a long and brutal war, simultaneously competing for my attentions as a child alongside the Vietnam War and riots following the assassination of Martin Luther King Junior. The Biafran War shocked the world for the unimaginable suffering and starvation it inflicted on the civilian population. Those startling images were imbedded in my mind, and I was very curious to see how much healing, if any, had taken place in the intervening years.

The roads we traveled, proper highways, really, were all freshly paved and well serviced. From conversation, I understood that this big investment in infrastructure was heavily underwritten by domestic crude, the end of the Biafran War happily coinciding with a dramatic rise in the world price for petroleum. If we craned our necks to look down at every major bend in the road, we could see piles of wrecked vehicles. Some of these may have been remnants of the war, but the vast majority were undoubtedly the result of too much money, too fast—people buying cars and trucks for the first time with their newfound wealth, but not adequately trained to drive them, especially at night.

We passed through Onitsha, a prosperous and rapidly growing city overlooking the river. The people looked healthy and vigorous, a far cry from the terrible images I remembered from my youth, effectively answering my question about the region's recovery. Here, much as anywhere that we stopped for a break east of the Niger, we were invariably approached by young people of about college age, largely Igbo, curious about us and eager to learn. I asked one of these students about the body of the man left beside the road in Bendel State. He confirmed for us the degree of banditry taking place on that side of the border and speculated that the NPF had summarily executed one of these outlaws "leaving him to rot as a warning to others."

---

[11] The political map of Nigeria has changed dramatically since our visit. Bendel State is now history, replaced by the states of Edo and Delta.

Apparently, the practice was common enough that it did not surprise him at all to know that we'd seen a dead man lying beside the road.

A very meticulously dressed and bespectacled fellow who had been listening attentively to our conversation interjected with an unexpected question: "Do you not associate with N%#gers?" he asked, in all seriousness. I wasn't the only one off the truck to hear this. Our heads swiveled toward him, the blood draining from our faces in unison. For a moment, we were all speechless.

"What would make you think that?" I asked.

"You have no Black people. Do you not allow Blacks to travel with you?"

As I recall, two or three of us babbled out an answer at the same time. I had to admit to the fellow, who told us his name was Christian Ogbonna, a student at the Institute of Management and Technology at Enugu, that I had no good explanation why not one single person of African heritage, from any country in which Tracks had advertised, had signed up for the expedition. It was, on the face of it, a very good question. One I had not thought to ask myself to this point. Each of us had our own reasons for signing up, but none of us could say that it was because we were interested in learning more about "our roots," unless it was in the context of our human origins and none of us could claim to be anthropologists. So, why not? Why were there no Blacks on our expedition? I had no good explanation for him.

"I would take this trip," he replied. "Someday, I will have the money." He sounded genuinely jealous of our ability to explore and learn about the continent that he called home and a bit bewildered to learn that only Whites, seemingly, had mustered enough interest to make the journey.

We drove for an hour and a half northeast and after a bit of combing about, camped in the village of Dodo, about 10 kilometers south of the town of Oji River.

Passing through Enugu, the short-lived capital of Biafra from 1967 to '70, and the towns of Ikom and Ekwatai, the more lush and abundant grew the landscape. The vast cross-border region south has since been fashioned into two spectacular national parks: Cross River on the Nigeria side and Korup on the Cameroon side, containing some of the richest rainforest in West Africa. We were able to traverse the narrow international suspension bridge over Cross River into Cameroon virtually unhindered but found that the Cameroonian customs and immigration post did not operate 24-hours a day. The agents, many of them women, kindly let us camp for the night on the grounds, a stunning location surrounded by palms, squawking birds, and dense jungle overlooking the sweeping river. I was so taken by the natural beauty of the place, the events that followed threw me for a loop.

When night descended, a public patio just down the street from the customs post lit up with swirling, colored lights to match the penetrating rhythms of disco and reggae. A press of people emerged from seemingly nowhere dressed to kill and ready to party. The female border agents who had officiously greeted us in their crisp and neatly pressed uniforms just a few hours earlier were now dancing side-by-side with us in slinky mid-thigh one-piece dresses, long fashionable earrings sparkling jewel-like under the dizzying strobe. They alternated with ease between any number of languages, English, French, and even German.

Unbeknownst to us, it was Cameroon's "Youth Day," a national day of celebration, commemorating the referendum that brought British Cameroon into union with French Cameroun, apparently doing double-duty as a holiday acknowledging the special place of young people in the fabric of the country. What better way to celebrate youth than an evening bobbing on the dance floor? The party went on until two in the morning. It was good wholesome fun.

The next morning, Valentine's Day, 1984, we packed and joined the queue at the border post. Our dance partners were back in uniform, dispassionate and professional. Our socialization the night before earned us no brownie points. It took hours to clear Cameroonian customs and the immigration agents gave us only nine days to cross the country, which left us with little time to do much exploring.

The road east of Ekok and then south to Kumba was hilly and narrow, littered with muddy potholes that slowed our progress. A dense temperate rainforest lined either side of the road, enough that you needed a machete to reach a place to relieve yourself with any privacy. I was disappointed to find that on leaving English-speaking Nigeria we were once again besieged with requests for cadeaux (gifts). On the other hand, the bank in Mamafé was highly efficient and police checks few and far between.

Technically still in West Africa, the winding mountain roads, lush jungle, bananas, teaming waterfalls, and chattering wildlife all pointed to having entered another realm, geographically speaking. Breathtaking, magnificent, spectacular, choose your adjective, they were equally applicable. We camped near Kumba on a lumber road that was part of a government preserve. Life in the enveloping forest appeared to have kicked into overdrive, ants were so large I could hear them walking atop the canvas of my tent, no exaggeration. There were tree snails as large as a man's fist, and beetles as big as a mouse. The nearby houses were of outwardly Western, you could say "suburban" design, but constructed from basic materials harvested from the forest and very roughly processed. I had my doubts about their long-term ability to withstand the elements.

The local inhabitants appeared to have mixed feelings about White tourists. I felt we were not particularly welcome. I did have an interesting conversation with a "commerçant" (merchant – pronounced 'cumair-sah') named Dickson Eseme who did his best to convince me that there was good money to be made in tomato paste and canned chicken. He swayed me enough that I passed his name and address on to my Mitsui contacts when I reached Nairobi. It was the least I could do for him.

Our next leg took us back down to the Gulf of Guinea on the Atlantic and to Douala, the economic seat of Cameroon, passing numerous banana, plantain, rubber, and palm oil plantations. Douala sits atop the Bight of Bonny (alternatively, Bight of Biafra), wedged between the estuary of the Wouri and Dibamba rivers. The port was modern and impressive, and the city boasted a sprawling market, the "marché du gros," with an abundance of dry goods from all over the world. I'd never seen so many shoes in my life, mostly Bata products, but there was no avoiding the vast shantytown on the outskirts of the city. Enormous Soviet-sized portraits of President Biya hung from every major edifice, in case anyone was in doubt about who was running the show. When I was a kid, every classroom displayed a portrait of the queen, so how different was that? A matter of degree, I suppose.

I bought a small brass Bamun amulet depicting a Cameroonian nobleman with a seriously maniacal grin to ward off evil, as well as a couple of other handsomely crafted souvenirs. We camped on the east-end of Douala in someone's yard. Mark passed around a bottle of homemade "Nigerian water," a palm spirit, colloquially known as kīe-kīe, that he'd acquired along the way. Naturally, I over-imbibed and was sick as a dog the next morning.

It rained for the very first time since we left Algiers, which was a refreshing treat for us, but played absolute havoc on the roads. For reasons that aren't entirely clear to me, the Cameroon government decided to forego the existing road between Douala and the capital, Yaoundé, to forge a new highway through the dense jungle heading northeast above Mandoumba. On either side of the sodden mud-red track that sufficed for a main road, lay the sawn-off remnants of once mighty trees that stood 50 meters high (160 feet) with girths of close to 1.5m (five feet)—trees, like the bongossi (Lophira alata), ekobem (Gilbertiodendron dewevrei), ngon (Klainedoxa gabonensis) and omang

(Desbordesia glaucescens) with fantastic cathedral-like buttresses.

We were not alone on the road. Aside from heavy construction vehicles, there were transport trucks laden with goods destined for Yaoundé. We bottle-necked atop the crest of a hill overlooking a steep valley and piled out to see what the trouble was. At the bottom of the valley below us sat two heavy mud-caked lorries that repeatedly failed to make it up the far slope, like soaped-up kittens trying to claw their way out of a bathtub. It was great fun for us to watch them back up and then attempt to make a run for it at full speed, slipping from side to side in hopes of breaching the distant crest, only to slide back down and start over again. Both drivers did eventually make it out of this trap. Malcom and the other drivers waiting with us watched and learned from their misadventure so that we had a somewhat easier time of it come our opportunity. It wasn't without effort and there was plenty of excitement, but we were able to make it to the top of the ridge in one go.

We camped for the night near the village of Ntang, then drove straight to the embassy of Zaire in Yaoundé, only to be disappointed. The embassy staff were unsure of their authority to issue visas to an expedition such as ours, suggesting that we try the Zaire embassy in Bangui in the Central African Republic. Holding out to the very last opportunity to obtain a visa was never a whole lot of fun, but there was precious little we could do about it. Poking about for a place to stay in Yaoundé we were told that we might be able to camp for a fee at the Presbyterian Mission. The mission compound was a simple establishment with basic, clean facilities that were both timely and welcome. In the three months since departing London I'd bathed and done my laundry, with few exceptions, out of a 10-inch basin. For the equivalent of a dollar twenty (500CFAF) I was able to luxuriate in a hot shower and give my clothes a thorough wash.

Knowing that the following day, February 19, my 25th birthday, was a Sunday and that we would be on the road again, Mark and Lila suggested a shopping trip into Yaoundé. We walked into the city and went our separate ways. A young man by the name of Bimi latched on to me and kept me company the entire afternoon. I bought a candy bar from a corner shop and polished it off as we walked along, but because of my poor planning found myself stuck with a gooey wrapper and no place to dispose of it. We walked together for a considerable distance while I kept an eye out for a suitable place to unload this sticky burden. Irritated by how distracted I was by this seemingly small responsibility, Bimi finally grabbed the wrapper from my hand and threw it down onto the street. "This is Africa," he chided.

Yaoundé was, however, very European in its own way. I had no trouble finding an upscale supermarket amply supplied with imported goods and I stocked up enough for a small self-indulgent birthday celebration. Back at the mission compound that evening, I served my companions a late-night snack of Lumpfish caviar on water crackers, anchovies, tinned cheddar, and olives. I also supplied the balloons. Mark and Lila produced a bottle of red wine. My "present," said Mark and Lila, tantalizingly, would be proffered the following day, my actual birthday.

It is fair to say that we were all, as a consequence, in good spirits, so it came as a great surprise when Bernard and Hazel announced that they would be leaving us, at least temporarily. It turned out that during their trip to the city, Bernard discovered that a significant number of well-heeled households in the capital owned pianos that had not been tuned in eons. A piano tuner by occupation, this was just too lucrative an opportunity to pass up. Moreover, it was timely. With all the unexpected additional fees we had incurred along the way, the couple were tapped out.

They weren't the only members of the expedition short on funds. Other members of the expedition who had brought along only enough cash and travelers checks to cover Tracks' rough estimate for visas and campgrounds were coping by simply sitting on the truck during our layovers or window shopping and doing little else. Jim was contemplating taking legal action against Tracks for having so grossly underestimated the personal expenses we were incurring. George supplied Hazel and Bernard with a predicted timeline, and it was agreed that they would "catch up" with us in Bangui. I nursed concerns about the viability of this arrangement given the unpredictability of things, but kept my thoughts to myself, and wished Hazel and Bernard well.

It was a long-haul the following day with few breaks from Yaoundé to Bertoua, passing a great many sugarcane and coffee plantations. I don't know if it was my imagination, but the people seemed to become friendlier, or perhaps less distrustful of us, as we traveled farther east. We camped that night on a logging road on the outskirts of Bertoua surrounded by massive, buttressed trees cloaked in roped creepers that you could swing from, Tarzan-like. It being my actual birthday, Alison and Kristine surprised me with a homemade pineapple pudding in lieu of a celebratory gâteau, produced rather miraculously on the fly and quite delicious.

Mark and Lila presented me with an attractive carving they were told depicted a messenger in the service of the Oba of Benin. It was quite heavy for its size and polished up midnight black, so there was no reason to doubt the vendor's assertion that it was made of precious ebony. Having stored it in my bag under that assumption, I was distressed to find it irretrievably broken into several pieces only a week later. The little messenger, in fact, was cleverly made of solid clay and fashioned in a perfect imitation of ebony that could only have been revealed by taking a sharp blade to it at the point of purchase, which the merchant undoubtedly knew. Lila was heartbroken upon hearing the news. She and Mark had spent considerable time selecting just the right present for me.

During the night, we were occasionally jostled from our sleep by the ground trembling beneath our beds and what sounded like distant thunder. This, we soon discovered, was caused by falling trees. Somewhere in these great forests, one of the countless monumental trees around us was always giving way to age. It would come down with a sudden and resounding "crack" and then, tumbling over, might strike another great tree which in turn might strike yet another, like titanic dominoes. Each of these events would cause a minor earthquake and you might be awakened several times throughout the night by such tremors. It was awe inspiring even just to imagine. Of course, you'd awaken after each treefall thinking to yourself, I'm glad that was far-off.

On sighting The Pig, the Bertoua police directed us to check in with "Tourist Control." The government-run tourist office fronted a small square. Like many towns and cities in West Africa, the national flag flying atop a high pole figured prominently in the center of the square. Jim, for reasons only he could understand, decided that the concrete platform beneath the pole was a suitable place to rest his butt while he waited to reboard The Pig. To make matters worse, he thoughtlessly made himself comfortable under the hot sun by removing his shirt. His indecent and disrespectful behavior did not go unnoticed.

In no time flat, he was surrounded by angry bystanders and several police officers. Jim was caught off guard, incapable of understanding what all the fuss was about. Instead, he met belligerence with belligerence. He was within a hair's breadth of being arrested when we all showed up to take him in hand. I think it was only the conundrum of having to deal with all eighteen of us that prevented Jim from spending a night in jail. Once aboard The Pig and safely out of town, Jim was unapologetic and, truth be told, indignant that he should be so rudely treated.

From Bertoua, we headed east and north toward Garoua-Bouaï, on the border with the Central African Republic. Beyond Bertoua, the great forests evaporated, replaced by dry grass-covered mountains where herds of cattle roamed. We camped early, near the village of Gado-Badzéré. Free from camp chores, with time on my hands and fine weather, I decided to explore alone the local foot paths and surrounding farms. It was, perhaps, the most peaceful and relaxed I'd been since starting out.

Walking atop a treed dike edging a farmer's field with hardly a soul about, I encountered a shoeless boy shouldering a school bag. This was far from town and anything remotely associated with tourism. There's no doubt I was an unexpected sight. The boy eyed me more with curiosity than trepidation. To my surprise, rather than pass me by, he blocked my path and introduced himself.

His name was Zaoro Vincent de Paul. He was fourteen years-old, he said in fine French, pointing to a farm in the distance as his home. Who was I? He wished to know and where was I going? And, moreover, did I enjoy football (i.e., soccer)? I invited him to sit with me beneath a tree if he had the time (in plain sight of anyone that might be concerned, I should note) and we could get better acquainted, to which he happily agreed. Discovering that I was an "Anglo," he was pleased to try out the few words of English that he knew. We talked together for no more than twenty minutes or so, and I think we both appreciated the serendipity of our connection. I left Zaoro with a promise that I would send him some newspapers or magazines when I returned home to feed his interest in the wider world. Without going into too much detail at this point, I'll share with you that Zaoro and I kept up our correspondence in the years to come.

We crossed into the Central African Republic (CAR) at Beloko unexpectedly hassle-free on the 21st of February. That marked the official end to the "reconnaissance" portion of our expedition. We were now back on Track's traditional route to East Africa. CAR didn't even bother with a customs inspection. That said, there were police check points coming in and out of nearly every town we passed through. It felt something like progress. We'd traveled, after all, through

North Africa, a chunk of West Africa and now had entered Central Africa.

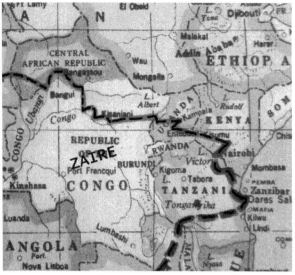

The author's route through Central and East Africa. The Republic of the Congo was renamed Zaire in 1971

The border region was mountainous, which always made for interesting views. My first impression of CAR was that the traditional villages, as a rule, were well-kept and orderly, rather picturesque and the major motorways in very good repair. With a little digging, I learned that these villages were a very recent legacy of the former emperor, Bokassa, who had forcibly relocated entire communities to their present sites along the major motorways so that he could better control the inhabitants. Bokassa had been overthrown only five years prior. Tales of his brutality were both chilling and macabre.

Unlike Cameroon, whose national parks were magnets for visitors, there was no tourism to speak of, nor much even in the way of inter-urban commerce, the economy being largely one of self-sufficient farming. Consequently, when we stopped in the town of Bouar, we found no public markets where people could gather to sell their produce, which made obtaining supplies a big challenge. There was no bank to be found in Bouar, although it was a reasonably sized town. I was surprised by just how extensive the French military presence was in CAR, armed Legionnaires a fairly common sight. This was the first time I'd seen any vestige of former colonial power still being flexed in Africa, with the sole exception of Ceuta, the tiny Spanish territory where we first landed. I imagine they were there as a "stabilization force." I'm not sure if these troops were the reason, but I found the people we encountered even cooler to our presence than in Cameroon.

The author, camping in the Central African Republic

We camped that night on a disused road amid dense clouds of mosquitoes. George suddenly collapsed on us, racked by chills and fever. It was malaria. Ronnie's nursing skills were never more appreciated. I dipped into my medical kit and shared a few tabs of Fansidar with George that the doctor had prescribed for me not so much as a preventative, but as a treatment. He recovered quickly enough, but his bouts were recurring, as happens with malaria. The next day, we made the long drive to the "chutes" (falls) at Boali, traversing rolling hills punished by scorched-earth farming, the smell of smoke filling the air.

The unpaved roads were in good repair, but the flip side was that we were frequently caught behind slow-moving graders. Our passage was also hindered by the many new bridges going up outside the town of Bossembélé, a crossroads of sorts. At Baoli, we were harassed by opportunistic police, who tried very hard to charge us a fee for looking about, parking, and certainly, camping. But they had no official authority to do so and backed down when we pressed the matter. The 50-meter falls outside of town were truly worthy of attention. I was pleased to see that their natural setting had been preserved. As we were the only ones about, the group went for a dip in the shallow pools beneath the plunge. I understand that a Chinese-built dam now stands upriver and that the water is periodically "turned on" for the few tourists brave enough to endure both the recurring cycle of violence and humanitarian crisis that now plague the country.

A hawker who went by the entertaining name of "Medicament Jean" pressed me to have a look at his handicrafts, an amusing collection of children's toys, gewgaws, baubles, and rough gadgets. Jean's mechanical flip-toys were remarkable really, fashioned from bits of odd cloth and pith-wood held together with simple pegs and a bit of corded fiber. I succumbed, although I had no need of it, to buying a toy that featured two women pounding imaginary millet when you pressed either end of the small board they were fixed to. It was a truly marvelous toy, an exemplary piece of folk art, and a perfect example of what can be achieved with very little.

It was a short drive from Baoli to Bangui, the capital of the Central African Republic. The city had a slightly austere feel about it, tidy and organized, but devoid of charm. Our vehicle was robbed of a few minor items the first day there, which put us on our guard. At the police check point entering the city, I saw two Soviet-made BTR-60s. Unlike the burned-out hulk of the BTR-40 we'd encountered in Mali, these armored vehicles were in operational use. For someone who'd trained so intensely for the Cold War, it was a kick to see them up-close.

We drove straight to the Zaire embassy with our fingers crossed, and, this time, were not disappointed. It would take 24-hours and 6,300CFAF (about $16 US) each for our visas. The highlight for me was finding eight cards and letters waiting for me at the central post office. We camped that evening at the "Centre d'Accueil Touristique" (Tourist Welcome Center) a few kilometers from the city center, where I shuffled off to read and re-read my precious letters from home. Sitting around talking with Lila and Alison that evening, the matter of Bernard and Hazel came up. Assuming they somehow managed to get themselves to Bangui in time, how would they ever find us?

Astonishingly, we did meet up with someone rather unexpected in Bangui—Sara, the Welsh woman we'd last seen in Niamey. By some miracle she'd got herself all the way to the Central African Republic. Sara had tales of her own to share and good reason to gloat over her achievement. She couldn't quite decide whether to head to the Sudan and up to Egypt next, or to mirror our own route to Nairobi. Incredible.

I walked downtown with Mark the next morning to cash a travelers check and mail a letter off to Edi. I had a connection, of a kind, with Bangui and the Central African Republic—an old and very dear friend of my parents, Arthur Woodruff, had served as the American ambassador to CAR from 1981 to 1983, along with his wife, my "Auntie Jean." I'd only missed seeing them by seven months, which was a real shame, but Arthur's staff were still employed at the embassy. Jean and Arthur asked that if I made it to Bangui (as if there was ever any doubt), I drop by and introduce myself, while extending their best.

Mark agreed that it might be interesting, so we ventured forth. The embassy was of an appealing modern design, but modest in scale. Identifying ourselves as a visiting Canadian and a New Zealander made no plausible sense, so I identified myself as a US citizen, which I was, after all (conveyed through my American-born father). Mentioning Arthur's name was indeed enough to elicit a reaction. Two staff members, Marion and Chris, invited us into their office and seemed sincerely pleased to make the acquaintance of someone close to their former boss. Not surprisingly, they were keen to hear about our travels and, in turn, described some of the work that the embassy performed. It was, all in all, a pleasant, if entirely inconsequential, visit.

While skulking about downtown, Mark and I made the acquaintance of "Tony," who evidently thought two visiting White men needed an escort, guide, concierge, or friend, "whatever the need might be," and latched himself onto us. Mark made it plain from the start that there was nothing to be had from us and that he was wasting his time. Tony shrugged that off without a thought, stating that he had "nothing better to do" and kept us company the rest of the day. He was, as it turned out, good company and eager to point out the things he thought we might find of interest. With Tony's help, we learned that the black market rate for currency ("Zaires," about 35Z to the dollar) in Bangui was so close to the official rate that it was neither worth the risk nor the effort.

Back at camp, Ronnie informed us that she was cutting short her journey, having accepted a nursing position in Melbourne. I gather she knew this might be necessary from the start, but was content to ride it out with us until she received final word. I don't think any of us felt particularly close to her, but Ronnie had been a stalwart companion and, to varying degrees, had nursed many of us along the way through unforeseen ailments. Like a doctor on an airplane who gets called upon to assist in an emergency she was hard-pressed to ignore our pleas for help, our meager expressions of gratitude her only compensation. With Hazel and Bernard still A.W.O.L. so to speak, her loss seemed all the more unexpected and poignant. A farewell party in her honor seemed only fitting.

It was my turn to join the grocery shopping squad the next morning, which proved to be a sizable challenge as there was precious little to choose from on the shelves, and what there was, was very expensive. In Central Africa our staples were banana, pineapple, papaya, manioc (cassava), and yam, which meant we'd become virtual if not literal vegetarians. Breakfast usually consisted of a porridge fashioned from either rice, cracked corn, or tapioca. The alternatives were toast with peanut butter, which I could no longer stomach, jam or banana. Lunch was invariably served cold, usually a salad of some sort or a vegetable sandwich. We always had the option of buying out of our own pocket a small 75g can of fish in tomato sauce to add to a meal. Dinner consisted of any of the above staples spiced up or embellished with whatever our shoppers could find in the local markets. The expedition members were imaginative cooks, for the most part, and the meals often quite enjoyable. Even so, when supplies ran short and the markets were empty, we sometime ate little more than a banana on a slice of plain white bread. Not terribly satisfying.

By happenstance, we stumbled on a restaurant, whose name, unfortunately, I can no longer remember, in a part of town known for its clubs, bars, and cool second-hand shops called "kilomètre 5," or even more informally as, "k-Cinq." The restaurant was busy, with happy, contented customers chatting amiably in every corner. But the menu is what stood out, bush meat for the most part: gazelle, monkey, boa (likely, Calabar python) and even elephant. We opted to play it safe and ordered a rich gazelle stew for lunch, which proved to be a brilliant choice, sweet and gamey.

I was sitting very near an older gentleman who took a kindly interest in us. Guessing that he'd witnessed a great deal in his lifetime, I girded up the courage to ask him what he thought about Jean-Bédel Bokassa, the infamous "emperor" of the defunct "Central African Empire." "He was a great man," replied the old fellow. "People respected him, and the world looked up to us." He seemed to consider this for a moment. "His only real fault," he added as an afterthought, "was that he liked to eat people." Bokassa always denied accusations of cannibalism, but his willingness to murder and dismember his opponents are pretty easily verified. I gather the k-Cinq district was later wrecked and then abandoned during the violence of 2014-'15. Today, it is no place for idle strangers to wander about—a painful thought.

That evening, the route forward was hotly debated. Should we take the Bangassou to Kisangani road or the Mobaye to Lisala road and a ferry up the Zaire River to Kisangani? The former offered "improved" rights of way but necessitated at least three trips across large rivers by boat. There were invariably issues associated with bringing The Pig and a large trailer onto a ferry, making multiple crossings problematic. Not to mention, multiple ferry crossings also meant multiple fees. Then again, word was the Mobaye-Lisala road was "muddy," which could mean a great many things. Even more troubling was that it was marked on our maps as a "difficult or dangerous section." There seemed no good solution. Moreover, where were Hazel and Bernard?

The following morning, most of our party traveled back into Bangui. The city was a hub for East Africa adventure travel. Encountering other Overlanders invariably led to interesting and animated discussions where fresh "intelligence" on places not yet visited was traded like a hot commodity. We learned on this occasion that the Tracks Nile expedition from Egypt to Kenya got caught out by the sudden closure of Sudan's border with Kenya and were forced to skirt all the way around to Bangui and then through Zaire to get to Nairobi. It took them an additional two months to complete their intended journey. Another overland company was delayed by the coup in Nigeria only to have their vehicle break down in Cameroon. It took seven weeks for the repairs to be completed by which time half the expedition members had given up and flown home. Despite our own setbacks, we were, it seemed, making good progress in relative terms.

I lazed about camp, washed a few items of clothing, and wrote letters home. By all estimates, we would soon reach a part of Zaire where the prevalent strain of malaria was Chloroquine-resistant. In anticipation, I took my first Maloprim tablet. For the remainder of the trip, I would alternate between Chloroquine on Mondays and Maloprim on Wednesdays, and, in this manner, hopefully avoid George's fate. If neither of these proved effective, I had a reserve of Fansidar for treatment.

The group returned to camp in drips and drabs. In retrospect, I was glad I hadn't gone with them. Both Mark and Julie had their shoulder bags snatched away in separate incidents. Thankfully, they kept their passports on their person, as did I, but this was little compensation for the loss or the trauma.

While we were busy catching up on the morning's events, Malcolm lay on a fold out cot with his shirt off, enjoying the sun, reading a book and tuning us all out as usual. As we were standing right next to him, it was impossible to miss the sight of a large jet-black scorpion landing squarely on his chest, having fallen from a branch above his head. There was a universal gasp and a moment frozen in time as we helplessly watched this play out. Malcolm hesitated for a mere second, reached over as if to scratch an itch and casually flicked the creature off. Sliding onto his side, he lopped its head off with the edge of his hardcover book. That was Malcolm for you.

We waited anxiously for Hazel and Bernard to show their faces that evening, but once again, they failed to appear. George made it clear that he had no intention of waiting any longer. We would get back on the road the next day, with or without them. There were mixed feelings about this. Some, including myself, were reticent to move on without at least learning their fate and gaining some assurance that they could get themselves home safely, knowing they were short on resources. Others felt the pair were responsible for their own destiny. It made for tension, in no way lessened by the pressing need for a decision on our route forward. The waters of the Ubangi were unseasonably low and the ferry over to Zongo (on the Zaire-side of the river) was subsequently out of service. George, already feeling put upon, left it up to the group to decide what to do. A consensus was arrived at, after much debate, to take the river crossing at Mobaye and then the drive almost due south to Lisala. I'm sure I wasn't the only one pondering the implications of "difficult or dangerous" as we went to sleep that night.

Tracks messed up and sent Ronnie a ticket to Moscow instead of London for some peculiar reason, so she forked out and bought her own ticket to Paris. Presumably, she flew from there to London and on to Melbourne. We said our goodbyes, packed up The Pig, and hit the road, sans Hazel and Bernard. It was, as it turned out, something of a false start. Exiting the city, the police turned us back, insisting that we get an "exit stamp" from immigration, which we duly obtained. I used the opportunity in town to purchase some additional one-hour passport photos for visas down the road. We encountered fewer police checks outside of Bangui and it seemed to me that the people we encountered north of the city were increasingly friendly towards us. I wondered if the reduced presence of French troops in the region was no coincidence.

The road was in excellent repair as far as Sibut (about 170 kilometers), then rapidly deteriorated into a painful sieve of flooded potholes. We camped the first night out of Bangui near Sibut. On the road east to Bangassou we encountered several more overland expeditions. The landscape improved with every kilometer, becoming increasingly lush and mountainous, dotted with picturesque villages clustered with white-washed mud brick homes with thatched roofs constructed in the round. The village men frequently shouldered spears. For what reason, I could only speculate. They moved with an air of dignity that I did not always observe amongst their counterparts in the city. One thing I could not fail to notice, and found rather disquieting, was the commonplace sale of monkey meat, in all varieties, large and small, smoke rising from their eviscerated bodies, often with the fur still on, pinned spread-eagle over wood-fired grills. Eating monkey is forbidden (haram) in Islamic practice, so the market was clearly not for the benefit of the region's Muslim population.

Tuesday, February 28, marked our 100th day in Africa, though it seemed to us like a year had passed. We camped just outside of Bambari, a prosperous and vital center on the Ouaka River. There were no mosquitoes or bothersome blackflies, which to my mind made for a paradise. I know Bambari to have since suffered badly in the see-saw conflict that has taken place between the government and an array of rebel factions since 2012.

At Kongbo, we turned south off the main road to Bangassou for Mobaye, on the Ubangi River. I felt we'd entered the African version of Shangri La, idyllic villages set in a tropical utopia. If I had my druthers, we'd have spent a few days or even weeks exploring the area, getting to know something more about the people and local culture. But George was adamant that we press on, arguing that we were a good two weeks behind schedule, plus the road ahead was uncertain at best. I have to wonder how this exceptionally stunning region, of all places in Central Africa, has weathered the recent upheavals. If there is any hope at all for the world, it has managed to slip under the radar, unnoticed and untainted.

Mobaye was an attractive city, perched on the edge of the great river with clear views across to Zaire (since renamed, the "Democratic Republic of Congo," or DRC). We made arrangements to take the ferry across the Ubangi very early the following morning. Our tentative plan was to by-pass as much of the Zaire rainforest as possible by taking the road south to Gemena, then heading southeast to Lisala where we would look into the possibility of shipping out by barge to Kisangani. An American Peace Corps volunteer in Mobaye shared with us over a beer that only a few days earlier another overland expedition had been turned back from Gbadolite by Zaire authorities after crossing the river and had to backtrack all the way to Bangassou before making another attempt—which meant a detour of at least 350 kilometers (or about 220 miles), plus an additional unplanned border crossing. Hearing this, we amended our plans. We would now cross the river and then track due east to Yakoma, by-passing Gbadolite and then trekking south to Bumba on the Zaire River.[12] I was disappointed by this decision, as I was looking forward to seeing Gbadolite, President Mobutu's reputed "Golden City" in the jungle.

Knowing that we had to be up early to catch the ferry, we attempted to find a campsite close to the river. George found a vacant lot partially concreted over that appeared suitable, a little way out of town and off the side of the road. None of the locals that we asked seemed to have any objection, so we settled in for the night. The sun had barely risen when I was stirred from a deep slumber by unfamiliar sounds and movements outside my tent. Not yet fully awake, I stumbled from my bivvy bag and pulled aside the flap to investigate. A herd of cows had moved in to occupy the space between our tents. This would have been amusing, in retrospect, except for the fact that the purpose of the concrete slab around which we had pitched our dwellings was now abundantly apparent. Not more than three or four feet in front of my face, the town butchers had already begun their grim work.

Still in my underwear, I watched dumbstruck as three men with expert hands pressed to the ground the bowed and resisting neck of one of these large beasts and proceeded to

---

[12] The Zaire has also reverted to its original and better-known name, the "Congo River."

slit its throat. Blood poured from the animal, steam rising from the pulsing tide in the cold of dawn. The butchers paid me nor the other members of our group, the slightest heed as we emerged. We were, after all, uninvited guests and they had their work to do. My mind fixated on the fact that the rest of the herd, all within breathing distance, stood passively by, seemingly oblivious to what was about to befall them. My eyes briefly met those of my horrified companions. In silent unison, we grabbed our belongings and got the hell out of there, not a single word or look exchanged with the three men engaged in their grisly task.

It was, to say the least, an inauspicious start to the day. While getting The Pig ready to board the ferry, the police approached us demanding 1,000CFAF each for "exit visas." George called their bluff, demanding to speak with a government immigration official and they backed down. The ferry across the Ubangi was an old self-propelled diesel-powered barge. We openly questioned its ability to handle The Pig, but the driver assured us it could. Besides that, the river was wide, swift, and clotted with large floating islands of beautiful but potentially hazardous water hyacinth (Eichhornia crassipes), an invasive species from South America.

The crossing to Mobayi-Mbongo, Zaire, cost us 25,000CFAF (or about $63 US) and proved, given the above, to be one of the more thrilling, if unnerving, transits I experienced in Africa. It seemed our departure was guaranteed, but not our arrival. As it turned out, there was no reciprocating boat launch or pier on the other side to receive us. The Pig sank right into the sand as we off loaded and was extricated with no little effort on our part.

The Zaire border agents were courteous and good natured. After letting us off with a very cursory inspection, we imagined we were good to go. What is it they say about the best made plans of mice and men? Our hotly debated plan to cut east to Yakoma went up in smoke with word that we were to be "accompanied" to Gbadolite to register with the state authorities. On the upside, I would get to see Gbadolite after all.

Gbadolite was the pet project of "President-for-Life" (Joseph) Mobutu Sese Seko, a new age city carved from scratch out of the jungle. Mobutu swiftly turned Zaire into his personal fiefdom after conspiring with Belgium in 1960 to murder-off the nation's first democratically elected prime minister, Patrice Lumumba. It was the most surreal feeling, tumbling suddenly out of the dense jungle into a city of broad paved boulevards, grand plazas, handsome brick homes, landscaped gardens, and capacious government buildings, even a European-standard supermarket. For all that, the city was largely devoid of populace and served no clear administrative or commercial purpose. We passed down the main avenue in bewildered uncomprehending slow motion, trying to make sense of our curious and somewhat disquieting surroundings. As directed, we registered with the state authorities, who struck me as polite and disinterested, and were thus able to shed our escort.

As Gbadolite had little to hold our interest after all, we headed right back the way we'd come, still intending to cut east to Yakoma from Mobayi-Mbongo. It was getting late by this time and there seemed to be few good places to camp, until one of our group noticed a well-used drive with a sign that read "Ferme laitaire de Nbzanga" (Dairy Farm of Nbzanga). After three months, most of us had all but forgotten the taste of milk. We needed to find a campsite before dark and this jungle ranch was just too intriguing to pass up.

The Ferme laitaire de Nbzanga was run by three Swiss contractors who were both surprised and elated to have us appear on their doorstep. On the face of it, the laitaire was a noble experiment. Mobutu had spared no expense in the effort to import a herd of some 200 world-famous dairy cows from Switzerland intended to bring a higher level of nutrition to the people of Zaire. Despite the expert skill of their Swiss minders, the herd suffered in the tropical heat of the Congo. Inadequate infrastructure (to transport and keep the milk chilled) plus an undeveloped market for their product, conspired to ruin the whole enterprise. With the dairy a failure, the ranch devolved into little more than an extravagant playground for Mobutu and his family.

We were told how Mobutu had a statuette of baby Jesus flown in by Boeing 747 for his nativity scene and kept a private fishery stocked with trout from Europe. I had little reason to doubt the veracity of these tales. Mobutu's reckless extravagance is legendary. Under international pressure to democratize the country, he turned the dairy ranch and the neighboring fishery over to "the people" in a symbolic and largely empty gesture just two months prior to our arrival.

There seemed little doubt in the minds of the Swiss managers that the operation's days were numbered. For our part our timing couldn't have been better. We had the run of the ranch's luxurious facilities, and moreover, were offered as much fresh milk as our hearts' desired. Once we'd had our fill of that, there was ice cold beer to satisfy any remaining thirst!

The most amazing part of this whole experience, at least for me, had yet to come. In passing conversation, we learned the managers kept a stable of fine horses to herd cattle in the less accessible areas of the ranch. Any of us were welcome to take the horses for a ride. Only Inger and I had any extensive riding experience. Naturally, we both leaped at the invitation. I saddled up a fine stallion named Hugo, and Inger, a gray mare named Sico. We spent an ethereal hour exploring the trails over the grasslands and the edge of the surrounding jungle, pausing to check out Mobutu's fishery, all on our own, unescorted. It was one of those serendipitous moments you tend to look back on, mystified that it ever happened.

As much as we all enjoyed our stay, it inevitably came time to move on. For good measure, our hosts saw us off with a bundle of fresh pork and beef. The road to Yakoma was off the tourist track, to put it mildly, even for overland expeditions. Consequently, our presence in the towns and villages we passed through created something of a stir. The reaction was occasionally overwhelming in the sense that the expectation of receiving a handout from us was very high and this made for some tense moments. The road was rough but passable, although we did have to stop and contend with a flat tire on the trailer. There were quite a few villages along the way, but very few towns of any appreciable size. I could not help but notice the number of people with prominent goiters, owing I supposed to iodine deficiency.[13] River blindness (Onchocerciasis) caused by a parasitic worm, was also common. The infected looked to us as though they had severe cataract damage.

Belgian troops were present in some of the towns, which I was very surprised to find, given their sordid history in the Congo. I suspected they were there to help prop Mobutu up in areas where the president's reach was not entirely assured, or where Belgian mining operations needed a little extra security. We camped outside of Yakoma near a small village. On my walk that afternoon, I came across a one-room school open on three sides. No one was there, owing, I think, to the time of day, so I was free to poke about. I can't say what the quality of instruction was like, but a more idyllic educational setting can hardly be imagined, like something out of Anna and the King of Siam.

Back at camp, Jim was bitten by a large insect and suffered a rather bad allergic reaction. A villager we spoke with was sure that it was the bite of a tsetse fly, a vector for sleeping sickness, so we kept an anxious eye on him.

We took the road due south to Bumba from Yakoma, heading deeper into Zaire. During a pit stop in Abumombozi I struck up a conversation with a young man, as often occurred, who was curious to learn more about us and our trans-Africa trek. In the course of our conversation,

---

[13] The primary reason we make use of iodized salt so extensively in the West.

it came up that I was Canadian. "Oh," he replied. "Have you heard the news about Trudeau?"

"No," I said. "I've heard nothing from home in weeks."

"He announced his resignation, two days ago."

"Really?" That was major news indeed. Pierre Elliott Trudeau had been the prime minister of Canada, except for one brief interlude, for the better part of my adult life, more than fifteen years. I was no big fan, not caring much for his imperious style or republican tendencies (a seeming contradiction), but I had to admit he single-handedly elevated Canada's position on the world stage, such that the country now routinely punched above its weight. It was clear to me after many conversations that Trudeau was widely respected in Africa as a leader who could not be bullied by the great powers and was willing to speak up on behalf of developing and non-aligned nations. The young man I was speaking with felt Trudeau's departure amounted to the loss of an important friend and advocate. Personally, I felt it was past time for him to give someone else a shot at running the country.

The villages we passed between Abumombozi and Bodala were almost too perfect, laid out in orderly lines, white-washed compounds with freshly renewed thatched roofs and tidy walled corrals for livestock. Wild pineapples grew between the lots in abundance. Termites contributed to the natural wonder of the landscape, building their nests toadstool-fashion, as we'd seen in Mali and elsewhere in the Sahel. You half expected to find a garden gnome sitting cross legged atop one.

When questioned about the curious lack of refuse, we were told that it was because just about everything was recycled or repurposed, leaving little to waste. Statuesque women in colorful wrap around skirts with loaded baskets skillfully balanced atop their heads walked with graceful strides along the road, the men either tending their herds or off to forage in the forest with impressive crossbows canted over one shoulder.

I'd hoped to have this sort of encounter in Central Africa—an eons-old society before the "march of progress" had erased it all from memory. In an ideal world, traditional practices allow people to thrive and operate in balance and harmony with their environment. I'd witnessed something comparable during our serendipitous visit to the Dogon village in Mali, but this was of a different character. While our Dogon experience was just as rewarding in its own way, there was no denying there was something rather wonderous about life in the Congo rainforest.

I was not wrong, however, to think this pattern of living was not long for the world. Between the villages, great swaths of forest were coming down to make way for coffee plantations. These bleeding gashes in the jungle shook me to the core. I was in no position to judge how this might or might not benefit the lives of those who lived there, but that did not lessen the profound sense of loss that I felt, and perhaps a deeper concern for the long-term health of the world. This great forest had withstood the ages. I was uneasy that after all this time, the final saga should be written by my generation.

I took a turn riding above the cab with Inger and wasn't particularly focused on her, until I saw some movement on the back of her right shoulder. "Inger," I said as calmly as I could. "I don't want to alarm you, but there is something crawling on you." Her eyes widened. It had reached her neck by the time I could reposition myself to offer any help. She instinctively grabbed at the thing with her right hand. This maneuver was not without personal risk as we were perched high atop the swaying cab traveling at a fair clip. The enormous bug clamped firmly in her fist was a locust, a giant grasshopper, no less than six inches long and a good thumb's width in girth. Inger screamed and tossed it way with a visceral shudder.

George shouted out the window, "Everything all right up there?"

"Fine," I answered, watching Inger scrub the side of her neck, a look of disgust stamped across her face. "It was just a bug. No worries."

We camped a little south of Bodala, near the banks of the Ebola (or Legbala) River. For all my preparation, medical consultations, inoculations, etcetera, the Ebola virus, for whatever reason, never once came up in conversation. We were all of us, I think, blissfully unaware that the Ebola virus was first detected just eight years prior to our passage, at Yambuku, less than 20 miles south of where we were camped. Of the 318 reported cases, 218 perished during that initial outbreak, a fatality ratio of 88 percent. In retrospect, not knowing was probably for the best.

A river crossing in Zaire

It was a long, long drive south to Bumba where we caught our first glimpse of the mighty Zaire River. It was a curious feeling to see high rise buildings once again. Our intention was to take a ferry upriver to Kisangani, but the best we could discern was that it would not arrive before Thursday, and this was only Sunday (March 4, 1984). Even then, there was no guarantee on when it might arrive. None of us were in any mood to hang about Bumba waiting on a chance connection, so we poured over the map and, as a group, eventually decided to take the "short cut" southeast to Basoko where we would cross the Zaire for a stretch, cross back again at Isangi, and then make the final leg to Kisangani. In theory, avoiding the main highway and the long way around would cut 140 kilometers (90 miles) off our trip.

We camped at the village of Yamawa, near the cut-off from the main highway to Lolo where we were royally received, the village headman deciding that our unexpected visit was excuse enough for a celebration. We joined the villagers in song and danced to the sound of marimba, tomtom, and shekere.[14] It was, for want of any other description, an intoxicating experience. Unfortunately, the festivities served as the perfect distraction for raiding our camp. A vacant tent went missing, which was tolerable, but Lynn and Gail lost a purse containing their precious passports, travelers checks, and about 800Z, a potentially devastating development for them and us. The swift and unexpected transition from high to low emotions was keenly felt. The village headman was embarrassed beyond words and swore to us that he would make matters right before the morning. As there was nothing we could do, we skulked off to our tents and hoped for the best. As if to underline the direness of our predicament, a tremendous rainstorm swept over us during the night, soaking more than our spirits.

A little after half past two in the morning, the headman braved the rain to let us know that Lynn and Gail's stolen property had been retrieved, abandoned about two miles up the road. He explained that the Nkanga, a traditional healer, had placed a curse on the perpetrators and this had been sufficient to get the offenders to re-consider their crime. The headman, however, was apologetic—fear of the Nkanga's curse failed to motivate the culprits to return Lynn and Gail's cash. In any case, our traveling companions were

---

[14] An instrument similar to a maraca or rattle, fashioned from a gourd filled with nuts, stones, or shells.

pleased to get their passports back and no more was said about the matter.

It was a short drive the next morning to the banks of the Itimbiri River. The government ferry at Bokata seemed capable and, moreover, on a regular schedule. What's more, since tourists were unheard of on this route, they had no system in place to deal with the likes of us, so we were permitted to cross free of charge. While waiting to board, we encountered an elderly Polish couple. Lila, as I mentioned, was fluent in Polish and translated their rather sad story. They had departed Poland after World War II and had spent the intervening thirty plus years in the Congo. For the first twenty, they toiled away at building a successful tobacco and pyrethrum (Chrysanthemum) plantation, Chrysanthemum containing a natural insect repellent. Their plantation was nationalized by Mobutu in 1974 and they'd been working as contractors on their own plantation ever since.

Now aged and seeing nothing good on the horizon, they decided to quit Zaire, attend a family reunion in France, and then head off on a trip around the world. Their Range Rover contained all their worldly possessions. We were fortunate to encounter them for other reasons. The couple shared with us an important piece of intelligence about our planned route. The ferry at Isangi was down for the foreseeable future. We'd have to find some other way to reach Kisangani.

The route forward to Basoko was rarely traveled by Whites. The few we encountered were employed on coffee or rubber plantations and inclined to keep their distance. A little more than 30 kilometers (20 miles) down the road we opted to break for lunch in an open area marked as Yamongumia (alternatively, Yamongbumia) on the map. It was a quiet spot, shaded by a few isolated trees. We were parked for maybe five minutes when it became all too clear that we had failed to fully consider the impact our presence might have on the local population.

A largish structure in the distance turned out to be a regional school. Once the children had spied us out, all hell broke loose. They immediately abandoned their classrooms, scores of children running madly towards us, schoolbooks still in hand and their teachers trailing helplessly behind. I thought for a moment that this must have been how Custer felt at the Little Big Horn, except that our purpose in being there was to prepare lunch. Uncertain of the situation, we immediately sought succor aboard The Pig. It did not take the children long to mob us on all sides, reaching up to shake our hands, shouting gleeful words of welcome.

Students rush to greet us at Yamongumia

Given past experience we were wary at first, but decided that there was safety in numbers and that the children, being just curious, posed no serious threat. So we dismounted, which caused the children to reconsider and run off. Our intention, of course, was not to frighten them. We gestured for them to come back, shouting words of encouragement to the teachers who helped to herd them back toward us.

We shook hands and embraced as many as we could manage and then broke off into smaller groups in an effort to answer questions and get to know one another just a little. I can't speak for the experience of the others on our expedition, but I recall asking one child if I could look at his notebook and was surprised to find that it was a "Gift from the People of Canada" endorsed, no less, by John

Diefenbaker, the prime minister from 1957 to '63. They must have been sent soon after the Congo gained independence from Belgium in 1960.

At some point, I found myself seated under a tree where children and one or two teachers instructed me on how to prepare a local delicacy. I was given a fine stick, just a twig really, split at the end to hold a fragment of leaf. This was inserted into a hole in the ground at the base of the tree, stirred about a couple of times and then quickly extracted. Clutched to the stick and leaf were a number of very large plump yellow winged ants. These were swiftly deprived of their wings, brushed into a shallow aluminum pan, then heated slightly over a tiny ad hoc campfire. Warm, but still very much alive, the insects were consumed much as other cultures might enjoy munching on pumpkin or sunflower seeds.

The ants, as I recall, were a tad on the bitter side. I ate just enough of them to satisfy my well-meaning hosts and my curiosity. They were evidently pleased to share this special treat with an unexpected guest. Crickets, grubs, and caterpillars remain an important, even essential, dietary supplement below the Sahel and consequently widely available, but not something I generally went out of my way to eat given my already sensitive tummy.

Each of us in our own way were moved in some fashion by our brief time with the students at Yamongumia, which made what happened next all the more perplexing. We said our goodbyes and mounted The Pig surrounded by a field of happy angelic faces. Waving farewell as we pulled away, the children scooped from the ground handfuls of dirt and mud and pelted us with it! I mean, really pelted us. Except for Lila who suffered a minor gash to her forehead, most of us managed to avoid the worst of it. "Perplexed" hardly expresses how we felt.

We questioned one another to determine if any of us might have done or said something to cause some offense at the very last moment but came up empty handed. Years and years later, I read a magazine account of someone who experienced something very similar in another part of Central Africa. The article revealed how it was a traditional albeit rare form of "farewell" in parts of Africa intended to ward off malevolent spirits that might harm the individual setting out on their journey. I'd like to believe that was the case. The experience proved unsettling and tempered our interactions even more going forward.

It wasn't long before the road was reduced to a mere track through dense rainforest, the heaviest and darkest we had yet to encounter. It pressed in on The Pig from both sides, the thick canopy often stretching over top of us creating a virtual tunnel through the jungle. For long stretches it would have been impossible for us to turn the Bedford around had we needed to, and nowhere at all to pass an oncoming vehicle.

I had my doubts that anything as large as The Pig had traveled this route in decades. The road was cut by an infinite number of narrow creeks spanned by rough cut logs. Each time we encountered one of these obstacles it was necessary for all of us to pile out and undertake an evaluation. If the bridge needed reinforcing, we took the time to do it rather than risk losing our only means of getting through this part of the Congo. The shrill sounds of insects, birds, and howling monkeys, which we rarely caught glimpse of, filled the humid air, in an unrelenting cacophony of sound. We occasionally encountered thick columns of ants on the move, flowing serpent-like across the road. Malcolm would gun the engine slightly to do as little damage as possible to them, but mostly to minimize the opportunity for them to get onto the vehicle, which they occasionally managed.

Most magical of all were the infinite varieties of butterflies that fluttered down in swarms from breaks in the forest canopy, like iridescent snowflakes. A smaller vehicle, probably a Land Rover, had obviously gone before us, leaving two infinite ruts in the soft earth that filled with rains at night. It was not unusual for clouds of butterflies to float down and drink from these long shallow pools, which created for us a real ethical conundrum.

Unlike the columns of ants that cut across our path from the side, the butterflies, just our rotten luck, were neatly aligned with our only path forward. At first, we attempted to walk ahead of The Pig and shoo them away, but they would only lift up for a moment and then settle right back down again. There was nothing for it, short of making a permanent home for ourselves in the jungle, but to run straight over them, murdering untold thousands in the process. It was heart wrenching to look back at the path of destruction behind us, so we got in the habit of only looking forward. If there ever was any single reason to keep tourists out of the Congo Basin, this was it.[15]

Navigating the narrow muddy track was exhausting work, so George would alternate with Malcolm, but George had thinner skin. Turning a bend in the road he suddenly encountered a kaleidoscope of the most incredible iridescent blue butterflies he or any of us had ever seen and instinctively swerved to avoid them. It took us hours to extricate The Pig from the mire we found ourselves in, with no certainty we would succeed. George grew a thicker skin after that.

We did occasionally pass small villages with the most fantastic gardens filled with pineapples, oil palms, coffee, bananas, papayas and heaven knows what else. It seemed as if you could put anything in the ground and it would grow in this part of the Congo. We stopped as usual to examine the span over a particularly large and swift flowing creek. It was in better repair than usual owing to its proximity to one of

---

[15] The Congo Basin, comprising both rainforest and tropical peatland, spans six countries in Central Africa. The Basin is critical to maintaining the stability of the world's climate. Although smaller than the Amazon in total acreage, it stores proportionally more carbon dioxide owning to the great size and longevity of its trees.

these villages. Several members of our expedition took the opportunity to strip down and go for a dip in the shallows along the bank, the water running too swiftly to harbor anything worrisome.

Standing on the bridge overlooking the deepest part of the creek I inadvertently knocked my eyeglasses off my face while taking off my hat and watched helplessly as they sunk into the depths of the creek. I had a spare pair, of course, but did not relish the idea of finishing my trip relying on a single pair of prescription glasses. Several young boys from the nearby village had wandered over to check us out. The one standing just next to me must have read the expression on my face because he dove straight off the bridge to fetch them out. It could not have been a simple task as he was under water long enough to make me uncomfortable, but he did succeed and made it clear that he sought no reward for his efforts.

We camped that night on a knoll overlooking fields cleared from the jungle. I was astonished to find no clouds of pestering mosquitoes. A storm moved across the distant fields a few hours later. Laying comfortably prone in my tent with the flaps drawn back, I was awed by the most incredible show of sheet lightning I have ever had the privilege to witness. It remained in the distance for a good long while with no apparent purpose other than to delight me and causing no more than a warm soothing wind to pass over our camp. I wondered if the electricity in the air had something to do with the absence of mosquitoes.

We finally reached Basoko. Situated at the confluence of the Zaire and Aruwimi rivers, it served as a major commercial hub for the region. We were now faced with another major decision. Knowing that the ferry at Isangi was down, we could either travel the main road to Kisangani, a full 850-kilometer circuit, or wait however long it took for a ferry to Kisangani, which we were being told might take a another month to arrive. There was, however, one other option open to us. That was to take the ferry across the

Aruwimi. But that way was fraught with risk and uncertainty because maps showed that the road continued past the far bank for perhaps 50 kilometers (30 miles) and then came to an abrupt end. Not a single printed map showed anything but impenetrable jungle for 100 kilometers the other side of Bomboma. We had only verbal assurance from those coming in by ferry that there was a "passable track" beyond that point connecting six or seven isolated villages. Malcolm, as always, was supremely confident and even relished the challenge. "A track is as good as a highway" he boasted. "It's only 60 miles."

There was sufficient impatience amongst the group to override our better judgement and risk the Aruwimi route. I could hardly contain my excitement at this unexpected opportunity to experience, first-hand, even a small part of Africa few outsiders had traversed since the Congo had gained independence. We would be entering the literal heart of Africa, potentially unspoiled and untamed, if only for a 60-mile stretch. If all went according to plan, we would connect with the road from Isangi in two or three days.

While waiting for the ferry to take us across the Aruwimi, we met two Belgians working for Scibe Zaire, an airline. They had managed to save an orphaned chimpanzee that couldn't have been more than a few months old and were torn over what to do with it. They'd named it, rather unoriginally, "Cheeta," having, I suppose, grown up with Tarzan films. While we talked, they allowed me to hold the chimp. It's a feeling I won't ever forget. Cheeta slipped from the Belgian's arms into mine, immediately wrapping itself around me and pressing its small furry head to my cheek in a desperate bid for love and safety.

I could feel the heat of its body against my own and its warm breath on my face, its tiny fingers clasped within my own. Life is difficult, to say the least, in many parts of Africa and it isn't fair, perhaps, to worry overly about the fate of a young chimp as opposed, for example, to that of a disadvantaged child. Yet, I could not help but feel a little extra concern for this poor creature, so utterly dependent on humans for its very life. I hope for its sake and our own, because humans were undoubtedly behind its misfortune, that Cheeta eventually found a caring home.

It was yet another exhilarating ride by ferry across a major river, and without incident. Once delivered onto the far bank the road shrunk to a narrow single lane track much sooner than we anticipated. Barely ten kilometers from the ferry landing we were already surrounded by dense jungle. If we were to encounter an oncoming vehicle, it would have required one of us to back up for several kilometers just to find a suitable place to pull aside. You might say it was pure luck that we never did meet up with another, but the truth of the matter is, we were the only ones mad enough to chance this route.

The terrain, for all that, was perhaps the firmest we'd come across in a good long while and would have been great going for a Jeep or Land Rover. The "issue," was the size and weight of The Pig. The rainy season arrived early, bringing torrential rains for a few hours every other night. A seemingly infinite number of streams criss-crossed our path and these were largely bridged with fallen timbers, many of them rotted through. As before, we had to stop and reconnoiter each passage which was exceedingly tedious work. It didn't take long for us to start taking larger and larger calculated risks. As a result, we crashed through two bridges and damaged the transmission on the second. Malcolm needed time to work on rebuilding it. With no other option, we made camp in the middle of the road where there was about as much chance of encountering another vehicle as there was for bumping into the president of Zaire.

As best as I could determine, we were camped somewhere near the village of Yamokanda, northeast of Bomese. Falling between camp duties, I had time on my hands, so I brewed up a cup of tea and with cup in hand, set off on my own to explore up the road for a short way, drinking in both the solitude of the jungle and the mesmerizing sounds emanating from the forest. I was well out of sight of the camp when I came upon a trail leading off to my right that might have been forged by a human or an animal. I had no way of knowing. Short of hacking my way in with a machete, I knew this could well be my only chance to get under the jungle canopy to have a peek at the interior of the forest for myself. I relished the idea of experiencing the jungle away from the others and didn't give it a moment or two of thought which the situation, in retrospect, really warranted.

Camping on the road near Yamokanda

I was, perhaps, ten paces into the forest when I encountered a man. He was as startled as myself and I only caught a glimpse of him as he ran off shouting something in his native tongue, but also—and this I found especially fascinating—employing a kind of bird call. This was a form of bilingualism I had never quite imagined. Obviously, it was a warning to others, which I really should have been more sensitive to. Yet, I managed to rationalize in my own mind that I was no threat to these people and simply carried on (possibly the stupidest decision I ever made in Africa), in my enthusiasm never thinking they might entertain a very different perspective on my presence.

I could hear the warning being passed from person to person deeper into the jungle, though I could see no one. The trail eventually opened on a clearing in the forest floor. It was still quite dark, however, owing to the dense canopy blocking out the sky some sixty feet above my head. At the center of the clearing was a small encampment, smoke still rising from the fire where the inhabitants were evidently engaged in making palm oil, that is until the point I strolled in with my cup of tea. It was a scene right out of National Geographic, less the people. I understood immediately that everyone had run off on my account and were probably keeping a close eye on me from a safe distance. If I'd any sense at all, I would have turned around and got myself out of there "Tout de suite!" Instead, I just stood there like an idiot pleased with my discovery.

Moments later, the man I first encountered reappeared. Apparently, he could also speak French and was visibly upset. "Que fais-tu ici?" What are you doing here? He demanded to know.

"Rien. Je veux juste parler," I replied. Nothing. I just want to talk.

"Es-tu fou? Tu es en danger! Tu-veux mourir?" Are you crazy? You are in danger! Do you want to die?

Die?! I was stunned. "Non! Je ne suis pas dangereux!" No! I'm not dangerous! I replied, defensively. I even showed him my teacup, as if that were adequate evidence. "Je veux juste parler." I just want to talk, I reiterated. Those last words had barely escaped my lips when a very young and very angry woman clad in nothing but a loin cloth jumped from behind a tree and dashed at me wide-eyed, nostrils flaring, machete in hand, before I'd any time to react. She screamed at me something that could only have been a threat and I felt the blade close to my neck.

"Tu-veux mourir?" repeated the man with growing vexation.

I finally got the message. "Okay! Je pars." Okay! I'm leaving, I said, slowly raising my arms in the air and taking a few steps back to put some distance between myself and the machete. Turning, I made my way slowly back up the trail one eye over my shoulder. The young woman, her machete still poised to cut me down, followed close behind until, I presume, she felt I was committed to leaving. The man, meanwhile, continued to emphasize his low opinion of my intelligence, suggesting that I must certainly have a death wish. He abandoned me at the trailhead and disappeared back into the forest. Shell-shocked, I walked back to camp, astonished to find that I hadn't spilled a drop of tea throughout my ordeal. To make my brush with death even more surreal, I found that foot traffic from the local village had increased along the road and, ironically, I was greeted by passing locals who wished me a pleasant "Bonjour!"

Back at camp, I warned the others to keep off the intersecting trails.

Malcolm managed to repair the transmission by the light of a kerosene lamp. The mosquitoes that had been ignoring us to this point experienced a sudden change of heart and descended on us with a vengeance. As we nodded off to sleep, we could hear the "tump, tump" of drums in the distance, one in answer to the other—villages sharing news of the day, and perhaps a warning about boneheaded White men strolling through the neighborhood uninvited. We could hear the drums each night from that point on, even as far as the outskirts of Kisangani.[16]

Villages of any considerable size along this route were few and far between, but even the most isolated boasted a central round-about fronted by a Mouvement Populaire de la Révolution (MPR) party headquarters with a large portrait of President Mobutu prominently on display. Communities without electricity or radio seemed unsurprised by our

---

[16] If you are interested in how the various peoples of the Congo Basin mastered this skill, I encourage you to read The Talking Drums of Africa by John F. Carrington, first published in 1949.

arrival, more than likely forewarned by the drums we'd heard at night. We were, for the most part, very cordially greeted.

My guess is that a small proportion of adults in the larger communities had occasion in their lives to visit Basoko or Kisangani and maybe travel on the Zaire or Aruwimi at one point or another, and therefore had some first-hand experience with the larger world. It was a completely different story for the youths we encountered in the very, very remote spaces between the larger settlements, who had yet to journey more than a few miles beyond their own communities. To these young people, most of whom had never seen a White person before and knew of us only from grim tales about the horrors inflicted by Belgium during its tenure, we were a danger—potential boogeymen sent to snatch them away. It broke our hearts to catch them off guard, dropping whatever burden they were carrying and running off in terror, which occurred all too often along this leg of our trip. The older people we encountered in the villages received us warmly enough, but seeing young children cling to their mothers in fear at the very sight of us was difficult to bear.

Back on the road, I was seated near the very back row of The Pig half daydreaming when a man leaped from the forest onto our trailer and began slashing at the ropes and canvas tarp with a machete. There was nothing we could do but shout up the rows to George and Malcolm in the cab. Malcolm had the presence of mind to hit the gas and aim for the nearest rough patch. The offender was immediately ejected, flying off into the distance less his weapon. In what condition he hit the ground, I couldn't say. Malcolm didn't slow down until we were well away from the area. The canvas was sliced through and some of Alison's kit damaged. Malcolm kept the machete like a prize taken in war.

It rained heavily that night, which, added to the challenge of crossing streams. Just west of Yambuya, we encountered the narrowest span yet. The stream was deep and moreover, just too wide across for us to find any fallen timbers both manageable and long enough to augment the structure. Malcolm figured he'd give it a go in any case and we held our breath as he drove The Pig across the creaking, bowing logs with perhaps an inch to spare on either side. Once again, he proved his skill as a driver, but just our luck, the track beyond had turned to soup during the previous night's rain and The Pig became mired right up to the axles. We spent the entire afternoon digging it out and only succeeded with the helping hands of many local volunteers.

The Pig mired in mud near Yambuya, Zaire

At Yambuya, we bid farewell to the Aruwimi and then headed due south, making as much time as we could before nightfall. Along the way, we caught sight of a large primate in a tree, likely a kinda baboon. More exciting still, Andy and someone else, I can't quite remember who, possibly Elaina, were riding up behind the cab, enjoying the sights when The Pig brushed up against some low hanging trees. From down below we could hear the two of them shouting in anguish. "Stop! Stop!" they yelled with terrifying urgency, and Malcolm came screeching to a halt. Chaos ensued as they bolted down and off the truck, rolling on the ground in evident agony.

"What's wrong?" we asked, confused, and concerned. There was real fear that they'd been bitten by tree snakes, which could be a deadly proposition in the Congo.

"Ants!" they cried, as they began to strip off their clothes and mercilessly swat and scrub at themselves. On closer inspection, we could see that they were covered in them—large red ants (probably a weaver ant, Oecophylla longinoda) with a bite made worse by their ability to spray formic acid in the victim's wound. Swatting at them accomplished little, as the ants clamped hold with their mandibles and remain clinging, even with half their body removed. Someone had the presence of mind to light up a few cigarettes and we used these to encourage the insects to let loose. We were attentive, after that, not to ride on top in places where the trees were hanging low.

We rejoined the main road running up from Isangi at Yangambi. Our timing couldn't have been more serendipitous. The man himself! President Mobutu! on a tour of the region, was due to pass through Yangambi in a matter of hours. The town was abuzz, thousands of well-wishers and minions streaming in from all over, entertainment venues, refreshment and viewing stands for VIPs being set up. There was a military band and a guard of honor performing Soviet-style drill. The crowds lining the road obviously thought we were part of the planned festivities, because many stood and waved to us as we passed by in The Pig. Most impressive of all, was a traditional Congolese dance troupe and choir. The all-male dance troupe wore leopard caps adorned with luxurious red feathers.

The dance was unambiguously phallic, but seductive rather than crass and pulsed like a heartbeat. The dancers wore ankle bracelets fashioned from tiny shells that rattled like bits of shaken glass when they shuffled their feet. In addition, they wore exaggerated wicker testicles and baskets to accentuate their hips. The testicles and hip attachments each contained small stones which the dancers, with consummate skill, could revolve within the wicker cages by gyrating their hips to the beat, creating a hypnotic "whirring" sound. They could, on demand, and in unison, cause a straw phallus to rise from their loins through some invisible mechanism. The choreography, creativity, rhythm, and energy displayed left us agog and wanting more. Which made the last-second decision by event officials to send us packing with the president's boat just minutes away, all the more disappointing. They made it plain that the decision had been made and no delay on our part would be brooked. We had to content ourselves with what little we were allowed to witness, camping that evening on the Catholic Mission grounds farther up the Zaire River.

The road between Yangambi and Kisangani was in fine repair, so we made the trip in good time. Kisangani, for a city of its size, had a relaxed and comfortable feel about it owing to the exceptionally wide boulevards and its many crumbling, but quaint, Belgian-era buildings. We camped behind the Hotel Olympia for 30Z each (about $1.10 US). It came as a shock to find Bernard and Hazel waiting for us. They had spent all the money they had earned tuning pianos in Yaounde just to catch up. They accused George of breaching his word to wait for them in Bangui and a verbal brawl ensued. Convinced, in the end, that nothing good could come from re-joining the expedition, the pair decided their best course, after all, was to take the boat to Kinshasa.

The whole incident left a bitter taste in my mouth. Worsening group dynamics aside, I was struggling with my own sense that I was missing out on opportunities to see and do the things I personally enjoyed by sticking with the expedition. If, for example, I'd been on my own in Yangambi when President Mobutu came through rather than with the group, I might have been allowed to stay and watch. I couldn't shake the thought.

There was a pleasant palm-shaded patio behind the hotel's restaurant for weary travelers to sit back and enjoy a cold beer. I was lounging there, entertained by a big parrot that could whistle the Colonel Bogey March with bewildering perfection, when I was surprised by a familiar and yet unexpected voice.

"Mind if I join you?" It was Sara! She'd caught up with us yet again.

She proceeded to regale me with astonishing tales of her adventures while traveling on her own. For all the hardships she endured, she seemed no worse for wear. There were downsides to her chosen mode of travel, but the advantages were obvious. She asked me about my own experience thus far, and I related both the good and the bad. "We argue too much," I admitted, "spend all our time worrying about money, don't stop to see the things I'm interested in, or spend long enough at them to really enjoy. I can't really relax either. There's always packing, shopping, washing, wood collection, or cooking duties. It was fun at first, but not so much anymore."

"Why don't you dump this lot, Old Boy, and join me?" she asked. I'd be lying if I didn't admit the idea had already crossed my mind. She fixed those strange amber eyes on me. "So, what's holding you back? Is the thought of traveling with me so much more frightening?"

"No. Of course not. It's just that you're heading north and I'm heading south to South Africa. Unless you've changed your plans? You do still plan to make your way up to the Sudan and then home from Egypt?"

"The fighting in the Sudan is getting worse," she replied, clearly disappointed. "I was rather hoping to see that part of the country. I was speaking with a fellow on one of the overland treks that just passed down that way and he said it's beyond dangerous. There won't be any more overland groups traveling that route, not for some time. I figure it'll be near impossible to hitch rides. I've decided to go through Uganda."

"Uganda?"

"Sure, why not? I'll fly home from Nairobi instead . . . if you'll tag along with me."

Uganda did hold a certain fascination. "You'd change your plans for me?"

"Of course, Old Boy. There's still a lot of interesting ground to cover and a good traveling companion is hard to come by. I'm leaving tomorrow, come hell or high water. Take a couple of hours. Think on it. And do, please, say yes!" She strolled off, leaving me with a crucial decision to make.

Mark found me soon after. "Care to catch a film tonight?"

"Say what?"

"They're showing a film tonight at the French cultural center. No idea what, but ought to be good for a lark. You in?"

"Sure, why not?" I replied, thinking only of Sara and what I should do.

On our way, I owned up to Mark that I was contemplating leaving the group. He was surprised, of course, but not unduly ruffled by the news. "Whatever you think is best, mate. Lila will be heartbroken."

The "cinema" behind the Centre culturel français de Kisangani turned out to be a capacious open-air structure with a grass roof, filled with folding chairs. The turn-out by Zairoise, Belgians, Greek merchants, and a smattering of Overlanders like ourselves was considerable. Once the sun went down, the tent was filled with mosquitoes to feed on us and bats zipping in and out of the projection to feed on them. The evening's entertainment began with a short black and white documentary on the introduction of the automatic pilot in prop driven aircraft, many years out of date even at that juncture. That this, of all films, made it to a showing at the Kisangani French cultural center was a curiosity in itself. The main feature was Le bois des amants, a 1960 drama directed by Claude Autant-Lara about a French resistance fighter and a German officer's wife who meet unexpectedly and fall in love. Spoiler alert—it doesn't end well for the couple. By the end of the movie, I'd made my decision—I was going to leave the expedition!

My decision to drop out surprised just about everyone. As Mark predicted, Lila took the news especially hard and cried, which I thought was sweet. I would definitely miss her, and Mark, for that matter. Despite our ups and downs, he'd been my companion through various adventures and misadventures. Lila, I think, had saved my life on more than one occasion just by keeping an eye on me and providing sound advice when I was at my lowest ebb.

I bundled up my kit and joined Sara at the commercial transport park where we took turns going from truck to truck trying to hitch a ride east toward Beni. That's when I realized how important it is to read the fine print before jumping ship and signing up with a stranger. Sara, as it turned out, hadn't shared with me her two-point "philosophy" on travel. One, first try to hitch for free. If that fails, then two, pay no more than what a local would pay for the same ride. The end result of this dogged conviction was that we spent a full day in a dusty truck park begging for rides and nothing to show for it.

We returned to the Hotel Olympia for a beer to lift our spirits and there I made the acquaintance of a twenty-five-year-old Kenyan journalist named Francis Wangila. Francis had what you might call 'star power.' He was a magnet for beautiful women and there seemed to be a perpetual buzz about him. For some strange reason, he was moved by our plight and pledged himself to seeing us on our way. More than that, he gave us the keys to his room and invited Sara and me to take hot showers and wash off the dust accumulated from a day spent at the truck park.

Coincidentally, my erstwhile companions, feeling the financial pinch of an extended hotel stay, chose that moment to move on to camp at the Saint Gabriel Catholic Mission, so I wound up saying goodbye to them, rather than vice versa. I gave Lila my annotated and hand-illustrated Lonely Planet guidebook as a parting gift.

Sara and I spent another day at the truck park, pleading for a ride to no avail, although a couple of merchants left us with the hope that they might have room for us the following day "depending." I went back to the Hotel Olympia and hung out with Sara and Francis, who did his best to teach us basic Swahili (or Kiswahili). The hotel, being the sort of place it was, we managed to strike up a conversation with a small group of Greek expat commerçants with deep roots in the Kisangani community. A fellow, appropriately named Odysseus, referred us to a part-Greek with a Belgian last name, Vincent Roumont. Vincent owned a transport that he contracted out to a trading company called SOCAM-NT and was apparently planning a run as far as Komanda. Odysseus thought we might improve our chances with Vincent if I let it be known my last name was "Dukas" (my propappoús, great grandfather, and proyiayiá, great grandmother, on my father's side were from the Peloponnese).

The next morning, Sara, Francis, and I, went to the home of Vincent to see if he might be persuaded. To my bewilderment and utter revulsion, Sara and I were invited inside to talk it over, but Francis, being African, was told he had to "wait outside." I stepped back and away from the door feeling sick and confused, but Francis derided me. "Do you want your ride or not, Dukas? This is the way it is here. You must go inside. Go!" He pressed me forward with an insistent wave of one hand. On principle, I should not have heeded my newfound friend. I should have done what was right and stood my ground, even if it meant an indefinite exile in Kisangani. Sara was more pragmatic and thicker skinned, although I daresay she was equally troubled by the situation. In any case, we needed a ride and had received Francis' blessing.

I think it was Sara's quirky charm and ballsey attitude more than my Greek heritage that convinced Vincent to take us on, and, to my even greater astonishment, at no cost! The truck would leave Kisangani that evening at 5 p.m. and we could ride above the cargo, although Vincent would not be accompanying us. To this day I'm at an utter loss to explain why a businessman who routinely charged locals a fare for such a ride would let the two of us ride gratis over 600 kilometers on a journey of no less than ten hours. I was beginning to see how Sara was able to get herself from London to Kisangani on her own and still manage to keep pace with our expedition. When I remarked on how this arrangement with Vincent made absolutely no sense, she brushed it aside with some implausible explanation about her background in psychology.

Francis, who had been waiting patiently outside in the mid-day sun, couldn't have been more pleased for us. He accompanied us back to the Hotel Olympia, teaching us along the way to count to 19 in Swahili. Back at the hotel we met up with Bernard and Hazel and Mark and Lila. Bernard and Hazel, always inclined to take each day as it comes, were in a party mood despite being flat broke and quite determined to spend their last dime celebrating my "liberation" from the Tracks expedition. I was surprised, however, to see Lila and Mark, having assumed the group had moved on. It turned out that George had underestimated expenses and the expedition had run short on funds. He'd wired the Tracks office in London for additional resources and now there was nothing for them all to do but sit and wait for the money to arrive. Lila and Mark, given the fresh circumstances, had hoped to catch me and see me off. It was a touching and unexpected gesture.

I bid Mark and Lila a teary farewell anticipating a 5 p.m. departure, but goods kept showing up at the last moment and it wasn't until the sun began to fade that our Swahili-speaking driver instructed us to mount up. After so much anticipation and build-up, it was an exciting moment indeed for Sara and me to clamber up the side of the truck and nestle in like cats atop the great pile of mysterious goods under canvas. We headed out with darkness settling about us and made it about 30 kilometers out of the city when the truck came to a halt and turned back without a word of explanation. Back at the truck park, we learned that they had forgotten to load "the boss's sardines." A decision was made to spend the night in Kisangani. Sara and I, not trusting that Vincent's men wouldn't change their minds and leave without us, shared a cold meal and spent an uncomfortable night atop the truck.

Sunrise the next day, we were instructed to dismount. The truck was partially unloaded and then reloaded with even more goods, mostly pre-wrapped and sealed away from curious eyes. Vincent showed up unexpectedly, announcing that he would be traveling with us after all. Two strapping young men joined us atop the pile of merchandise. For reasons I never understood, their front teeth were filed into sharp points, their gums stained ruby red from chewing betel nuts. Their appearance caused us some anxiety. They turned out to be quite amiable fellows, which proves the old saw about a book and its cover.

At 10:30 a.m., we set off once again. It was not a pleasant ride. High wood panels hemming in the cargo prevented us from looking out over the countryside for more than a moment or two at a time by standing on our toes while the truck bounced along the heavily rutted road. If you were not quick about it, you soon found yourself rudely thrown down, battered and bruised by the hard-edged cargo. So, we contented ourselves to laying with our legs stretched out, backs to the panel walls, either eyeing one another out of sheer boredom or studying the blue cloud-flecked sky overhead.

We made a pit stop at Bafwasende, an epicenter for Simba rebels fighting to overthrow Belgian rule during the early 1960s. Vincent invited Sara and me to join him at the home of another commerçant for a beer and small talk. Our fellow passengers and Vincent's East African driver did not receive similar invitations. The conversation was all in French. Sara, to my embarrassment, wound up translating some of this, as I struggled to get a handle on our host's vernacular and accent. Frankly, her linguistic dexterity surprised me.

We were soon back on the road, which became increasingly narrow and challenging. At one point, we nearly collided head-on with another vehicle as we rounded a blind corner. We stopped several times to assist other trucks either stuck or broken down. An incredulous driver asked if Sara and I were tourists, evidently a novelty in those parts, to which she replied, "Non, nous sommes juste fous" (No, we're just crazy). Unable to look out and bouncing around so much that it was impossible to even doze, I succumbed to motion sickness. Vincent took pity on me and allowed me to ride in the cab until we finally stopped for a few hours' sleep at Nia-Nia, somewhere between 3 and 7 a.m.

East of Nia-Nia, where the Ituri and Epulu rivers meet, we crossed some of the largest and densest tracts of unspoiled lowland rainforest in the Congo Basin. It is or was a region of indescribable beauty and home to hundreds of species of butterflies, forest elephants, chimps, antelope, buffalo, leopards, and one of the rarest and most curious animals in all of Africa, the okapi (O. johnstoni), which looks like a cross between a zebra and a small giraffe (perhaps the inspiration for Dr. Doolittle's "Pushmi-Pullyu").

The Ituri Forest is also home to the Mbuti and Efe Pygmy people. The term "Pygmy" is actually derived from Greek, but there is no good consensus on an alternative term. An enormous wildlife preserve was created in 1992 covering much of the Ituri watershed to protect the okapi, other vulnerable species, and a fast-diminishing way of life, but it has been an uphill battle against poachers, illegal mining, and Mai-Mai rebels. We made another pit stop at the Station de capture okapis (today Epulu Station, about 6 kilometers west of the village of Ka) where Vincent treated Sara and me to ice cold cans of soda pop.

Somewhere between the villages of Ka and Yakele, our progress was halted by a big tree that had been cut down straight across the road. We were the only vehicle passing through at the time. What seemed to us like an entire Pygmy village—men, women, and children—swarmed over the tree with machetes like ants on an invading insect. This was a boisterous community of Mbuti (or Bambuti) people. Most were clothed traditionally, in materials gathered from the forest rather than the worn out hand-me-down Western rags that, sadly, seemed to be gaining traction in the region. They sang without interruption, a chaotic yet pleasing sound, like a windchime in a storm. They ignored our presence and set about their task with determination and humor. They would have made good time clearing out the felled tree, but this was apparently just one of several they intended on bringing down.

The Mbuti gained more energy and enthusiasm for the task with every felling, letting out a triumphal cry each time they succeeded in bringing one down. Vincent was fit to be tied and cursed them in French and Greek, at the same time pleading with them to stop and clear the road. Sara and I, on the other hand, were captivated by the whole encounter and felt blessed by the opportunity to witness the Mbuti at work.

It took hours for them to complete their project. While all this was taking place, we opted to walk ahead, informing Vincent that we would rendezvous with him farther down. I was adamant with Sara about keeping to the road and not wandering off, but otherwise reveled in a rare opportunity to take in the great forest at our leisure. Emanating from deep within the surrounding jungle we could hear drums over the usual cacophony. Sara turned to me invoking an old explorers' trope, "I say, Carruthers, the drums have started."[17] I was "Carruthers" to her from that moment on.

---

[17] Sara was playing on the plot of an old adventure novel by A.E.W. Mason. Captain Frank Carruthers was a fictional character in Mason's 1937 novel, The Drum. Set in India's Northwest Frontier, disaster befalls anyone who lays eyes on a phantom drummer who beats a mysterious and haunting rhythm in the night on a legendary drum.

We helped ourselves to wild raspberries and passed the time spying out monkeys chattering in the trees above our heads. A clutch of young Pygmy girls singing in perfect harmony passed us by without a pause or curious glance in our direction. They were clad only in loin cloths and tattooed from head to toe. They showed not the slightest interest in our material possessions or culture, and I instinctively admired them for it.

On our way again, east of Kibimbi, the topography became increasingly mountainous and the road increasingly slow going. We stopped to eat supper in Mambasa and Vincent treated us to tins of beef and fish with beer to wash it down. It rained quite heavily that afternoon. Vincent managed to squeeze both Sara and me into the cab until it stopped raining, leaving our less fortunate African (and paying) companions to weather it out on top. We reached Komanda, the truck's final destination, about 8 p.m., thanked Vincent profusely for his generosity, which seemed to amuse him, and parted company. It was dark and raining hard, so Sara and I chose someone's back yard at random and prepared a hootchie-style shelter for the night.

It continued to rain through the morning, which provided an excuse for us to sleep in. Although tempted to scout out the nearby grottoes, we agreed that we hadn't enough time or funds remaining to squander on an optional excursion, which was admittedly paradoxical (maybe even hypocritical?), given that was one of my excuses for bailing on the Tracks expedition. Instead, we sat on a wall outside of Komanda for almost five hours attempting to hitch a ride. While waiting, I learned that Sara was the casualty of a failed attempt at a Ph.D. in biochemistry and more than a little bummed about the experience. She was also a huge admirer of British writer, H.H. Munro, renowned for his macabre sense of humor.[18] This, in part, accounted for her calling me "Old Cabbage," and other curiously Edwardian pet names.

A number of vehicles stopped to pick us up, but the drivers gaped at us as if we were a couple of lunatics and moved on when Sara informed them that we had no intention of paying for a ride. Passing the time, we briefly crossed paths with Steve, a Brit returning home after working for some time in Zimbabwe. Eventually, we were rescued by a group of evangelicals/commerçants traveling in a rundown pickup truck who evidently valued good deeds over money, lucky for us. They sang songs of the gospel as we bumped along in the back of the open pickup.

One of our fellow passengers, as it happens, was a Pygmy heading to a wedding accompanied by a rather large pig. The latter, we were informed, was to be a gift for the bride and groom. The pig, I must say, was well behaved. I couldn't say the same for our vehicle. The pickup was short on power, requiring us to get out and push over each small incline, stretching the 100-kilometer trip from Komanda to Oicha (or Oyija) to several hours. The pig, of course, remained on the truck each time this occurred. The wedding guest as well, as the pig, he asserted, was too valuable and too precious to leave unattended, even for a moment. Round about the fifth or sixth time we got out to do push the truck, Sara turned to me with a mischievous smile and said, "Do you realize we're pushing a pig and a Pygmy in a pickup? How many people do you know will ever be able to say that?" It wasn't exactly profound or representative of what I came to Africa to accomplish, but it made me smile too and I was happy Sara was there to bring it to my attention. I doubt the thought would have otherwise occurred to me.

The evangelicals dropped us off at the local protestant mission, a neatly ordered and conspicuously tidy compound

---

[18] Munro went by the pen name "Saki." He was killed in 1916 by a German sniper during the battle of Ancre. His last words, reputedly, were, "Put that bloody cigarette out!."

on the edge of town, a center for treating Hanson's Disease and providing desperately needed medical care to the Pygmy population. The lone missionary on duty at Oicha was an Australian who was, to say the least, cool toward us. I gathered from the little he shared about himself that he found life to be pretty serious business and, consequently, thought our escapade across the heart of Africa to be a frivolous self-indulgent waste of time. From his perspective, I suppose it was. All the same, he laid out the rules quite precisely and pointed us toward our room.

The next morning, we had much better luck catching a ride on a coffee transport headed for Kasindi. I say "luck," but we bartered for the ride with a few items of clothes each. Sara, it turned out, was "okay" with barter in a pinch. We were excited to learn that the driver planned to make a brief detour for a delivery to Mutwanga at the foot of the Ruwenzori Mountains—the Mountains of the Moon! We were no less fortunate in the fact that we could ride safely perched atop the huge, cushioned sacks of coffee with sweeping views of the countryside. We shared this space with fourteen other passengers including three armed soldiers and several chickens.

South of Oicha was beautiful fertile country, tamed from the jungle for agriculture. Our first stop was Beni, a prosperous town amidst rolling hills. The market was overflowing with the plumpest, juiciest, sweetest pineapples you can ever imagine, which we took the opportunity to enjoy and seriously over indulged. From Beni almost all the way to Mutwanga we passed through the boundaries of Virunga National Park. I thought I'd seen plenty of beautiful country in Africa by this time, but nothing, simply nothing, before or after, compared to the Ruwenzori Mountains for sheer unspoiled majesty—emerald-green valleys blanketed in exotic floras juxtaposed against snow-capped crystalline mountains and plummeting waterfalls. Our necks hurt at the end of the day from swiveling back and forth between one breathtaking vista and another.

We pulled into a modest depot serving the coffee plantations surrounding Mutwanga as the sun was beginning to fade. High above us, dozens of small red stucco homes sheltered under verdant palms along the terraced foothills, thin plumes of gray smoke rising from their chimney pots. The passengers stepped down and mostly went their separate ways, except for Sara and me and the three soldiers.

The commerçant winked at us conspiratorially and motioned for us to come have a look at the heavy sacks being off-loaded. We should have realized from the get-go that it made no sense to be shipping coffee to the plantation rather than from it. He opened one of the sacks just a hair to let us see what was inside. Cash! Cash, in sacks so heavy one man could hardly lift them. We'd been riding all along on top of tens of thousands in Zaire notes, pay for the plantation workers, disguised as coffee! Our three soldiers weren't just hitching a ride to base, they were the payroll guards. If word had leaked out along the way, we'd have been easy pickings for bandits or rebels. I could see the commerçant was much relieved to see his delivery safely completed, and in retrospect, so were we.

We slept in the truck that night. The next morning, March 17, 1984, marked four months to the day since departing London and my 107th day since arriving in Africa. We made an early start on the road to Kasindi, theoretically a short ride of only 50 kilometers, but it rained heavily and the road turned into a treacherous mire that threatened to overturn our vehicle at any moment.

The entire ride from Oicha to Kasindi was such an incredible experience that I felt I needed to reward the commerçant with something special, although he could not have known how much the experience had meant to me personally. I'd been dragging along a framed British commemorative coin set I'd picked up in London with the intention of giving it to someone who might appreciate it and yet never expect it. It was a small thing, but the commerçant was clearly thrilled with it and almost hugged me in gratitude. He promised me that it would hold a place of honor atop his mantel. Sara wondered openly at what other interesting items I had hidden away in my bag, but that was really it as far as unusual gifts.

We soon learned that relations between Zaire and Uganda were distinctly frosty and although crossing was permitted, it was not much encouraged. Sara did not improve the situation. She was snarky with one of the Zaire customs agents. As a result, we were searched more thoroughly than usual. The agent I was subject to was "suspicious," he said, of my tube of toothpaste. I wound up squeezing the entire contents onto a large leaf for inspection. Satisfied, he handed me back the empty tube, rolling up the leaf and setting it aside with such care there was little doubt he had some further use for it.

A considerable no-man's land existed between the outskirts of Kasindi and the border crossing at Mpondwe, on the Ugandan side. We would have to walk through open fields carrying our bags for over two and a half kilometers in the rain. I had one enormous convertible backpack and two shoulder bags, which were easily manageable over short distances. I'd never planned for an actual cross-country hike with all that baggage. Sara was only slightly better off. It was hard going. I felt like a refugee, following the long line of men, women, and children over rolling hills hauling all manner of goods and belongings stored in curiously innovative containers.

The border was closed for the night by the time we reached it. The Zaire border police kept a small post on the edge of no-man's-land that we camped behind. We could hear the police inside cooking up a hot meal over a charcoal stove, obviously enjoying themselves. Cold, wet, and hungry, Sara fixed up the courage to ask if they could spare a little something for us, a thing that would never in a million years have occurred to me. To my astonishment, we were invited to join them for dinner like long-lost friends.

At sunrise, with dew still on the ground, we trudged the remaining distance over to the Ugandan customs and immigration post. It was perched astride a shallow river where a few women were already hard at work washing clothes. Owing to the early hour we were the first ones awaiting processing. The customs check was superficial, the agent going through the motions as if he had better things to do and wondering why we were wasting his time. He gestured toward the door with a jerk of this thumb, directing us to report to immigration, but the door to the office marked "IMMIGRATION" was locked with no one about. "Maybe we should just skip it?" offered Sara.

I wasn't so confident that avoiding an immigration stamp wouldn't wind up biting us in the ass. "Let's try around the back," I prompted, and sure enough there was an open doorway. Inside were the missing immigration officers, engaged in a game of cards. "We were told to report for an immigration check," I spluttered. They glared back at me, laying down their cards and leading us back to unlock their office. "Open your bags," ordered the senior-most officer. The two men proceeded to go through our belongings with a fine-tooth comb. Finding nothing of particular importance, the officer looked at me with accusing eyes, "What about currency?" he asked.

"What about it?" I responded. I had a hundred plus US dollars hidden in a secret zippered pouch behind my belt, a few Zaires and leftover CFA francs in my wallet, plus travelers checks. I wasn't about to volunteer that information. "Isn't that a customs matter?"

"It is illegal to bring Zaires into Uganda. If you have Zaires it is a police matter." This was news to me. There was no way for me to confirm or deny the assertion.

"I have a small amount of Zaire notes," I admitted. About 15Z in total, worth about 55 cents. I opened my wallet and handed over the notes. He turned the small clutch of fractional banknotes over in his hand, inspecting them front to back.

"I am doing you a favor by confiscating these. You could be in big trouble for attempting to bring illegal currency." He looked at me with hungry eyes. "Is this all?" I didn't like where this was going.

"That's all the Zaire notes I have," I replied. There was a commotion out the door that redirected his attention. Several heavy vehicles had pulled up, army trucks loaded with Ugandan troops. A moment later, a very large dark-skinned man with deep traditional facial scars entered the room. In the blink of an eye, the immigration officers turned into wet toast, literally withdrawing to the corner of the room. The newcomer was wearing a crisp camouflage uniform, sleeves rolled up tightly against his oversized biceps. His British-pattern rank identified him as a second lieutenant. He ran his eyes over the two immigration officers and then over to Sara and me, sussing up the situation quickly.

"Is everything all right?" he asked.

"Fine," I replied. I glanced at the immigration officer. "Are we done?" I asked.

He nodded sheepishly, seemingly happy now to be rid of us.

We quickly repacked and dragged our bags outside. The obliging customs agent was standing to one side, careful to remain aloof from the unfolding events. I asked him about getting a ride into Kasese, nearly 60 kilometers to the northeast. "No rides," he replied. "The border is closed. No lorries coming this way." Disconcerting and potentially troubling news for us.

"Well, is there any place I can change money?" We needed Ugandan currency if we were going to buy food to eat.

"No banks. They are all closed for the weekend." Just our luck to arrive on a Saturday. Sara and I huddled together to talk over the pickle we'd evidently got ourselves into as the troops remounted their transports. I had an unpleasant vision of being left alone with Sara at the border together with a belligerent and moreover vindictive immigration officer. The second lieutenant must have read my face. Halfway into the cab of his truck, he stepped back down as an after-thought and walked over to us.

"Would you like a lift into Kasese?" he asked. There was no hesitation on our part. He directed his soldiers to make room on one of the benches at the back of his truck. Sara loaded in first. I was about to reach for my bag, but the second lieutenant reached for it first and heaved it up. It was heavier than he expected, and he looked at me appreciatively.

I can tell you, it was a "trip" for me, and Sara, I suppose, to hitch a ride with the Uganda National Liberation Army (UNLA) and to see the countryside around Lake George on what turned out to be a wonderful sunny day from the vantage point of an open flatbed truck. Of course, traveling in this manner had the added advantage of allowing us to by-pass numerous police and military checks. The diesel engine and gravel road made for noisy going and making it difficult to carry on a conversation, but I was able to learn that these were troops from a frontier detachment of the 31st Battalion out of Fort Portal. I wanted to take photographs, but we were cautioned to keep our cameras out of sight.

Across the fields surrounding Kasese, I caught sight of one of the strangest things I'd ever seen. It looked like a group of stoop-shouldered men in gray suits promenading back and forth, but their faces were long and distended with a slightly yellowish tinge, like cartoon characters from Spy vs. Spy come to life. I could not imagine what these beings were. The sight of them gave me the willies. It wasn't until we got right up close that I realized they were storks, marabou storks to be precise (L. crumenifer). These remarkable birds grow up to five feet tall with a wingspan of over eight feet. At a distance it's difficult if not impossible to tell them apart from humans when they walk.

We were delivered to the military post in Kasese and unexpectedly ushered in to meet the "OIC" (Officer in Charge) of the Ruwenzori District, Lieutenant Dennis S—

(probably best if I don't mention his full name). The second lieutenant that rescued us at the border was dismissed rather gruffly and departed. The office was elegantly appointed, and I couldn't shake the feeling that it had once served as part of a British East African garrison. Lieutenant S. broke out a bottle of Johnnie Walker and introduced us to his adjutant, "Gems," who had obviously been sharing a drink or two with his commanding officer before we were brought in, though it was yet early in the day.

The lieutenant proceeded to politely interrogate us from the comfort of his leather armchair. Although he wore the rank of a junior officer (the same rank as myself, as it happens), Lieutenant S. was in charge of a substantial military district and commanded, I was given to understand, the better part of a battalion. First and foremost, he demanded to know if his subordinate had abused us in any fashion, which threw Sara and me for a complete loop. "On the contrary," we assured him, the man had undoubtedly saved us from a costly shakedown. The lieutenant remained skeptical, however, and it became clear that there were serious tribal divisions within his organization. The second lieutenant had been nothing but courteous and professional the entire time we were with him. Suspicion and mistrust based solely on ethnicity, I thought to myself, is a piss poor foundation for a national army.

What I did not understand or appreciate at the time was that UNLA was a purely political construct forged together from competing political "Fronts" in opposition to ousted president, Idi Amin. It was not a "national army" in any sense of the term. President Milton Obote was just as guilty of retribution politics as his infamous predecessor. In fact, unbeknownst to Sara and myself, UNLA forces were enmeshed at the time in a brutal civil war with the National Resistance Army (NRA) just north of Kampala that would result in the forced relocation and deaths of thousands of civilians. Obote was ousted from power a year after our visit.

Lieutenant S. was all sweetness and honey. Somewhere in the midst of our conversation he slipped in a request to exchange a substantial quantity of Ugandan shillings (Sh) for American dollars. We would be doing him a "great favor," he said. This was black marketeering at its most obvious and I wasn't at all sure that he wasn't just testing us. It became clear very quickly, however, that he was in earnest. The man was an opportunist, pure and simple. Because we arrived on a weekend and the banks were closed, I did offer to change $20 with him, which he accepted. I wasn't about to risk more than that, which clearly displeased him. But he let it go for the time being and invited us back to continue the conversation later that evening.

In the meantime, we set about finding a place to stay for the night. Camping out in Kasese was not recommended for safety reasons, but the few hotels in town were all booked up. Sara once again wielded her magic, and we were given permission to camp out in the hallway of the Modern Lodge for free. What business does that sort of thing? Not to sound ungrateful, but the "Modern Lodge" was a pretty threadbare establishment. I figured we'd catch a few winks there and move quickly on.

Once we had our accommodations sorted out, we scouted about for a place to eat and found the Travel Bar where we chowed down on perfectly prepared fried fish with a side of chips all for the princely sum of 280 Ugandan shillings (or about 86 cents). We then made our way back to the military post and picked up on our conversation with Lieutenant S. while he plied us with bottles of White Nile beer.

Although still very much on duty, he got progressively drunk. Now and again, we were interrupted by Gems with matters that required the lieutenant's deliberations. I understood from the few snippets I caught that we were in the presence of someone whose word was law. As much as we were enjoying this strange and unexpected twist of events, even reveling in a rare, privileged moment, there was danger at hand. The lieutenant was clearly up to something, and I wanted to remain alert enough to figure it out. Doing my best to hold my liquor, the good lieutenant made it clear that there was no brooking his hospitality. After a couple of hours of this, I was hardly able to stand up. Sara, if at all aware that some great game was afoot, cared not a smidgen and got so drunk that neither of us could understand a word she was saying.

Lieutenant S., not so drunk as he seemed, eventually got round to a proposal. Ugandan rebels, he explained, had established bases in Zaire and he was eager to suss them out. His thought was for us to return to Zaire and work as his spies! He figured, rather shrewdly, that if we simply carried on under our existing "cover" our real purpose would be hard to discern. He was quite serious. In return for our services, he would arrange for us to be placed on the books of the Ugandan News Agency and fittingly compensated. Sara was too far gone to comprehend his offer, muttering something about it being 'all very interesting and exciting.' Nothing good, I felt, was going to come of this.

"You don't have to decide this minute," said the lieutenant. "Let's meet tomorrow at noon and we can firm things up."

"Good by me," I replied, happy to be away from him.

He rested one hand on my shoulder. "And tomorrow when you return you can help me exchange more shillings for dollars."

The sinking feeling in the pit of my stomach grew larger. I politely explained to him that I could be arrested at the border if I did not have the supporting documents to prove I'd changed the money legally at a bank.

He smiled at me in a way that sent chills down my spine. "That's okay," he replied. "It was only a request, not a demand. I'll see you tomorrow." He arranged a ride for us back to the motel, as Sara was in no position to walk. Our "room" in the corridor didn't need much preparation. We were tucked well out of sight in an open utility closet so as not to interfere with the movement of paying guests. I helped put Sara to bed, then stretched out as best I could, unable to sleep. I knew from passing that there were a couple of young Scandinavian women in a room up the hall. They had traveled to the Ruwenzories to see mountain gorillas. I was just beginning to doze off when I heard shouts and the sound of fists pounding on a door.

"Go away!" screamed the young women, repeatedly. "Leave us alone!" But the pounding continued amid slurred and heated voices. I made to get up, but Sara placed a cautioning hand on me.

"They can't get in if the girls don't open the door. Stay still," she whispered.

She was right, of course. Alone, unarmed, and clad only in my briefs, I wouldn't have stood much of a chance. At best, I would have been laughed at. Still, I listened attentively to hear if they gained the door. If they managed it, I told myself, then I will go out there and do whatever I can to help. As fortune would have it, the intruders were not bold enough to attempt breaking down the door and eventually stumbled off into the night. The walls were thin enough that even from down the hall we could hear the women consoling one another amidst frightened sobs. I went back to sleep.

We grabbed just enough winks to function, gathered our kit, and cleared out come sunrise. Sara had a massive hangover and listened impatiently as I summarized the potential for big trouble if we did not skip town before noon. There was no telling, in my opinion, how far our friend the lieutenant would go to entangle us in his affairs, and I didn't want to wait around to find out. A few discreet questions, however, revealed there were a good many military check points along the road to Kampala. Given the circumstances and the unpredictability of the soldiery, I managed to convince Sara that it was worth spending a few bucks to take the train.

A ticket agent downtown sold us two second class overnight train tickets to Kampala for 1,800Sh (about $5.50 US apiece). The station was some distance out of town, but the train wasn't due to come through until 3:30 in the afternoon. We grabbed a bite at the Travel Bar where we ran into Gems, of all people. Fortunately, he had no inkling of what his boss was up to.

Thinking it was prudent to put some distance between ourselves and Lieutenant S. before noon, we hitched a ride to the outskirts of town, walking the rest of the way to the station. 3:30 came and went, still no train. The station master told us it wasn't unusual for delays due to overcrowding or mechanical issues. To while away the time, we taught ourselves to play Mancala, an African game played with stones. Much to our relief, the train pulled in at 5 p.m. and we were on our way, men and women assigned to separate cars. I wasn't sure if that was quaint or prudent. I shared a sleeping compartment with five other men, four businessmen, and a 66-year-old Uganda People's Congress (UPC) party official.

Many of the passengers that boarded the train with us at Kasese were women netball players, a hugely popular sport in Africa and parts of the Commonwealth. If you aren't familiar with netball, it sort of resembles basketball, except there is no dribbling or running with the ball, and no backboard. Kasese was host to a regional championship, hence the lack of available rooms.

An hour down the line the train came to screeching halt. I figured technical problems and looked to my traveling companions for confirmation. One of them stuck his head out the window, then turned to us and announced, matter of factly, "We must get off the train."

Get off the train? I thought to myself. We're in the middle of nowhere, empty fields on either side. But I could see people quietly filing through the corridor. I followed along, wondering what was afoot. By the time I reached the carriage door, I could see hundreds of people standing in the grass beside the tracks, but that isn't what concerned me. Moving forward through the crowd of detrained passengers was a company sized unit of armed men in uniform. I craned my neck to see if I could spot Sara amongst the throng, but no luck. The soldiers took up positions at each carriage door. A few boarded the train.

A loud whistle from up near the engine broke the awkward silence and the passengers began to re-board. The soldiers checked IDs. It was obvious that this was mere pretense, an effort to give an air of respectability to their extortion, each passenger handing whatever cash they could spare to the soldier who might otherwise bar their way. It was a shakedown on a monumental scale. I stood in the queue like everyone else until it was my turn to come face-to-face with what passed for a soldier in Uganda. He was a good head taller than me, nervously fingering the Kalashnikov rifle in his hands. He looked at me as if pondering his options, then gestured with two fingers to his lips, puffing on an imaginary cigarette.

"I don't smoke," I said apologetically. He rolled his eyes ever so slightly, then twitched his head to one side.

"Go to your compartment. We will come see you later."

Back in our compartment I reclaimed my place in the upper birth and waited all alone, listening to the sounds in the corridor and imagining the worst. But no one came to follow up with me. The other occupants of my compartment returned, and the train pulled away. Evidently, hitting up a foreigner for cash was potentially more trouble than it was worth.

Looking down from my bunk, I asked the old party official what this was really all about. I could sense his embarrassment. "The troops haven't been paid in months," he explained. "They rely on the good will of the people to help out. No one gives more than they are able," he said, as if holding up a train at gunpoint was the most normal thing.

Quite the system, I thought to myself. The four businessmen broke out a bottle of home brewed liquor distilled from banana. It didn't take long before they were plastered. Doing my best to ignore them, I struck up a conversation with the UPC party member. By Ugandan standards, 66 was very old (in 1984, the average life expectancy in Uganda was just 50). Because of both his age and his position in the party, he commanded respect. I discovered that he was a veteran, having served with the 4th Battalion, King's African Rifles during World War II. I shared with him that I was on leave from the Canadian Army, thinking that it might help to bridge our worlds. That, perhaps, was a mistake.

"Canadian?" piped in one of the businessmen, an obese and overbearing fellow, that I had taken an immediate dislike to. "I was in Canada. Wainwright, Alberta," he said with distinct disdain.

"Really?" I replied. "Why was that?"

"Commonwealth training program. Cold, miserable place, Wainwright. Canadians are assholes. Racist shits." He looked up at me as if daring me to challenge him on the point. What little I could discern of this fellow, I daresay he'd brought on his own troubles.

"You were in the military?" I asked.

"Yes."

"I'm sorry you were so badly treated. Not all Canadians are 'racist shits,' but, yeah, some are."

He gazed at me through half-lidded eyes. "Have a drink." He staggered toward me, thrusting the bottle they'd been sharing in my face. I foolishly hesitated, not only because these four men had been slobbering over the same bottle, but because of my previous run-ins with homemade spirits. My stomach had barely settled after months of discomfort. I was instinctively reticent. He pulled back, "Won't drink from the same bottle as a N%#ger, eh?!"

"No! That's not it at all!" I stammered. "I've had a bad experience with homemade liquor recently. My stomach can't take it."

He looked to his drunken pals. "What do you say we toss this piece of Canadian shit out the window?" He turned his attention back to me. "What's to prevent us from throwing you out the window right now? No one would know and no one would care." I knew he meant it.

"Look, I've got nothing against you. I'm telling you the truth. I just had a really bad experience with homemade liquor. If it means that much to you, I'll take a drink. Just not too much. Okay?"

The old party official stepped in, calmly addressing the drunken businessmen in what I presume was Bantu. They listened respectfully, then returned to me. "Father, here, says we should let you alone. He's 66, you know. That's very old for us. If he says to leave you alone, then we'll leave you alone. That's all."

I breathed a sigh of relief and nodded gratefully to the old man. "Let me have a swig of that, but just a sip, okay?"

He grinned at me with one eye open and passed me the bottle. I tried not to think about it and quaffed back a mouthful. I was surprised to find that it didn't taste anything like banana. They left me in peace after that.

The train rumbled on through the night. The car was quite modern and comfortable for second class. I slept comfortably, it being an actual bed. The train stopped one more time just outside of Kampala, about 7 in the morning, for a military inspection. This time, actually searching for rebel sympathizers. We reached Kampala an hour and a half later. I met up with Sara at immigration, where we were instructed to register. She told me that she'd slept right through the train being stopped and everyone herded off, and only learned about it afterward. The women in her compartment didn't want to disturb her.

There was a place to store our bags at the station, which was very liberating. I loved Kampala from the moment I stepped off the train, a modern vibrant city, with a distinctly African beat. The women's dresses amazed me, reminiscent of garments from the antebellum South (less the hoops, of course), with big puff shoulders. The Mascot Restaurant across from the main post office, looked like a good choice. Sara and I chowed down on a big breakfast of eggs, chips, and coffee for just over a buck. For another two and a half dollars a night, I was able to get a shared room at the Mukwana Hotel near the taxi park and bus depot. The Mukwana must have been a beautiful building in its day, exquisite woodwork. Like the train, men and women kept to their own rooms. The entire South Asian population of Uganda had been expelled by President Idi Amin in 1972 and were slowly beginning to return. My roommate was an Indian national, a Sikh named Don, in Kampala on business.

I went over to the Kenya Airways office to ask about flights to Nairobi and wound up booking a flight for $90 US from Entebbe the following day on Uganda Airlines. It would be a short hop, but a chance to experience what it's like to fly in Africa. Moreover, the airport at Entebbe held a kind of curiosity for me, owing to the Israeli raid and connection to Idi Amin. It was only after I purchased the ticket that I learned a young Brit had been murdered at Entebbe the prior weekend. The motivation for his killing was never clear.

I spent the rest of the afternoon window shopping with Sara, who decided in the end that she would take the train to Nairobi ("Why would I fly" she persisted, "when the train is cheaper?"). We spotted a beautiful monochrome batik of grazing zebras in a shop at the same time and wound-up bidding against one another for it. I won the bid at 2,700 Shillings. It hangs on my wall to this day. As a consolation prize, I gave her a superbly crafted slingshot I'd picked up in Zaire.

The shops all closed by 5 p.m. Although technically there was no curfew in effect at the time, soldiers roamed the street at night and robbed anyone they could corner. My stomach began to bother me again, so I went back to the hotel, took some meds, did some sewing and re-packing. In the pocket of one of my shirts I found a tea bag that had been given to me as "change" back in Mali. Don returned to the room one night after a visit to the Sikh temple, steaming mad. He'd been held up by soldiers, for the second time, and robbed of 5,000Sh ($15 US). He warned me that he was occasionally woken up in the night by gunfire in the street, so I was surprised to have been woken up in the middle of the night not by gunfire, but by a terrible row over privacy between a couple of Australian women and the hotel manager.

I got up early the next day to meet Sara for tea and to wish her safe travels. We'd meet again in Nairobi, God willing. She was catching the 9:30 a.m. train together with the Australian women. As a parting gift, she gave me her Hitchhiker's Guide to the Galaxy "DON'T PANIC" button. I caught a matatu (a shared minivan) to downtown Entebbe, a 40-kilometer trip, for less than a dollar, and then a "special cab" to the airport for a couple of dollars more. Entebbe seemed to be a well-heeled community, rather posh, including a first-rate botanical garden. The famous airport, however, was very run down. I only caught a glimpse of the actual terminal from the historic raid. It had never reopened. Given political affairs in the country, I was surprised to find the airport security and customs rather relaxed.

Waiting for my flight, I struck up a conversation with an agrochemical salesman from India. The equivalent of a business commuter flight, it was, on the whole, very professionally run. It was, however, immediately evident that no one had serviced the interior of the plane between flights. I knew this because on the floor right in front of my seat was an American $50 bill! Some businessman likely let it fall from his wallet while paying for his drinks. My $90 flight, for all intents and purposes, was now $40. It literally paid to be first to my row and in my seat. The view from the plane was amazing. Kenya appeared as a vast arid plateau broken by hills running down to Nairobi. The man seated next to me turned out to be an American diplomat. He enjoyed the few tales of my travels thus far, enough that I was unexpectedly rewarded with a chauffeured ride into Nairobi.

Nairobi was, and I presume, still is, a world-class city. I enjoyed hearing Swahili spoken so widely in the street. It is very easy on the ear and relatively simple to pick up, but if you thought Canadians used "eh" a lot, you haven't heard someone speak Swahili.

The city had everything you could possibly want and at unimaginably affordable prices. For 150Sh ($11 US) a night, I was able to get a modern well-appointed room with a hot bath at the Solace Hotel on Tom Mboya Street. The Burger House restaurant, just next door, offered an all-day breakfast consisting of juice, eggs any style, toast, baked beans, and coffee perfectly prepared and all for 15Sh (about a buck ten). If I wanted, I could order a hamburger, banana split or a chocolate milkshake. The first time they served me coffee, however, I nearly choked to death. The local practice of putting a big chunk of fresh ginger at the bottom of the mug took me utterly by surprise. My first thought was that some gargantuan insect had fallen into my cup. Only after I fished it out and gave it a good sniff did I realize that it was ginger intentionally used to flavor the coffee. I've prepared my morning cup of java with fresh ginger ever since. It gives the coffee a spicy kick and is altogether habit forming.

I'd pre-arranged to meet up with Sara at the Solace, assuming our plans would align. I was certain there would be mail waiting for me at the poste restante, so I was devastated to find there was no word from home or Edi awaiting me at the main post office. The post office only kept poste restante mail for so many weeks and then trashed it. I presume the delay reaching Nairobi cost me my precious mail.

It then occurred to me that my father might have sent me something via the Mitsui office. I introduced myself to the Assistant General Manager, Mr. Hayashi, but there was nothing for me there either. Mr. Hayashi generously offered to send a Telex to my dad, letting him know that I'd arrived safely in Nairobi, keeping in mind, he had no idea that I'd jumped ship on the Tracks expedition.

I wandered about town, enjoying the sites. Blue Thunder, a 1983 action flick starring Roy Scheider was playing at the 20th Century Cinema and I thought, heck, why not? It was fun, and the theater was one of those Art Deco classics. Later, back at the hotel, I learned that someone named "Steve," was trying to find me. I tracked him down and learned from him that Sara had beat me to Nairobi but had to return to Kampala because the poor girl had left her passport behind.

The following day, I paid a visit to the Canadian High Commission because I was down to the last remaining unstamped page in my passport. They refused to add another extension to it (I'd used up seven of the eight additional pages provided by the embassy in Upper Volta), but for 255 Kenyan shillings ($23 Canadian) I was able to obtain a brand-new business size passport on the spot. Impressive.

Surmising that I was going to be in Nairobi at some point, a friend of my mother passed along the name of the daughter of a mutual friend before I left for Africa who, coincidentally, worked at the Canadian High Commission. Her name was Margo Schwartz and she was new to the diplomatic service, a job that I incidentally coveted. I introduced myself and Margo suggested that we get together for lunch the following day. Checking back with the Mitsui office, I learned that my father had replied with a Telex. As pre-arranged, he had wired $1,100 US to me via the Standard Bank on Kenyatta Avenue. This was money intended for my airfare home from South Africa, or if I should choose to cut short my trip, to return via Nairobi.

The money was waiting for me at the bank, and I had no difficulty cashing it out in the form of VISA travelers checks. The Telex included a request for me to call home. It was a quick call and my mom and dad seemed much relieved to hear my voice. My father surprised me, however, with news that he'd paved the way for me to interview for a position at the Mitsui Bank of Canada in Toronto. My mother insisted that the "intelligent thing" to do was to cut short my trip, take the interview, and start my career.

They played the guilt card saying that my trip was taking too long and that it was beginning to take an emotional toll on Edi. Could that be? I somehow doubted it. I'd endured enough to know that I would never have another crack at this. If I passed on the opportunity to traverse the continent from top to bottom, it would be lost forever. I could see all the signs that this sort of trek would be next to impossible to complete in the not-too-distant future and in my heart I knew that I would curse myself for not having the tenacity to finish what I set out to do. I would regret it to my dying day.

The job interview would just have to wait. I gave them my love and let my mother and father know in no uncertain terms that I planned to keep going all the way to South Africa. It would only be a few more weeks. Just in case, I jotted off a letter to Edi.

I found Sara back at the hotel. Steve had got the message muddled. It wasn't her passport that she'd left behind. It was all her travelers checks. She'd left them under the mattress at the Mukwana Hotel. Lucky for her, the hotel cleaning service was not terribly thorough. The checks were still there. It was Sara's turn to do something to decompress, something utterly mundane. I don't know if it was a deliberate theme, but Thunderball (from 1965), with Sean Connery was playing at another cinema and since she was in the mood, I agreed to a second movie-night. This time, for the last time, we said our good-byes and parted ways, promising one another to keep in touch.

I slept in the next morning, read the paper, updated my journals, then prepared for my "date" with Margo from the diplomatic service. We met at the Stanley Hotel and then went for lunch at the African Heritage Restaurant. It turned out that Margo was a Queen's University politics grad, like myself, and close enough to my own age. I was looking at the living embodiment of all that I'd striven to become and failed to attain.

The restaurant's live band was great and because Margo paid for the meal, I was a guest of the Government of Canada. We talked a little about her experience as a Canadian diplomat in Africa. This was a wakeup call for me. Canada was big into supporting mega-projects that were, in all probability, a form of tied aid. It seemed to me that Margo did a lot of driving about in black four-wheel drive Suburbans to observe the progress on these projects. At least, that was my impression. She'd been to Uganda more than once and felt that a lot of good was being done by Milton Obote. I didn't share her optimism or feel that she had a firm handle on what was going on in that country. I'd twice sat for the foreign service exam and thought to myself, it's probably a good thing that my ambitions for a career in the diplomatic service have come to naught. Was I just being petty? Possibly. It wouldn't have been a good fit for me.

In any case, Margo had plans to visit with a Canadian couple that afternoon, Geraldine and Patrick Robarts. Geraldine was an artist and Patrick, an architect. She thought I might find it interesting and wondered if I'd care to tag along. "Absolutely," I replied, and I'm very glad I did.

Geraldine and Patrick owned or rented, I'm not sure which, a posh estate out in horse country. It was all quite extraordinary. I enjoyed tea and cake with Geraldine overlooking their extensive garden. The conversation, inevitably, came round to horses—they had four. "If I cared to," offered Geraldine, she could arrange to have one saddled up and I could go for a ride. A chance to go horseback riding in Kenya? Does an elephant have a trunk? Yeah, you bet!

I could tell from his body language that their stable manager, Paul, who was built like a professional jockey, didn't like the looks of me from the start and had some nefarious plan in mind. He saddled up an especially skittish horse named Netta for me and another for himself, peppering me with questions all the while about my level of experience. Once out of the stable, he instructed me to follow on and then proceeded to ride off like a bat out of hell.

Of course, he knew the terrain intimately while I hadn't a clue what was ahead, but I clung to my animal and kept right on his tail. He was evidently hoping I'd take a tumble, if only to teach me a lesson in humility. We galloped along the trails over rolling hills through trees and bush. I had to pinch myself each time we came across a startled giraffe. Once it became clear that Paul couldn't shake me off, he eased the pace a bit and we rode together, side-by-side, like old friends, for a two-hour hack. I thanked him profusely back at the stables for an unforgettable experience. Margo drove me back to my hotel and I promised to send her a post card from South Africa.

My final day in Nairobi, I breakfasted at the Burger House where the wait staff, to my great delight, brought me exactly what I wanted without my saying a word. Not far from the hotel, I stumbled on a man with his skull partly bashed in. I couldn't say from what, but there were obviously some unsavory elements lurking about. Nairobi was not a safe city at night. It was probable the poor fellow had been wandering around like that for some hours. Sadly, not a soul passing by was willing to offer aid. I certainly had no idea what to do in this situation, and felt, quite frankly, that by intervening I would only create insurmountable problems for myself. It pained me, but I left him to his fate.

It rained for the first time in a long while. I located where I could catch a matatu to Namanga, across from the old "OTC" (Overland Transport Company) bus station, then returned to the hotel where I puttered with a variety of household chores and studied the map going forward for the umpteenth time. The next day, March 26, 1984, I would hit the road entirely on my own for the first time. I felt a pang of uncertainty, like a newly fledged baby bird about to take its first flight. Inevitably, there would be that sudden frightful drop, then, hopefully, a chance to soar.

"MY TRIP" – JOURNAL No. 3

I CAUGHT THE MATATU TO NAMANGA AS PLANNED but had to pay an extra 10 shillings to get the driver to move after sitting on his duff for two hours hoping for one additional passenger. Outside of Nairobi the landscape quickly turned to arid grassland. It was a inspiring sight to see the Maasai wearing their traditional robe (a Shuka), spear canted over one shoulder as if it were the most natural thing. How superior, to my mind, than tattered Western hand-me-downs.

This, perhaps, is an appropriate place to comment on men's affinity for hats in parts of West, Central, and East Africa at the time. Hats of almost any make and style. Woolen toques were especially prized. Red, white, pink, or blue winter hats were a common sight. I once saw a man wearing a crocheted doily as a hat and another sporting a New England bonnet together with dark sunglasses. These individuals obviously had their own fashion sense and I've no doubt "couldn't give a rat's arse," as the Brits are wont to say, about what we in the West thought of their take on style.

Not to convey the wrong impression, I need to point out very clearly that the upwardly mobile segment of society dressed, generally speaking, the same as we're accustomed to, jacket, tie, skirt and blouse, as the case may be. Today, woolen toques have largely given way to baseball caps amongst working class males, worn together with a good pair of jeans, while the well-heeled are inclined to be seen in clothes by trendy African designers.

Giraffe, antelope, gnus (wildebeest) were a frequent sight on the road to Namanga. I was able to spend a little more time than expected observing the native flora and fauna because our matatu got a flat and the driver kept no spare. It was only by the good graces of another matatu driver willing to risk lending us his, that we were able to reach our destination.

It was, moreover, only by sheer luck and good timing that I was able to make the crossing from Kenya to Tanzania. The border between the two countries had been closed since 1977 and only recently reopened. Tanzanian president, Julius Nyerere, had tried, without much success, to forge an independent socialist-oriented path in East Africa. Concerned that his struggling nation might be "economically emasculated" by its relatively powerful neighbor, he cut off nearly all ties with Kenya. Relations were just beginning to thaw. Consequently, crossing the border was a breeze. The only negative, and a minor one at that, was that I was required to exchange all my Kenyan shillings for Tanzanian shillings at a piss poor rate.

I caught another matatu for Arusha, a little over 100 kilometers south. Police checks were again the norm, although somewhat perfunctory. I booked into the Safari Hotel and got a simple room for 168Sh a night (or about $14 US), pricey in comparison to Nairobi. The view of Mount Meru, the fifth highest peak in Africa and a dormant volcano, was impressive. Arusha promoted itself as a tourist hub, but there was an overwhelming atmosphere of stagnation. I contemplated making the detour to see the famous game park at Ngorongoro, but everything offered seemed geared to group tours and the prices inflated for the tourist market. It was clear that it would take too long for me to reach the park on my own hook, there being too many variables involved. Of the $2,400 I'd started out with from London, I was down to less than $1,500, not including funds reserved for my flight home. Would it be enough for me to reach South Africa and any expenses I might incur there? I debated back and forth with myself. I didn't want to leave myself penniless on my return to Canada.

Two things ultimately combined to rule out a trip to Ngorongoro. The first was a conversation with a fellow at the hotel bar who said he'd been to Ngorongoro and enjoyed seeing the flamingoes and the big cats, but found the experience undercut by the caravan of minivans that circled the animals. "It was difficult," he shared, "to take a photo without getting a vehicle or another tourist in the shot." The second was a warning from another traveler about an increasingly common scam in Tanzania employed when trying to pay for something in US dollars. A vendor would proclaim the proffered note "counterfeit," summon a conveniently available plainclothes officer, and your money summarily confiscated with words to the effect that the officer was doing you "a favor" by not pressing charges. That sounded frighteningly familiar.

I decided to test the waters by asking the hotel bartender if he would cash a $50 bill for me. Sure enough, just as I'd been warned, the bartender held the note up in the air to examine, declaring it "suspicious." "Never mind," I said, and snatched back the note.

That was enough for me. If not Ngorongoro, there was always Kilimanjaro. This time I caught a bus, taking me from Arusha to Moshi and the foot of the legendary mountain, some 80 kilometers to the east. I sat squashed between a convivial woman from Ethiopia dwarfed by the huge bundle of groceries on her lap and a very old man who thought I was completely nuts to risk my life "just to see Africa."

I walked to the YMCA at the foot of Kilimanjaro and was able to get a room with breakfast for a song. Naturally, I came with the intention of climbing the mountain—more like a vigorous hike, I'm told. I don't know if it was the time of year or just my rotten luck, but the peak was shrouded in cloud and only visible for about one hour each morning. I was reticent to fork out a lot of money just to gaze down at a cloud bank. More importantly, the train from Dar es Salaam to Lusaka only ran once per week leaving me with no room to hang about waiting for the weather to clear, so Kilimanjaro was out as well.

Down hearted, I walked to the train station to see about getting a seat on the next day's train, but it was completely sold out. Back at the "Y," I picked up a copy of Laurens van der Post's The Lost World of the Kalahari on a shelf of "Take one/Leave one" books. Two pages in, I just knew I had somehow to make the time and effort to visit the Kalahari. It would compensate for missing out on Ngorongoro and Kilimanjaro, or at least I hoped it would.

The following day, I went again to see if I could get a seat on the train to Dar es Salaam on the coast. In Tanzania they still relied heavily on classic steam engines, the great "iron horses" that I remembered fondly from childhood, and I was looking forward to the trip. The lineup just to purchase a ticket three days hence, however, was beyond my patience or timeline. I failed miserably at hitching a ride. I just hadn't Sara's inexplicable luck. So, I bit the bullet and bought a ticket on a "luxury coach" (i.e., bus) leaving that evening for 400Sh ($33 US). Waiting for the bus, I dug deeper into van der Post's Kalahari, my imagination stirred by a Bushmen song:

Women:

Under the sun / The Earth is dry
By the fire / Alone I cry
All day long / The Earth cries
For the rain to come / All night my heart cries
For my hunter to come.

Men:

Oh! Listen to the wind / You women there;
The time is coming / The rain is near
Listen to your heart / Your hunter is here.

Rain is something joyous in the southern reaches of Africa, something to be celebrated, to dance and sing about, not treated as something somber or sad as is more often the case in the West. Inexplicably, I'd never heard Toto's mega hit song about the rains in Africa until I reached southern Africa and heard it playing on a shop's PA system.

The luxury bus, when it arrived, was jammed beyond capacity, with young men hanging out the open front door. There were problems with the fuel pump, and we had no choice but to cool our heels for an hour and a half past the scheduled departure time while the mechanics tinkered with it. It was 550 kilometers between Moshi and Dar es Salaam.

As it turned out, the fuel pump was never properly fixed, and the bus kept stalling out on the hills. Fortunately, there were enough of us on board willing and able to get out and push whenever that occurred. Most took it in stride. So long as you didn't have a tight deadline, it was sort of fun to do and an enjoyable break from riding inside the cramped and stifling interior, but the road was rough, making for a long, uncomfortable night. I hadn't counted on the police checks when opting to travel by bus. With so many on board, it took ages to process us through each stop. What should have been about a 9-hour trip took 13.

Most of the buildings in Dar es Salaam were from the 1940s or earlier and incorporated Islamic architectural features. I booked into the Clocktower Hotel and shared a room with a young Tanzanian. The mosquitoes at night were fierce and carried with them the potential for real harm. This was a Thursday. I walked the 4 kilometers to the train station and purchased a first-class ticket for Kpiri Mposhi, Zambia, just north of Lusaka, departing Saturday, which set me back about $75 (904Sh). Pretty reasonable for a journey of almost 1,800 kilometers, though it required changing trains at the border.

Waiting in the queue, I met a fellow Canuck from Cobourg, Ontario, named Rod, "going the same way." He had an uneasy vibe about him, a bit young and cocky for his own good, but I let it go since I had no intention of hanging with him.

Canned goods in Dar es Salaam were in very short supply, only a handful of tins on the shelves in any of the shops I went in. It was easy enough to obtain something to eat from the street vendors, however, and the food usually well prepared. Chicken and chips became my mainstay. The most prosperous shops, I noticed, were run by South Asians, referred to as "Hendis," in East Africa, the same body of entrepreneurs that Idi Amin expelled from Uganda so precipitously in 1972. By coincidence, dry good shops, hardware stores and the like, are often called a "Dukas" in East Africa, the Urdu word for shop being "Duka." My name thus becoming a topic of conversation and an occasional ice breaker.

With a couple of days to spend in Dar es Salaam, I needed some pocket money, if only to eat. The official exchange rate of 12.10 shillings to the US dollar was painfully below the black-market rate of 60 shillings to the dollar. I was made to feel a chump by my fellow travelers for not skipping the banks and "doing the sensible thing." At the same time, I was wary of asking a hotel bartender for change given my experience in Arusha. But three times that day, the same fellow, a big man in a black leather jacket, clucked at me as I walked by, "Change?"

I thought to myself, maybe I should give it a try? It was an undertaking fraught with risk. I had no idea who this guy was. He could be an undercover cop for all I knew. Or a chiseler, like the one that took advantage of Mark, or worse. He had a pleasant smile, so there was that.

I started down the street doing my best to look nonchalant, pausing ever so slightly as I passed him, enough to make eye contact. "Change?" he asked.

This time, I nodded.

"Dollars?"

I nodded again, adding, "60 shillings?"

He rocked his head from side to side, the universal gesture for 'I'm thinking about it,' then shrugged submissively. "Not here. Follow me. But keep back."

Follow me? Where? I hadn't thought this part through. My mind was in turmoil. I guessed it didn't make much sense to conduct an illicit transaction in the middle of a busy sidewalk in clear view of everyone, but where would this fellow lead me? He already had his back to me and was several paces ahead, slicing his way through the crowd. Do I follow him, or not? I followed.

He turned left at the first intersection, never glancing back, and I did the same. Half a block farther, he turned left again down a quiet alley. I followed. There was an open door two buildings down. He turned left into that. Again I followed, finding myself in a working kitchen where no one seemed to take the slightest notice of our passing. Emerging out the far door into the building lobby, he took the stairwell up. I followed up two flights to a corridor lined with what looked like office doors. He glanced over his shoulder to see if I was still keeping up. Stopping at one of the doors, he gestured with one hand for me to go in.

What in hell was I doing? I was completely at this man's mercy. If there were a gang of cutthroats behind that door, if he slit my throat here and now and took all my money, God in heaven would know that I deserved it for being so friggin' stupid. But I did as he directed, stepping inside. The room turned out to be a men's washroom. We stood there alone, face to face.

"How much?" he asked, his voice echoing in the empty room.

"20?" I offered, tentatively.

"What? That's all? 20 dollars?" I shrugged, and he rolled his eyes at me in exasperation. "Okay, my friend."

That's when it hit me. I didn't carry US dollars right on me. Too much of a temptation for scoundrels and pickpockets. I had the money, but tucked away in the secret zippered compartment behind my belt!

"Do you mind if I use the loo for a moment?" I asked, sheepishly.

He laughed. "Go ahead, but no funny business."

I ducked into one of the stalls and nervously extracted a 20 from my belt, then stepped out and handed it to him. He reached into the interior pocket of his big leather jacket and extracted a large roll of bills and counted off in front of me 1,200 shillings. "Do you need to count it again?" he asked.

"No. We're good," I replied, at this point not caring if he'd palmed any for himself or not. I just wanted to be out of there.

"Wait two minutes then you can leave," he said, and disappeared out the door. I waited two minutes, descended the stairs and exited via the front door of the building, merging into the busy pedestrian traffic on the sidewalk. There was no sign of the black marketeer. I'm guessing he never staked out the same site of a transaction more than once or twice on the same day. I did count the money later on, and it was precisely 1,200 shillings.

With a bit of cash in my pocket, I could afford to explore the city at my leisure. I first checked out the National Museum, formerly, the King George V Memorial Museum. It was filled with fascinating exhibits on the history of the country, but I don't think the museum had been renovated since it was first opened. The labels below the artifacts were all yellow with age and peeling away. The building grounds, however, were lush and garden-like. I could imagine Hemingway being inspired by this place.

I parked my bottom on a park bench and savored both the beauty of my surroundings and the fragrant air. An ornate wrought iron lamp post just off to my left caught my eye. It was emblazoned with the German Imperial Eagle, dating it back to when the city was part of German-colonized East Africa. I can only think that my intentions were misconstrued, because I was there just a few minutes when two policemen approached me and asked me my business. Although satisfied that I wasn't up to mischief, they politely asked me to move along. In the remaining hours before sunset, I scouted about for fresh fruit to bring back to my room and arranged for my laundry to be done for 40Sh (about 70 cents using my ill-gotten gains. It would have cost me $3.30 US if I'd gone with the official exchange).

With no particular agenda in mind, I decided to pay a visit to the Canadian High Commission, where I was able to sit and read in their small library and catch up on news from home. There was an old copy of the Globe and Mail newspaper from Toronto containing a reference to The Journeyer, a historical novel about Marco Polo written by Gary Jennings. I was struck by a similar sense of unexpected adventure, disorientation, and discomfort, although our respective journeys took us through very different lands separated by 700 years.

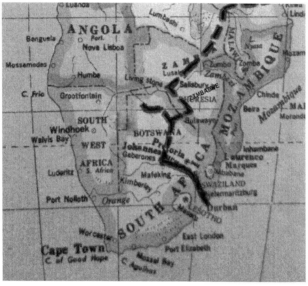

The author's route through southern Africa. Rhodesia (misspelled "Rhoresia") was renamed Zimbabwe-Rhodesia in 1979, then briefly Southern Rhodesia, and, finally, Zimbabwe, in 1980

Come Saturday morning, I took a cab to the railway station, passed through immigration control, and boarded the train. I was riding the Uhuru Railway or "Freedom

Railway," officially the TAZARA Railway, a joint venture of Tanzania, Zambia, and the People's Republic of China, and operated, for the most part, by the Chinese. The railway was constructed to provide landlocked Zambia with access to ocean ports in Tanzania for copper exports, a mainstay of its economy, and to circumvent the apartheid nations of Rhodesia and South Africa, hence the unofficial name. At the time it was inaugurated in 1975, it was the largest single foreign-aid project ever undertaken by China at a cost of some $500 million US, employing 50,000 Tanzanians and 25,000 Chinese construction workers. The train was fast and efficient, making only brief stops at stations along the way. I shared a compartment with two others, one of whom happened to be Rod. He'd spied me out of the crowd and figured we were natural companions. I did my best to ignore him, as the views from our window were frequently remarkable.

The thing about trains, no matter where in the world, is that they cut through country that is otherwise inaccessible. You can see the most astonishing things from the comfort of your recliner. In this case, we passed right between Mikumi National Park and the Selous Game Reserve. The animals, including elephants, giraffes, wildebeest, zebra, and herds of antelope, are used to the train's passage and pay it no heed. Sadly, the police aboard the train insisted, for their own paranoid and inexplicable reasons, that we could not take pictures. There was more to these incredible vistas than game. We crossed through winding mountain passes, past stunning waterfalls, over towering trestles spanning verdant valleys, great swathes of swamp, and bamboo forests. The sun burned red gold as it set over mountains to the west. Then, as darkness settled in and we passed over a vast stretch of marsh, the sky lit up with flashes of blue-green ball lightning. When things went quiet during stops at isolated stations you could hear the crickets, not 'chirping' as they do in Canada, but "clinking" like crystal glasses striking one another.

We crossed into Zambia at Nakonde. Customs and immigration filed through the train preoccupied with currency smuggling. Even so, I had to declare every non-household object in my possession, no matter how small, which proved to be quite a list and took some time to prepare. I volunteered to hand in my few remaining Tanzanian shillings rather than having to account for them. Rod tried to hide the fact that he was carrying Kenyan shillings. His deceit must have showed on his face because they insisted on searching his bags and found them. That resulted in an immediate fine of $30 US, which made him seethe. They then discovered his Canadian Tire Store "money," coupons actually, made to resemble banknotes and issued in fractional denominations from 3 cents to a dollar and emblazoned with the portrait of a thrift-minded Scot. Rod, to his great personal amusement, had been flogging these bills on gullible individuals to pay for drinks and such like. He had to do some fast talking to convince the customs agent to not fine him for failing to declare this "currency" as well.

After clearing customs, we deboarded to change trains. A few enterprising vendors showed up with corn and cabbage to sell, but I had no Zambian money on me. The train set off a little after midnight on April 1st. One o'clock by my watch, as the time zone changed at the border. I was plenty hungry by this time. I managed to convince the cook in the restaurant car to change $10 to Zambian kwacha (or ZK, receiving about 15 kwacha and 90 ngwee in change), which meant I could at least get a bite to eat. Sometime in the middle of the night the train came to a lurching halt. There were shouts outside the car window. I wondered, at first, if this was a repeat of Uganda. Several men with flashlights walked down the length of the train checking the under carriage. A man sharing the compartment with us rolled down the window to ask what was up. Apparently, the driver thought he'd struck someone walking on the tracks, but no body was found, and we were able to move on after a brief delay.

Whatever it was I'd eaten late at night came back to haunt me. There is no good time or place for the runs, on a train in Africa no less. I would have been better off going hungry. Our train arrived at Kpiri Mposhi at 9:00 in the morning, right on time, despite the delays en route. I walked with Rod into town, changed $50 to kwacha, then went off in search of a decent meal. From the shops, it was plain that Zambians were openly trading with South Africa, despite the embargoes in place. I suppose the country was captive to its geography and had little choice in the matter, despite its better angels. Rod was "done with the authoritarian attitude" on the train, opting to take the bus on to Lusaka. So much for Rod. I was happy to be rid of him, and purchased an onward ticket to Livingstone, another 12-hour train ride, so that I could spend some time at Victoria Falls. Something I was especially looking forward to.

This time, I went for a "standard seat" on the train, which meant catch-as-catch-can for comfort and location, but it only cost me 15.90ZK ($10 US). It was an uneventful trip, much of it through urban areas. The train, for some reason, kept making long unscheduled stops. We didn't pull into Livingstone until 2:00 in the morning and at that hour no one was going anywhere. And yet, there were at least a couple of hundred people on hand, no amenities, and the station house closed. With the temperature dropping by the minute and a light rain falling, everyone bundled up as best they could, huddling together for warmth on the railway platform and the surrounding yard, trying to get in a bit of shut eye before sunrise.

At sunup, I gathered my belongings and headed into town on foot, following a thin line of early birds with the same destination. Livingstone was a lovely Art Deco-ish resort town, immaculate, all the buildings colorful and freshly painted. I'm generalizing for sure, but the Zambians I encountered struck me as especially mild mannered and polite. I relaxed and had a wonderful breakfast at the Northwestern Hotel, a charming building dating back to 1907. I caught a minivan to Rainbow Lodge on the shores of the Zambezi and was put up in a comfortable thatched hut of my own for the equivalent of about $10 (17ZK), a big change from sleeping on a railway platform.

I walked along the east bank of the Zambezi without a soul in sight, startling crocodiles hidden in the tall grass and sending them slithering into the water. I figured I'd gone far enough when confronted by a troop of wild baboons, a dozen or more, lined up across the road, their attention unmistakably focused on me. They are large and altogether intimidating creatures. Nothing to mess with. Anyway, I managed a good view of the falls from the international bridge. Well worth the effort, everything you might imagine. Powerful, majestic. Unlike Niagara Falls, these cataracts were set against a backdrop untouched by human hand, and there was something special about that. There were, however, a few modest shops discreetly situated along the road to the falls with carvings in heavy dark mahogany by local artisans, some of them at work. I bought a couple of very small beautifully rendered figures of women grinding maize, making extra sure that I did not repeat Mark and Lila's unfortunate mistake, then went back to my hut to relax and enjoy the sunset over the river.

It was something of a trudge with my bags, but I made the walk over the bridge and crossed into Zimbabwe the following day. I "parked," to use the local term, at a campsite just the other side of the border and then took a launch with a handful of other tourists down river. The launch stopped at a craft village where a Nyanga kraal had been recreated. The tepee-like huts within the kraal were ingeniously designed and very solid. I thought to myself that one of these would make for a very nice cabin in Northern Ontario. I bought a small soapstone carving of a chief of the Batonka people, which maintains an honored place on my mantel.

Thinking over my travel plans and inspired by what I read in van der Post's book on the Kalahari, I decided to make my way by one means or another to Maun, Botswana. Having shifted my plans, I spent the night under the stars very near the railway line, unexpectedly, but rather pleasantly, disturbed from my sleep from time to time by the dreamy sound of a whistle coming from a passing steam engine—an interesting vestige of the former (Rhodesian) regime's efforts to circumvent international trade embargoes by eschewing oil imports. As a result, they kept a bevy of old steam locomotives in service, modified in creative ways to create new efficiencies. 'Steampunk' had yet to impact popular culture, but these fabulous machines were a Steampunk enthusiast's dream.

I was up early the next morning to catch a 7 a.m. luxury coach to Bulawayo. The bus, in this case, was the height of modernity and comfort, but I could sense real tension on board. It took time for me to puzzle it out through bits and pieces of conversation. It seemed that I had blundered into a war zone, a brutal conflict colloquially known as "The Gukurahundi" (a Shona term, with rather sinister connotations). We were traveling through the heart of Matabeleland, home to the Ndebele people, where the notorious Fifth Brigade of the Zimbabwe National Army were actively engaged in a ruthless suppression of alleged Ndebele rebels affiliated with the Zimbabwe People's Revolutionary Army (ZIPRA).

Young Ndebele men were being rounded up and summarily shot on mere suspicion. ZIPRA was fighting back and the situation in Matabeleland was chaotic and volatile. This was the same road that six young tourists near enough my own age—two Americans, two Brits, and two Australians—were kidnapped at gunpoint in July of 1982 and never seen again. In fact, our bus passed through the very town where they were seized. I tried to take some comfort in the thought that this had happened two years prior. My fellow passengers, Black and White, were on pins and needles. How did I not pick up on this while making my plans, I had to wonder? To make matters worse, if that were possible, it looked like the entire region was suffering from a serious drought.

The bus stopped at the Gwaai River Hotel for brunch. It was an enchanting colonial-style inn, emblematic I suppose, of "the old regime." But I had a chance to chat with the aging owner, Harold Broomberg, a White or "European" Zimbabwean and as gentle and selfless a man as you could ever hope to meet, who told me he'd been running the hotel at a loss since the Lancaster House Agreement, which led to the ousting of the apartheid government. When I questioned him on why he kept the hotel running, he replied, "for love, and to benefit the local economy. There are few opportunities here," he shared, "for people to find good jobs." Harold was immensely proud of his country and had nothing but high hopes for the future of Zimbabwe. It broke my heart to learn that the Gwaai River Hotel was later ransacked and burned to the ground during Robert Mugabe's mismanaged effort to settle Black subsistence farmers on European farms.

The trip to Bulawayo, thankfully, was uneventful, except for a flat tire along the way. We arrived early afternoon and I found a room at the Roslington Villa on Wilson Street for 11 Zimbabwean dollars a night. The US dollar and Zimbabwean dollar were close to par at the time. In sharp contrast, Zimbabwe suffers at the present from extreme hyperinflation, 100 US dollars equal to about 36,000Z$.

I walked around town for a time and was impressed by the wide clean avenues and the crisp-looking policemen. There were plenty of ruddy-faced White Zimbabweans still about, dressed cliché fashion in Bermuda shorts, knee socks, and bush hats. The city boasted one of the most magnificent old cinemas, which I was keen to see from the inside. The feature film, Aces High, with Malcolm McDowell, was from 1976. Tucked into the shorts before the main film was an ad for Excedrin headache tablets, only the poor sod with the classic "Excedrin headache" was driving a noisy overcrowded gas-guzzling bus in some part of rural Africa, filled with unruly passengers holding live chickens in their laps and carrying way too much baggage. A bit over the top and filled with awful stereotypes, the ad did remind me a bit of my bus trip from Moshi to Dar es Salaam. The audience, both Black and White, certainly found it amusing.

Since experiencing that astonishing performance by the dance troupe in Yangambi, I had it in my head to bring home one or two cassette tapes with music that would remind me of Africa. With the end of my African journey in sight, I spent part of the morning scouring the shops in Bulawayo, hoping to find something that would fill the bill, but I was severely disappointed. There were plenty of music tapes available, but they were virtually all reggae. Bob Marley had conquered Africa! On the upside, I passed an FTD florist shop and it got me to thinking, so I went in and asked, "Can you arrange for flowers to be sent to Canada?"

"Of course," replied the helpful clerk. "Do you know the name of a local florist? If not, I can easily find one in our catalogue." This was 1984. I did not expect a florist from Kingston, Ontario to be listed in a printed catalogue in Bulawayo, Zimbabwe, but sure enough, her voluminous FTD catalogue had all the contact information for Pam's Flowers on Princess Street. I arranged for a dozen roses to be sent to Edi and hoped they would be well received. Time would only tell.

Bulawayo was only a pit stop. I bought a 2nd class ticket on the 1:30 train for Francistown, Botswana on National Railways of Zimbabwe (NRZ) for the criminally low price of 7.50Z$ ($6.80 US), about three times the price of my cinema ticket of the night before, keeping in mind, this was a trip of nearly 200 kilometers across national boundaries.

With time to spare before my train I paid a visit to Douslin House, a Bulawayo landmark, impossible to overlook. Built in 1900, the original contractor, George Harker, poured his heart into the design and construction of the building, went bankrupt in the process and took his own life. It housed the Bulawayo Art Gallery (today, the National Gallery of Zimbabwe in Bulawayo), a truly priceless venue, highlighting the art of Zimbabwe and southern Africa.

I was curious to see what my 7.50Z$ bought me when the time came. What I got was the train ride of a lifetime. The engine that pulled up to the station was a modified steam locomotive of burnished brass and jet-black iron. The conductor informed me that the whole train had newly arrived from South Africa after an extensive refit. Behind the engine stretched a line of priceless Pullman-quality cars, all lovingly and painstakingly refurbished.

My compartment consisted of polished wood panels and beveled mirrors, brass and gold-leaf labels identifying the former owner as "R.R." (Rhodesia Railways). Pulling out of Bulawayo, I was able to see something of urban Zimbabwe and the vestiges of the old apartheid regime. Sadly, one form of terror had morphed into another, the fear of rebel attacks requiring continued vigilance on the part of the police and military. Screens on windows to protect against grenade attacks, 10-foot wire fences, elevated and reinforced trucks on the roads to reduce the impact of land mines were still very much in evidence.

We crossed from Plumbtree into Botswana at 4:30 in the afternoon. I was surprised to find the border between the two countries was almost seamless. I found a room at the Hotel Tati in Francistown for 18 pula (or P) per night, or about $17, and that was with a shared bathroom and toilet down the hall. Quite pricy in comparison to what I'd got myself used to. More importantly, I was starving, hungry enough to eat a horse, but didn't have a pula to my name. The hotel would only agree to cash small denomination notes, insisting that I needed to change larger bills at a bank. The catch was the banks were all closed for the day. I was in the horns of a dilemma. The most I could get my hands on was 5 pula. So, with only 5P in my pocket I went to the restaurant next to the hotel and scanned the menu for anything I could afford that would fill the big hole in my belly. The situation didn't look promising until I spotted it. "French Onion Soup," for 4.50P!

I placed my order and impatiently bided my time until my evening repast arrived. Imagine my chagrin when I was served a bowl of plain brown broth with a few caramelized onions floating in it. Where was the cheese that put the "French" in French Onion Soup?! The big glop of sticky gooey Swiss Gruyere topped with a thick tranche of baguette and parmesan au gratin? I beckoned the waiter over. "I ordered French Onion Soup," I explained. "This is a consommé."

"I beg your pardon sir, this is French Onion Soup."

"I'm telling you it isn't. French Onion Soup comes with cheese and bread. This is not what I ordered."

"One moment please." He went off to the kitchen and returned with the chef. I calmly, but firmly, restated my complaint. The chef considered for a moment. I could see his professional pride kick in.

"You are absolutely correct, sir. My sincere apologies. This is not French Onion Soup. I will fix it for you immediately. Thank you for your patience." The onion broth was removed from the table, and I was served a basket of bread rolls with fresh butter while I waited. Twenty minutes later, I was presented with a piping hot bowl of French Onion Soup, made to order and to perfection. The chef himself came out to ensure I was satisfied.

"Absolutely. Thank you. This is much better."

"Again, please accept my apologies," said the chef.

"Think nothing of it," I replied. I savored every drop of my soup, trying not to spill it down my chin as I wolfed it back. I paid my 4.50 pula and even left a 50 thebe tip for the waiter.

The next day, after exchanging the money I needed, I sniffed around town for a ride to Maun without success. At the bus terminal, they suggested I should wait on the road near the airport where I "might" be able to catch a bus out of town. So, I forked out for a cab and had the driver drop me off at the likely location. To my surprise, a bus did eventually pass and I flagged it down, the driver informing me that I could pay when I reached my destination. We hadn't traveled ten miles when the bus was pulled over at a government weigh/inspection station and summarily "condemned." Everyone was ordered to get off.

In the midst of all this, I struck up a conversation with a Zimbabwean who claimed to have recently seen four of the missing kidnapped tourists—that they were alive and well and, in fact, had "gone African" (meaning, gone native). He claimed that they were being held as political pawns and would be released unharmed at the next election. I learned the truth a year after returning home. The bodies of all six hostages were discovered in March of 1985. Five had been shot and one strangled. Apparently, they'd been put to death after shouting for help from a passing government helicopter.

A bunch of young men in a beat-up pickup truck offered to take me as far as Mosetse for 2.5P, which was about a third of the way to Maun. I figured it was better than waiting around. Trusting to fate, I threw my kit in the bed with a couple of them and squeezed myself into the cab between the driver and one other. We talked about this and that for the hour and a half it took to get to Mosetse, passing miles of parched grassland and dry shrubs devoid even of game. It all seemed rather innocuous.

The village of Mosetse was little more than a loose collection of buildings, gathered about the local watering hole. We piled out of the vehicle, and I grabbed my kit to keep it within arm's reach, pleased to see that it had not been tampered with. The store/bar had a frontier feel about it, rough-finished, a few bulk necessities on the shelves for sale, a handful of tables, and a counter from which to order your drinks or buy tins of peas. The leader of the men I'd hitched with tapped me on the shoulder and announced that he was able, after all, to take me farther up the road toward Maun. I shouldn't wander too far off. They were just going to grab a cold drink and then head out again. He went off with his mates to talk over whatever it was they needed to talk about, leaving me to stare out the window.

In the corner near the window, sat a very old man with a walking stick, who had hardly taken his eyes off me since I'd walked in. His face was so deeply lined, you could see the gray stubble from his beard where the razor would not pass. His eyes were yellow with age, and rimmed in red. Having nothing much to do, I edged over to him and wished him a "Good day."

"Where you from?" he asked.

"Canada," I replied.

"Umm. And where you headed?" he asked.

"Maun. I want to see the Kalahari." He nodded knowingly, and we got to talking. It got round to me saying that I was in the Canadian Forces. He owned up to being a veteran himself, and that he had served with the "Assault Engineers" at Normandy during World War II.[19] He laughed, remembering how "the Canadians got the shit kicked out of them near Boulogne" (likely, Operation Undergo, at Calais in September 1944). A couple of other patrons, regulars I suppose, came over to join the conversation, emphasizing, in case I didn't realize it, that I was speaking to a "grand old man" and an important member of the community. I assured them I had no doubt of that. The old fellow stood up with some effort, looked out the window and gestured for me to stand close beside him. He whispered to me. "Don't go with these men. They will rob you and leave you for dead."

I looked at him askance, searching his face for confirmation. He was deadly serious.

"Look out there, across the field. Do you see those buildings in the distance? That is Dukwe, a refugee camp.

---

[19] Presumably, the 1st Assault Brigade, Royal Engineers.

The men you are traveling with are from there. They are not supposed to be on the loose. Don't go with them if you value your life."

I was, otherwise, very likely to have gone off with them, and who knows then what would have become of me? I learned later that Dukwe was "home" to over 6,000 refugees from failed revolutions in Angola, South West Africa (Namibia), Zimbabwe-Rhodesia, and South Africa. It wasn't a prison, per se, so the enclosure was porous enough for the more audacious members of the camp to get out.

Once my would-be traveling companions were finished their drinks and ready to go, the leader slapped me on the back and told me to mount up. I muttered something about having changed my plans and stood my ground, which took him aback. There was precious little he could do about it, save kidnapping me in broad daylight with a handful of locals on hand. He shrugged dismissively and they drove off. Naturally, I thanked the old vet for his concern and offered to buy him a drink, which he was pleased to accept.

I hung about the watering hole at Mosetse waiting for someone to come through on their way to Maun, managing to catch a ride for 2P with someone the old man was willing to vouch for. The one minor complication was that the driver was only going as far as the end of the paved highway, below the village of Nata, less than an hour up the road. I accepted the ride anyway and was let off at the side of the road with nothing but scrub grass and low-lying shrub around me in all directions as far as the eye could see.

For the first time since leaving London, 139 days gone by, I was utterly alone with only the sound of the wind for company—and I relished the moment. A feeling of contentment and overwhelming satisfaction swept over me. Perhaps it was relief at not having died by misadventure that afternoon. I think, rather, it was because I was in Africa. And, for the first time, shielded from constant inputs and having to make split-second decisions, away from always having to second guess myself and never quite mastering it.

I laid out my gear in the culvert beside the road and sat back, soaking in the peace and quiet. I must have dozed off. The sound of tires on gravel nudged me awake. I was surprised to find the sun was setting.

It was a police car. The door opened, a lone cop stepped out, gazing down at me, hands on hips. "Good afternoon," he said.

"Good afternoon," I replied.

"Are you in need of assistance?" he asked, cautiously.

"No, thank you, constable. I'm fine," adding, as an afterthought "But, I am trying to make my way to Maun and having some trouble catching a ride."

"So, it would appear," he said, with a quick glance across the empty landscape. He resisted a smile. "I have to tell you, this isn't an altogether safe thing you are doing."

"I tend to agree," I said. "But this is where my ride dropped me off."

"There is a filling station about a mile up the road. I'm sorry I'm not allowed to give you a ride, but you should be able to get there on your own and catch a ride from there."

"Thanks, I'll do that," I replied, reassuringly.

Not surprisingly, he was curious about me and eager to hear of my travels. He didn't seem to be in any hurry, so we chatted for a time, while I fixed myself a bite to eat. He spied amongst my larder a large fresh apple I'd brought all the way from Lusaka, commenting that imported fresh fruit was very hard to come by in the district, at least of any quality. I happily gave up my apple, which he was pleased to accept, adding that he would bring it home to his family to enjoy. He told me that the situation was about to change in the district, they were expecting a great "boom."

What sort of boom?" I asked, my interest piqued.

"Electricity," he replied. "That will make a big difference here."

"I'm sure it will," I said in complete agreement. Botswana, and southern Africa for that matter, struck me as being quite "up" on things. I'd never given any thought to very rural districts. The constable wished me well with an added caution to "be safe," and headed off. Once darkness fell, I gathered my kit and headed up the road, walking alone under a star-filled sky.

Despite the late hour, I was able to arrange for a ride the rest of the way to Maun for 11P. It was a cramped, uncomfortable ride, again in the back of a pickup, but the night sky proved to be a riveting diversion and somewhat made up for it. I was dropped off at Riley's Hotel—right from the pages of van der Post's book!—at 2:00 in the morning. For 32P ($29 US) I got a room with a bath, breakfast included. I overslept owing to the late hour of my arrival and missed the programed breakfast hour, but they served me anyway and I was glad for it, as I was famished, and it turned out to be a wonderful full-course spread.

At Riley's, I had a surprise encounter with three White South Africans who had been on the condemned bus with me back in Francistown. Curiously, finding out how I could get up to the Moremi Game Reserve in the Okavango Delta was like pulling teeth. I only wanted information, but there seemed to be an unspoken rule that business wasn't even talked about on Sundays, the Lord's Day of Rest.

Since the only way into the Okavango Delta was by air, I walked to the airport hoping I would find someone there to speak to or at least pick up some informational pamphlets. No such luck, so I walked back to the hotel. A tourist shop named "Bushman Curios," by chance, was open for reasons I couldn't understand. They carried some promotional material for safaris into the delta, but these were all too rich for my blood. The sort of thing movie stars, multi-millionaires, and royalty would go on. I felt sure there had to be another more reasonable way to reach the game reserve and was doggedly determined to do so after all I'd been through to get to Maun. In any case, this was evidently going to cost me more than I'd anticipated, so I asked the hotel management if I could downgrade my room, which they obliged, dropping it to 25 per night ($21 US, but still including breakfast). Completely knackered, I slept the rest of the day.

Monday morning, I got up extra early, enjoyed a healthy breakfast, and went off again in search of transportation into the delta. The hotel desk suggested I try out a firm by the unlikely name of "Maun Offices Services." I located the MOS office with a bit of effort. My first thought was that it didn't look anything like a travel agency. The manager, or owner, was outside engaged in an animated discussion with a young couple. I got the impression most of MOS business was conducted in the street. When I finally got a word in edgewise, the manager/owner told me, somewhat gruffly, to "come back later." No time was specified. I went to the bank and cashed a couple of large travelers checks on the hunch that only cash would be good enough for purchasing a trip to the delta, then I went back to the MOS office to see if I could make any more headway.

"Plane leaves in 40 minutes to Delta Camp, take it or leave it," said the manager/owner.

"40 minutes!" I cried. "Seriously?"

"You're wastin' time jawin' with me, sport," he added, with a wry smile. "You might want to pick up some supplies before we head out." I ran back to the hotel as fast as my legs could carry me, tossed my kit together, and then out to the hotel lobby to clear my bill. The desk clerk could not have been less empathetic, fulfilling his duty to the hotel with long accustomed formality. I wanted to throttle him. Grabbing the receipt from his hands, I dashed out and down the street, my shoulder bags whacking me in the thighs and the small of my back with every alternating step. I didn't even take time to think about what the bill came to.

I popped into the first dry goods store that was open. Three nights, I thought to myself, grabbing a handful of packable non-perishables, whether or not they made any sense, and rushing up to the cashier. I arrived at the MOS office in a complete sweat, panting and out of breath. I was not the only passenger ready to depart. The three South

African lads had beat me once again, leaning comfortably against the wall, bags neatly stacked, sipping hot coffees. They smiled mischievously, the embodiment of schadenfreude.

"You made it," quipped the owner/manager. "Come in. Settle up. Then we're off."

It's only by happenstance that I arrived in Maun at the opening of the season. While that explained the patchy access to resources and information, it also meant far fewer tourists and the chance to secure a trip to the delta at a reasonable rate. He hustled us into a waiting van and then over to the airport where a Cessna was fueled and waiting.

There was room enough for perhaps three more passengers in the plane. We flew low over the delta. What sets the Okavango apart from most other river deltas is that it sits within an arid desert, the Kalahari. Flood waters stream down from the highlands in Angola, fanning out into the desert sand, creating a vast fan-shaped network of freshwater channels and lagoons that are a seasonal mecca for wildlife as the sun evaporates away their water supply. Seasons are reckoned differently in the delta, partly because it is in the southern hemisphere. Late April to September/October are the hot dry "winter" months, but somewhat counter-intuitively, this is when the waters rise, eventually submerging large swaths of the delta.

We landed at the airstrip supporting Delta Camp. The outfitter arranged for me to go exploring with my own "poler" and mokoro (dugout canoe) for three nights. He was a San Bushman (probably Wayeyi or "Bayeyi," from the little I could discern) and went by the name "Kwet" (pronounced "Ket"), apparently abbreviated from Kwetsaura or Kwetsani, the island village his family called home.

Kwet gave me the impression that there were only two Bushman villages in the delta of any size, and even these must have been modest. His first stop was for a short visit with his sister. She greeted us with cups of milky homemade beer, called "tho-tho-tho," made from fermented sorghum seeds, excellent and quite refreshing, even served warm. Her home was a traditional hut, or mogwafatshe, similar to a North American wigwam, but fashioned from long grass and papyrus reeds and no more than about four feet high. Kwet's sister, like the Pygmy people I'd encountered in Zaire, exhibited steatopygiaI, an ancient genetic trait that causes a peculiarly prominent accumulation of fat around the buttocks. San Bushmen see it as a sign of beauty, so I'm quite sure my flat bottom was as nasty as it gets from their point of view.

Kwet stood upright at the back of the mokoro, poling us down narrow channels hemmed in on either side by towering papyrus reeds. Crocodiles and hippos inhabited these waters. The hippos were a particular hazard and Kwet was always on the alert for their presence. When I asked him why, he pointed to a large crack down one side of the mokoro that had been mended, explaining that hippos could be extremely aggressive. They apparently have an instinctive dislike for mokoros, and I wondered if that was because they resemble crocodiles from below. Kwet's mokoro leaked like a sieve and I was constantly bailing using a tin cup.

I was fixated on spotting rising bubbles in the water that might indicate the presence of hippos, when a large brown snake swam out of the reeds bumping against the side of the mokoro, and wouldn't you know it, right where I was sitting. The snake was obviously as startled as I was. It raised its head eye level with my own, extended its hood, and stared me down. Time stood still for me, until it dropped down and swam back into the reeds.

Kwet, who had frozen mid-pole, shook his head in a way that indicated to me, 'that was a close shave.' "Poisonous?" I asked. He nodded, confirming my suspicions. I later researched the snake that faced me down. It was an Anchieta's cobra (Naja Anchietae), not the most venomous snake in the Okavango (that honor belongs to the Black Mamba), but then again, it would have bitten me smack on the kisser, had it not thought better of the situation.

The author with a new bush cap, photographed during the side trip to the Okavango Delta

Kwet was a man of few words, so there were long periods where it was serenely quiet, except for the gentle sound of his pole stirring the water, and bird song. Traveling through the reeds would have been the most pleasant diversion were it not for the infinite number of rope-like webs and giant spiders that thrived among them, large enough, I dare say, to catch small birds in flight. We made camp the first evening on a small island Kwet called "Kru-Kan." You won't find these smaller fringe islands on any map because they are ephemeral, submerged below the surface of the water with the winter floods.

Kwet prepared an open fire and set up his tent. For all the traditional ways he and his family lived, his gear was high end. I remarked on this, with a hint of admiration, and he told me that he often played host to professional photographers and naturalists from around the globe who returned each year to the delta. They would sometimes "tip" him with "A-one" gear. A-one was his favorite expression. He used it in response or reaction to just about anything. He left me to my own devices, indicating that I should walk about on my own. I should clarify that I had paid for an "economy safari" and that meant no food or accommodation, and the bare minimum in terms of animal tracking. Kwet seemed well aware of this arrangement.

The island was small, dotted with palms and flowering shrubs, the shoreline profusely populated with cranes, plovers, and a few storks. When I returned, Kwet showed me how he made bracelets fashioned from the thick black tail hairs of kongoni (hartebeests). I kept a spare inexpensive watch and traded it for two of them. That night, I slept under the stars. Once or twice from a distance, echoing across the water, an animal would 'cough,' a deep baritone cough that prompted you to sit up and pay attention—it came from a sitatunga, an elusive aquatic antelope (Tragelaphus Spekii).

Perhaps it was out of habit or an abundance of caution, but Kwet kept the campfire going all night. I woke several times to see him tending it, snorting from between his thumb and index finger the snuff he made from a local herb that could easily have passed for catnip. He was plainly addicted to it. I had to wonder about this man, wedded to the Okavango. He was undoubtedly better off here, in his own element, than the big city or even Maun, able to pick and choose at his leisure what he cared to adopt from the "modern" world.

The largest island in the delta was Chief's Island. We steered toward it, but Kwet landed me on a smaller nearby island that he called "Toma-O." A few hippos appeared as we approached the shore. He was furious with himself for not remembering they were there. As I was getting out of the mokoro a male red lechwe (a type of antelope, K. leche leche) stampeded across the shore almost running me over. There were a great many large birds on the island and a number of giraffes.

Kwet repaired his net and went fishing, again leaving me to my own devices. He returned with a large catch of bream, which resembles an oversized tilapia, and a half-dozen big catfish. Another poler joined us, and together they prepared and cooked their feast over the open fire. I didn't do much of anything that afternoon but enjoyed watching them go about their task and just generally chillin'. We were besieged by blackflies at sunset. It's possible that the remains of the gutted fish were partially responsible.

My guide surprised me with a serving of the cooked bream together with cornmeal mush for breakfast. The custom was to eat it off your plate with your fingers. Gawd, it was delicious! It took all my strength not to beg for seconds. We packed and made the trip over to Chief's Island, a permanent fixture in the delta. Even though the winter floods had not begun, the island was teaming with wildlife. Kwet led me on a walk all the way to noon. A good part of the island was mopane woodland—a mix of acacia, savanna grasslands, and shrubs. I saw baboon, giraffe, zebra, tsessebe (a type of antelope), wildebeest, and a magnificent kudu (again, a type of antelope, but one that rivals a moose for size). If I'd come to the Okavango closer to August and September, I could well have seen lion, leopard, cheetah, elephant, hyena, wild dog, and buffalo, as well. August to September is also the season for tiger fish—imagine a carp with piranha-like jaws and you'll get the picture. As if crocodiles and hippos weren't enough reason to stay out of the water.

We returned to Toma-O. Kwet went off to make himself a new pole and I went for another walk. Coming out of the shrubs into open grass I saw in the distance what at first looked like three giant apes, but that made no sense, as there were no giant apes in the Okavango. Yet they swung their arms from side to side, jumped up and down and beat their chests. I could just make out the sound of their threatening cries, "Ooo-ooo, ah-ah!" I held back just to be on the safe side. It didn't take long for the "apes" to reveal their true identity. The three South Africans. Who else? They thought it was hysterical.

"Just having a bit of fun, is all. Care to join our party tonight? We've got plenty of beer." I told them I'd think about it and thanked them for the invitation. Actually, I helped Kwet haul in his catch for the day and chatted for a short bit with a French couple also camping on the island (practicing my rusty French), then sat about the fire after the sun went down listening to the wood spittle and pop, mesmerized by the burning embers. In the distance, the South Africans partied, blaring disco tunes on a portable boom box.

My final day in the delta, I was up early and went for a walk to the south end of the island. On the spur of the moment, I carved "Neil Dukas '84" on the stump of a dead tree, on the assumption that I was doing no real harm. It was my way of celebrating having successfully crossed the continent, or very nearly so. I imagine Kwet would not have been impressed. I hope the stump has long since rotted away.

We set off next for "White Island" and went for another walk. This time, I saw warthogs, tiny imp-like steenboks, and giraffe, and was lucky enough to catch sight of an African fish eagle soaring overhead.

When it came time to head back to Delta Camp, I thanked Kwet for making my stay so memorable and wished him well. He noticed my stash of English toffees and asked me if he could have some for his children, which I was pleased to share. I boarded the Cessna together with the South Africans and the French couple. We were hardly in the air when the South Africans started needling the pilot about his flying skills and the capabilities of our aircraft. Obviously, they knew which buttons to push. An "old-time" bush pilot, he was not about to let this go unchallenged. We immediately banked hard to the left, headed down fast and leveled off so low to the ground I could swear our wheels were grazing the tops of the grass. He buzzed several herds of antelope and we watched them scatter with fractal-like precision. Although I'd left my stomach at 3,000 feet, I had to admit it was pretty thrilling and magnificent to behold.

On the ground, I bid the French couple, Barb and Michel Cabioch, a safe journey home. To my surprise and delight, they asked if I'd like a lift to Gaborone. Yeah! And how! Gaborone, the capital, was a good 850 kilometers (530 miles) to the southeast, so their offer was no small gesture. I checked back into Riley's for the night and treated myself to a roast beef dinner fit for royalty. We were on the road the next morning by 8 a.m., crossing the Tropic of Capricorn, and didn't get into Gaborone until 5:30 p.m., averaging 100 kilometers an hour in their brand-new Toyota.

The highway was as good as the best we had in Canada and the car was air conditioned, although we often just drove with the windows down. This was unaccustomed luxury and convenience, on a road of a quality that I had not previously witnessed in all of Africa. We chatted along the way and listened to the Voice of America on the car radio. I was back in the world I knew, so to speak. One of the first bits of news I heard was that there had been an attempted coup the prior week against President Biya of Cameroon, 70 dead and thousands arrested.

I tried to focus on the scenery outside my window. Below Maun, on the fringes of the Kalahari, the earth was bleached and rugged, mostly thorn bush dotted with gnarled trees tinged with small shiny green leaves. Curious white obelisks, as tall as a man, punctuated the landscape, ancient memorials to once thriving colonies of termites. In the culverts, here and there, were clumps of wispy grass with fluffy golden heads, swaying in sharp contrast to the harsh unmoving environment. South of Nata, where I had shared an apple with a policeman, were the vast Makgadigadi salt pans, the remains of an enormous prehistoric lake, and the presumed cradle of Homo sapiens. This was also a region that had suffered badly from an outbreak of Foot and Mouth Disease. Consequently, cattle inspection stations were a regular feature along our route.

Outside of the Bushmen, the other group of people that stood out in this part of Botswana were the Mbanderu (or Herero, after their language). The Mbanderu were the descendants of refugees who fled to Botswana after an unsuccessful revolt in 1904 against the German colonial administration in South West Africa.[20] The Mbanderu women wore stunning period dresses influenced, apparently, by the ones they'd seen worn by German colonists back in 1900. This was topped with an elaborate and distinctive headdress swept forward much like a bull's horns.

Gaborone was picturesque, surrounded by fields of red earth and rippling hills on the horizon draped in lush green bush. Barb and Michel put me up for the night in a spare room. Their life was an eye-opener for me. At 25, I hadn't yet come to grips with being an adult. I was still "figuring out" what I wanted to do in life. A couple of years younger than me, they both had steady well-paying jobs working as teachers in Botswana with Alliance Française. They lived in a good neighborhood, rented a spacious modern townhouse, owned a new Toyota, and could travel easily to amazing places like the Okavango Delta. They could even afford to have someone fix meals and clean house. It gave me real pause to think about my own life and accomplishments.

---

[20] The German government issued an official apology in 2021 for its role in the near extermination of the Mbanderu people, together with an offer of reparations.

Barb and Michel didn't have to return to work until Monday, it being a Saturday, so Michel volunteered to drive me to the train station to see if I could purchase a ticket to Johannesburg for the following day. The ticket agent told me that reservations needed to be booked a week in advance. But he did provide a glimmer of hope saying that I "might" be able to get a last-minute seat on the Sunday morning train if a cancellation came up. It was better than no hope at all. Michel said not to worry, I would be their guest if need be. In the meantime, I could spend the day with them and see some of the local sights. Barb was not the least put out, seemingly happy for the excuse to enjoy an additional "play day."

So, off we went, first to visit a small game park under construction on the edge of town. We couldn't go in, but the ostriches were free to come up to chain link fence along the highway, obviously as interested in us as we were in them. Unbelievable creatures, especially up close. Then lunch at Georgina's Restaurant, an upscale eatery, where we were joined by their friend, Sylvie, employed at the French embassy. Sylvie was the epitome of French bohemian style—colorful and fancy-free. She suggested we spend some time at the Oasis Hotel pool, which was more about lounging poolside than swimming. I was witness to a funny conversation between Sylvie and a waiter, straight out of a Pink Panther movie.

Sylvie to waiter: "Waiter, I want a coop."

Waiter: "A coop?"

Sylvie: "A coop, for my thé."

Waiter: "Oh. You mean a cup?"

Sylvie: "That's what I said, you silly man, a coop for my thé."

Then, it was on to the New Oasis Roller Rink. I have to admit, I never expected to go roller skating in Africa, but what a wonderful, unexpected bit of fun. I should add here that Botswana was and remains a fully integrated society. By that, I'm referring to Black and White integration. There was no inkling of any tensions or even a thought about the color of people's skin at any of the venues I attended. If you do not know the history of Sir Sereste Khama, the first president of Botswana, and his English wife, Ruth Williams, I highly recommend their story, which has since been released as a major motion picture. It was not without sacrifice and struggle that an exceptional coming together of people and cultures was achieved in Botswana, but the payoff was there for anyone with eyes to see. It was remarkable and uplifting and I was overjoyed to experience it.

There was a bon voyage party that night for a French expat at the home of another couple. I was invited to tag along. The party went on to 4 in the morning! Michel was blitzed beyond redemption. I had to be at the train station by 5:30 if I had any hope of obtaining a seat and I was beginning to wonder if I would make it. A friend, Christoph, came to the rescue, offering to drive me, plus an opportunity to refresh myself at his apartment beforehand. I said farewell to Michel and Barbara, whom I couldn't thank enough, and went off with Christoph who was true to his word.

I really, really liked Gaborone and would have enjoyed spending more time there. Less than a year later (June 14, 1985), South African forces conducted a day-time raid on the offices of the African National Congress in the heart of Gaborone. Twelve people were killed, only five of whom were ANC members. By most accounts, the South African authorities were more interested in teaching Botswana a lesson for playing host to the ANC, which they considered a terrorist organization, than forestalling any impending security concerns, therefore not too particular about who might be harmed in the assault.

The White apartheid government under P.W. Botha ruled South Africa with an iron fist. Pretoria maintained an embassy in Ottawa, but leisure travel to the country was not something someone with any lick of sense wanted to advertise. I had mixed feelings about visiting the country. I had no interest in supporting an apartheid regime, but there was no other way to complete a true cross-continent trek. Besides, for some perverse reason the political scientist in me felt that it might be "educational" to witness the brutality and injustice of apartheid first-hand.

I knew from my studies that possessing a South African visa would not be well-received in most parts of Africa and could seriously hamper my plans if discovered en route. Tracks, in fact, specifically barred customers with passports containing a visa or entry stamp for Israel, South Africa, Portugal or any Portuguese Territory. I understood the prohibition on travel to Israel and South Africa well enough, but the embargo on travel to and from Portugal, frankly, puzzled me. It was, I suppose, testament to the sordid legacy of Portuguese rule that this level of enmity and suspicion persisted nearly ten years after Angola and Mozambique had achieved independence. I had always planned to give Portugal's former possessions in southern Africa a wide berth. I wanted to see what I could of Africa but venturing into a proxy war between the Soviet Union and the United States, with South Africa and Cuba thrown in for added measure, was a bit much, even for me.

Canadians did a lot of business with South Africa on the QT notwithstanding the supposed sanctions and cultural boycotts, so it came as no surprise to me that I could apply for a "second passport" good only for travel to South Africa. To accommodate my travel plans it was valid for six months and stamped with an effective date of December 10th, so that it wouldn't expire before I arrived. I received the passport in a timely fashion and then sent it off to the South African embassy for a one-year multi-entry visa. I then tucked it safely and discreetly away until the time it would be needed.

The train for Ramatlabama departed at 6:50 (Ramatlabama as a destination needs some explanation, but I'll get to that in a moment). The fare was a very reasonable 8.40P ($7.70 US). There seemed to me to be lots of room on the train, so I don't know what all that business about needing a week's advance reservation was about.

This is the point where I have to pause to make clear a few things about the last-gasp efforts of the South African apartheid regime to legitimize its existence and the inane lengths to which it went to demonstrate it. First of all, it is important to understand, their axiom was "separate, but equal" suggesting that there was no overt discrimination involved in the separation of races. To prove their case, they created a number of ostensibly independent "homelands" (or "bantustans") loosely modeled on the Native reservations in Canada under the Indian Act, the "nation within a nation" concept. But the bantustans were a complete farce. At every turn, anything allocated to the Black constituency was inferior to what Whites received. Comprised of a scattered collection of non-contiguous enclaves rife with political dissent, the bantustans were, for all practical purposes, unviable.

Technically, under the constitutional arrangements of the time, I was crossing from Botswana into the "Republic of Bophuthatswana," although Ramatlabama was only 25 kilometers (16 miles) from Mafeking, South Africa. Moreover, the purported capital of Bophuthatswana was Mmabatho, virtually a suburb of Mafeking.[21] In fact, the two cities were eventually and sensibly merged post-apartheid into the City of Mahikeng and declared the new provincial capital.

Nothing, absolutely nothing, the Bophuthatswana government did, occurred without the approval of Pretoria. When the train pulled into Ramatlabama, a Bophuthatswana customs and immigration official came through to stamp my documents, accompanied by his White South African

---

[21] An interesting aside if you have any interest in Scouting, Mafeking is where it all began. Robert Baden-Powell modeled the Boy Scout movement after the Mafeking cadet corps, established while he was commanding the town garrison during the Boer siege of 1899-1900.

counterpart who reviewed and approved my entry into the country. For all that, I experienced no problems entering South Africa, but was only permitted a two-week "Holiday" visa.

My trans-African adventure was coming to an end, whether I wanted it to or not. The same train continued from Ramatlabama to the "border" with South Africa for an additional 1.20P, where we had to disembark owing to a different gauge in rail lines. I had the option of boarding another train for Johannesburg, but it was 11:30 in the morning and the train to "Jo'burg" wasn't scheduled to depart until 11:30 that night. I didn't relish sitting around the train station for twelve hours, so I looked into taking the bus, but it being Sunday, there was none to be had.

A sympathetic greengrocer changed my remaining pula to South African rand (R). I then tried my hand at hitching a ride. It took two and a half hours before someone in a hot candy apple red sports car pulled over to pick me up. Mike was headed to Jo'burg, a three-and-a-half-hour ride east, and apparently happy for the company. A young White South African, he'd spent six years in the Royal Air Force and was readjusting to being back in South Africa and civilian life.

Discovering that I was Canadian and fresh off the boat, so to speak, Mike took it upon himself to "educate" me on how to get by in South Africa. "The first thing," he said, "was not to hitchhike, unless I had a death wish." I won't repeat the language he used to describe Black South Africans. He pointed to his glove box. "Open it," he prompted. I did as he said, revealing a Glock semi-automatic pistol, presumably armed and ready. "That's what you need to get around in South Africa."

He then prepared me for the possibility that if our way was blocked by "terrorists" at some point, he might just have to run them down and make a quick escape. Hence the fast car. Wonderful. I had the distinct and creepy impression that he found using his gun or running down people on some thin justification an enticing proposition. That worried me, too. I'd like to be able to say that Mike was just a "character," but that would misrepresent how truly dangerous and misguided he seemed. In any case, we made it to Johannesburg without incident and he dropped me off outside of the Braamfontain train station. I wished Mike good health and thanked him for the ride.

Johannesburg, of course, was a sprawling, bustling city, the largest in South Africa. From what I could see, it appeared neat, trim, and cultivated, with plenty of 'Old Dutch' architectural influences still apparent, which made the contrast with the numerous mining dumps skirting the city all the more jarring.

The Boers, Afrikaans-speaking descendants of Dutch settlers, were, for the most part, devout church-going people, so almost everything was closed on Sundays. I had an easier time understanding the English spoken in Botswana than I did around Johannesburg, the Afrikaans accents were so thick. I noticed, while I was there, that Boney M., a popular Euro-Caribbean disco group, was playing at Sun City, Bophuthatswana, despite a United Nations' cultural boycott in place at the time. Dolly Parton, Elton John, and Queen were among a long list of artists performing at Sun City, perhaps because the money was just too good to turn down or because of some idealistic notion that music, like sports, is above politics. As White performers, perhaps they did not grasp the enormity of apartheid's impact on Black South Africans. But a Black vocal group touring South Africa at that point in history? I had a hard time getting my head around that.

I booked into the Hotel Springbok for 30R including breakfast (about $25 US a night). First thing, the next morning, I went to a Standard Bank branch to cash the VISA travelers checks I obtained from the funds my father wired me. I almost collapsed from shock when the teller informed me that the checks weren't "cashable" in South Africa, due, I suppose, to the economic sanctions.

The bank manager was summoned, and I pleaded with him that this money was my only way to purchase a flight home. To my huge relief, he agreed to waive the policy and cash them. I have to think that South Africans were quite adept at evading sanctions by this time and that the bank would somehow find a way to collect its due.

My old friend, Mike (Michel), had wanted me to return home via Paris and spend some time with him there, which was tempting, but I was reticent to return penniless to Canada. Besides, my leave from the army was nearly up (my authorized leave from the Canadian Forces was set to expire on April 30th) and I was anxious to reunite with Edi. Cash in hand, I went to the South African Airways office and booked a flight to New York on the 24th of April, eight days hence, and four days before my South Africa visa was due to expire. What to do and see with my few remaining days in Africa?

I considered making the trip to Cape Town, but my timing was off. We were heading into Easter and everything, including hotels, trains, and busses, were booked to Cape Town all the way through Easter Monday. The prices were also jacked up for the holiday weekend. To be able to legitimately claim that I'd "crossed Africa" from north to south (on a secant line from Ceuta to Durban), I felt I needed, at the very least, to dip my feet in the ocean.

My parent's neighbor back in Canada, Angela O'Neill, was South African born and raised. Angela had spoken with her mother in Durban before I'd left and had passed along an open invitation for me to put up at her home for a few days. It would save me a chunk of change and I'd get to see a little of what life was like in a (White) South African home. So, I booked a return ticket to Durban, returning on the 23rd.

The train wasn't due to depart until 6:30 in the evening, leaving me the remainder of that afternoon to window shop for souvenirs. I was drawn to a high-end jewelry store displaying some unique and very attractive African-inspired pieces in the window. I splurged, unplanned, on a gold necklace with a stylized depiction of hunters chasing down an antelope, thinking that Edi deserved an extra special souvenir from my time in Africa.

There were actually two side-by-side train stations in Johannesburg, a decrepit old station for Blacks and a spanking new station for "Europeans" with all the modern conveniences. I was loath to participate in this absurdly artificial separation of the species, but there simply was no alternative. Directly above my head was the sign in English and Afrikaans that still sends chills down my spine: "WHITES ONLY / NET BLANKS."

It took a good 15 hours to cover the 725 kilometers between Johannesburg and Durban. I shared a compartment with a fellow named Steve, close enough to my own age, on a week's leave from the army. We compared notes on military service and questioned one another about what life was like in our respective countries. Steve was of English descent and had a far more balanced and realistic opinion of South Africa than Mike, who had given me the ride into Johannesburg. He was also hopeful that some kind of political accommodation could eventually be reached between Black and White South Africans to end apartheid, but not at all optimistic about the timeline.

I took pictures of the rippling landscape from out the window of our carriage as the train passed through the "Valley of a Thousand Hills," a largely unspoiled range between Pietermaritzburg and Durban that forms part of the Zulu kingdom. Time permitting, I hoped to have a closer look at the valley before departing South Africa. Arriving in Durban, I paid a quick visit to the tourist bureau to pick up a map of the city. The local cinema was showing Yentl with Barbara Streisand, of all things, but I only had one objective in mind and made a beeline for the beach where I waded into the Indian Ocean, "officially" completing my trans-African odyssey (April 17, 1984).

A French dentist working in Soweto, the impoverished Black township outside of Johannesburg, was on hand to witness my achievement and volunteered to take my picture. He was raising a family in South Africa and was beginning to doubt that it was for the best. He grilled me on life in Canada, thinking it might be an option. After listening to my stories about the winters, I doubt he seriously considered it. Five months later (September 3, 1984), marked the start of the "Soweto Uprising," leaving thirty dead, and that was just the beginning.

I found a room for 23R ($19 US) at the Killarney Hotel, just to settle down and get my bearings. Then I called Angela's mother, Joy, to let her know that I'd arrived. When Joy picked up the phone, she claimed to have no idea who I was. Surprised, and taken aback, I carefully explained my situation. "I'm sorry," she said, "I have other guests at the moment, and it would not be convenient," and hung up. Well, that was that, but I was seriously low on funds by this point and more than a little concerned about it. I momentarily regretted my decision to buy Edi that expensive neckless. Don't panic, I told myself, remembering Sara's gift. I tallied my remaining funds and calmed down. There was enough to see me through, and even a little extra for some judicious tourism.

I tried the music shops again and fared a bit better, picking up three cassette tapes, none of which, however, featured truly traditional African music. There was an album by Zulu artist Moses Mchunu, however, described as "neo-traditional" and, over the course of time it has become one of my favorite go-to recordings of African music. I went to see Yentl, despite the weird juxtaposition of cultures, if only to check out the cinema. When I emerged and got back to my room, the weather had dramatically changed for the worse. Durban was experiencing the peripheral effects of Tropical Storm Kamisy, a storm that destroyed 80 percent of the cities of Diego Suarez and Majunga in Madagascar, leaving 68 dead and 100,000 homeless.

I relocated to the Miramar Hotel the next morning for half the price per night, then walked to the Old Fort. It was a pretty spot within town, that included a small display on the military history of Durban. Durban, as it happens, has a tangential connection to Canada. It is named after Lieutenant General Sir Benjamin D'Urban who served as the governor of Cape Colony, South Africa from 1834 to '37 as well as Commander-in-Chief of the British Forces in North America from 1846 to '49. There is or was a plaque in his honor at the Old Fort. An Englishman from Suffolk, he typified the itinerant careers of British soldiers, having served in the Napoleonic Wars, Antigua, British Guiana, the Cape Colony, and eventually Canada. While governor of Cape Colony, he exceeded his authority, unilaterally annexing Xhosa lands, and therefore has the dubious distinction of being the first person to bend Africans to British rule. D'Urban died while serving in Montréal and is buried at the Champ d'honneur national in Pointe-Claire, Québec overlooking Lac Saint-Louis.

One of the most troubling things I witnessed in Durban were Zulus employed at pulling rickshaws. Tall, powerful, athletic men, warriors you could say, splendid to behold, dressed in traditional Zulu garb, but hauling White tourists around at a fast trot under the hot sun. It made my skin crawl. I gather there are only a handful of rickshaws still operating in Durban, but the magnificent Zulus, thankfully, have been replaced by commonplace capitalists wearing fanciful costumes of their own devising. You see as much in San Francisco. I was, however, super lucky to stumble on a small traveling circus passing through.

"Circus Brian," a.k.a., Brian Boswell Circus, was an intimate 1-ring South African show, the highlight of which was an incredible musical ride featuring riderless Arabian horses. Sadly, no one was minding a baby elephant and camel tied outside the main tent and a young boy who'd got too close was trampled and seriously injured by the camel. I discovered too, that there was a very fine amusement park right on the seaside. I enjoyed myself at the circus and the park but missed not having anyone to share them with.

I must have over indulged, because I awoke the next day with a tremendous headache and opted to spend most of the day in bed, just listening to the radio. Coming from Canada where radio programing was extensive and super slick, South African stations were sparse amateur productions by comparison. No matter which station I dialed in, it seemed like they were willing to put just about anyone on the air without preparation or planning. The news was read off as a series of headlines without any background or depth. I found this all very peculiar.

There was a television in the room as well, but I could not follow the Afrikaans shows, and the rest of the programing seemed to be re-runs of American shows that had absolutely no appeal for me. From what I could see on television and in print, Hollywood's distorted betrayal of life on the American frontier, with its emphasis on independence, resiliency, and self-sufficiency (coincidentally, tamed by White men) resonated extremely well with White South Africans. Ads featuring characters unambiguously modeled after the 'Marlboro Man' of American cigarette fame figured prominently in South African media. "Coke is Reg!" (Coke is it!) proclaim the roadside billboards in Afrikaans.

The next day was Good Friday. As expected, just about everything was closed. The weather being warm and sunny, I spent most of the day lying on the beach, watching the women, surfers, sail boats, and ocean-going freighters. Everyone around me was White. I watched anxiously as a Black family strayed onto "our" beach from farther down the shoreline. How do people cope with this constant tension? I wondered.

I was relieved to see that no one paid them any heed. Perhaps, I thought, the barriers are beginning to come down in parts of the country? One could hope. With everything closed, I went back to my hotel room to soothe my sunburn.

The evening's news included a report that the South African Ministry of Health and Welfare, an oxymoron, if I've ever heard one, had forbidden the collection of funds for a Gandhi memorial.

On Saturday, I walked to the Durban Museum and Art Gallery. You wouldn't have known from the collection that there was much in the way of Zulu culture or history in Natal Province (today, KwaZulu-Natal), or any contribution made by the South Asian community.[22] The displays were all about the triumph of White settlement over wilderness and barbarism, and earlier British and Dutch history. Naturally, there were displays on the Zulu Wars as well as the First and Second Anglo-Boer Wars. The Second Boer War was of some personal interest. My Militia regiment, the Governor General's Horse Guards, had a South Africa "battle honor" emblazoned on its standard, members of the unit having served with the Royal Canadian Dragoons and the 2nd Canadian Mounted Rifles in the Second Boer War (1899 to 1902), the first authorized deployment of Canadian forces overseas.

Canada sent three contingents to South Africa, more than 7,000 volunteers all told. The pros and cons of Imperial politics aside, British and Colonial forces waged a particularly "grim" but effective strategy to defeat the Boers, pioneering the use of civilian internment camps where the prevailing conditions were the stuff of nightmares. Canadian troops performed admirably in battle, but frankly speaking, were also complicit in some of the worst abuses of the civilian population.

I flitted about the displays, until at one point nature called, as they say. A member of the museum staff pointed me to the stairwell where I could find the "men's public amenities," but imagine my chagrin at having to choose between a door marked "Whites," another marked

---

[22] Indians first arrived as indentured laborers in the 1860s.

"Coloureds and Asians." To take a simple whiz, I had either to deliberately disregard the sign and risk the chance of discovery and subsequent punishment or compromise my ethics by conforming. I'll let you ponder what I decided to do given the circumstances. I assumed the same pattern was repeated on the opposite stairwell to accommodate women and could not help but wonder at the resources expended on multiple lavatories for the supposed sake of racial propriety by such a small and rarely frequented museum. I was even more perplexed by the pamphlets I saw lying on the museum counter promoting "voluntary euthanasia." I'd landed in an Orwellian dystopia.

For my last full day in Durban, I caved in and joined a tour group headed to the Valley of a Thousand Hills overlooking the Umgeni River. If you are a fan of the 1964 epic Zulu! starring Michael Caine and Stanley Baker, you'll understand why I was looking forward to it. The Zulu people have called the valley home for centuries and have managed to endure as a distinct society despite the pressures. For me, the most interesting part of the tour was the kraal homesteads—large, fenced enclosures built on the downward slopes of the rolling hills with several beehive shaped huts with thatched roofs (a "rondavel" or iQukwane) grouped inside.

Unfortunately, the cultural performances were canned, lackluster affairs. Zulu women sang and danced topless in what may have been traditional fashion for us, but it seemed to me their hearts weren't in it. They were accompanied by a single "warrior" and a traditional healer who double hatted as the village chief. When all was said and done, we were encouraged to purchase curios. A classic tourist trap. Anyway, I did appreciate the opportunity to experience even a tiny bit of the culture and history they were willing to share. You extract what you can from such experiences. On the bus back to Durban, I sat next to an unapologetic "Rhodesian" expat, who feared that South Africa would "fall next" and this time he'd have to "stand firm and fight."

I returned to the beach and finished a spy thriller I'd picked up somewhere along the way, giving it to a young Black South African that had engaged me in conversation. I packed, checked out of the hotel, grabbed a light dinner, and headed to the train station for the ride back to Johannesburg. Waiting for my train, I watched, for the last time, the gleaming hunter green and brass steam engines get watered and fueled up, chugging and puffing with each sip, then a long sleepy ride through the night. We pulled into the station at Johannesburg a little after 8 a.m. All told, I'd spent 145 nights in Africa. Now it was time to head home. In some ways, I wasn't prepared to leave, and in other ways, I couldn't wait. I took two photos of the infamous "Whites Only" sign to remind myself in years to come what extreme intolerance looks like and moved on.

Johannesburg was a bit unusual, in that you confirmed your flight and checked your bags with the airline at their office in the city, then boarded a bus to Jan Smuts International Airport, which required a separate ticket. I had only 5 rand left of the 200 rand I'd started out with before traveling to Durban. At 7:45 p.m., on April 25, 1984, I boarded a 747B for New York and left Africa behind.

The meal onboard the South African Airlines flight was a relative feast. The plane made a pitstop on Isla do Sal, in the Cape Verde Islands to refit the aircraft, then was back in the air. Midway through the night we were treated to a magnificent lightning storm in the clouds some 10,000 feet below. It seemed to go on forever. Curiously, there wasn't the slightest bit of turbulence. It's something I've never experienced in air travel before or since.

We arrived at Kennedy International Airport just after 6:00 in the morning. I zipped through customs and immigration and caught a helicopter ride to Newark, New Jersey. The helicopter stopped at La Guardia airport and the United Nations Headquarters, then flew right past the Statue of Liberty, which was a kick in itself. By sheer luck and good timing, I got the last seat on a People Express flight to Syracuse, New York because some poor sod missed his connection. Moreover, the flight cost me just $38, cash!

From Syracuse to Kingston, Ontario (and Edi), it was 204 kilometers or just under 130 miles. It doesn't sound like much, but there was no public or private transportation service across the US-Canada border. I walked the mile and a quarter it took to get from Syracuse Airport to Interstate 81 and stuck out my thumb. I was out there for perhaps 20 or 30 minutes when a New York State Highway patrol car pulled up. The trooper got out and looked at me askance. "You do know you're not allowed to hitchhike on an Interstate?"

"No. I didn't know that," I replied. "I'm sorry, Officer. I just want to get home. I've had a long trip."

"Where you comin' from? And where you headed?" he asked.

"Africa, and Kingston," I said.

"Africa?"

"Yes, Sir." That generated a conversation, which left the trooper shaking his head.

"Okay, son. I suppose if you can handle hitching rides in Africa, you can handle whatever we can throw at you in New York. You be safe now." He left me to my fate, no citation.

My first ride got me as far as Pulaski. My second ride happened to be from a Queen's University student also heading to Kingston, but would only take me as far as the duty-free shop at Alexandria Bay because he didn't want to chance any hassle crossing the border with a stranger, let alone someone just arrived from Africa. I couldn't fault him for the decision and was grateful to get that far.

I actually walked across the border, something I'd never done before. The Canadian customs and immigrations officers at Lansdowne were more interested in hearing about my trip across Africa than concerned about what I had in my bags. I was given a cursory examination and allowed to enter the country. I still needed to get to Kingston, however, and was out there for hours walking backwards along Highway 137 with my thumb out and getting nowhere. In growing desperation, I pulled out a marker and a sheet of paper and wrote:

KINGSTON
IT'S GETTING DARK
PLEASE PICK ME UP!

A few minutes later an 18-wheeler pulled over a good 10 or 12 meters beyond me. I was sure he'd just stopped to fix a tire or something and kept my thumb out, but the driver got out of his cab and beckoned me to join him. He helped stow my bags and up into the passenger seat.

"I didn't think truck drivers ever picked up hitchhikers," I said, mystified, but pleased.

"They don't. Too risky and the insurance wouldn't be happy to know. First time I've ever done it. Not sure why I stopped, tell you the truth." He seemed suddenly puzzled by his own behavior. "Maybe it was your sign."

"Well, thanks anyway."

"Sure. You're going to Kingston, right? Where you comin' from?"

The trucker, whose name, unfortunately, I can't now recall, reacted much the same as the state trooper. When he learned that I was going to Kingston to re-unite with my girlfriend after 5 months in Africa he felt totally vindicated, you could say, exonerated, for his inexplicable decision to pick me up. He said I should look him up if I was ever in Sandbanks—if he were home, I'd see his rig sitting in the drive. He dropped me off at Division Street and Highway 401. I took a cab from the bus depot that used to be a few blocks down from there and booked a room at the Quality Inn on Princess Street.

I fretted about Edi. Would I be a welcome sight? I wonder if she ever got my flowers? I was by no means certain. Her last letter to me was a terse postcard sent four months earlier to a poste restante in Central Africa. Tomorrow, I said to myself, will reveal all. I was beyond exhausted, but meaningful sleep eluded me. Visions of Africa intruded haphazardly on my thoughts and dreams for weeks after my return.

Epilogue

I MOVED ABOUT KINGSTON AND TORONTO FEELING DISORIENTED, like someone who's suffered a stroke and is learning to use a knife and fork all over again. I couldn't shake the strange sensation that I'd been let in on a secret that few people could possibly understand and would probably be wasting my time trying to explain. I felt I'd aged as well, as if each month in Africa was somehow equivalent to a year in Canada. I couldn't decide at first whether it was best to go back to school or take up a career. That invitation to sit for a job interview with Mitsui Bank was still out there.

I did feel confident that I'd achieved the goal I'd set out for myself, to fill the gaps in a purely academic education, and took some satisfaction if not pride in that. But I also learned an awful lot about myself during my journey across Africa. Although I faced tough physical and mental challenges in my youth, much of it in service of Her Majesty's Canadian Armed Forces, nothing, before or since, quite compares to my time in Africa. Primo Levi famously posited, and I'm paraphrasing here, that it is constructive to measure yourself at least once in your life under truly formidable conditions and to enter into it with a mindset of feeling strong, while not necessarily being strong.[23]

---

[23] Levi endured the horrors of Auschwitz. I don't purport for a moment to have faced that "Lord of the Flies" level of challenge, nor do I think Levi was recommending it. His point, rather, is that everyone, at least one time in their life, should have to struggle and thereby come face-to-face with the person they really are deep down.

To be honest, I'm not proud of how I measured up in every instance. Of course, I'd never been in a situation where I was the visible minority. You quickly learn that there is no way to escape the stereotypes associated with the color of your own skin. It is a salutary thing, to be frank.

Under these reversed circumstances, it was pointless on my part to give much if any thought to other people's skin color for large segments of my journey, just as you don't make a deliberate mental note of every tree you pass that it has green leaves, although I suppose my brain must have subconsciously processed the fact. If anything, short of an actual conversation, I tended to rely on the clothing and the accessories that people wore to make some sort of judgement about them. The notable exceptions were, of course, South Africa and Zaire, where I was compelled by the prevailing society to take note of skin color, and worse, accept judgments based on that sole criterion. The experience left me feeling sullied.

Africa, I have to say, also took a heavy toll on me physically. Aside from having battled pneumonia early in the trip, I lost a great deal of weight and suffered from debilitating stomach ailments. The latter frustrated me no end because I was far more cautious about what I put in my mouth than most of my traveling companions. I discovered some years later that the combination of anti-malarial drugs that I was taking (Chloroquine and Maloprim) may have been responsible for the nausea, diarrhea, stomach pain, headache, and fever I endured. Little consolation. Once I reached Botswana where the toilets more closely resembled those in Canada, I discovered that I had bigger issues. My stool was grotesquely and rather alarmingly interlaced with blood and mucus.

A return trip to St. Michael's Hospital Department of Infectious Diseases in Toronto identified my intestinal hitchhiker as Entamoeba histolytica, both cysts and trophozoites, a feces-transmitted parasite, as it happens, also associated with abdominal pain and diarrhea. Left untreated, the disease might have resulted in irretrievable damage to my colon or liver. Prescribed treatments of the antibiotic Iodochlorhydoxyquin, normally used to treat ringworm, as you can tell, were effective. But periodic migraines, which I did not experience before my trip to Africa, trouble me to this day.

On the lighter side, having traveled almost exclusively with Brits, Aussies, and New Zealanders for so long (Ronnie, the notable exception; even the French Kristine spoke English with a British accent), I'd picked up a number of words and expressions without even thinking about it. Lorries, torches, loos, and petrol became entrenched vocabulary. Banana was pronounced bah-nah-nah and tomato, toe-mah-toe. From the Aussies and Kiwis in particular, I picked up two phrases: "sussed" (to have sized up or studied a situation), and "I reckon" (meaning, in my opinion). I had to make a conscious effort to shake off these unconscious affectations.

In the thirty-eight years that have elapsed since I was last in Africa, much has changed, and much has not, some things for the better. First and foremost, the apartheid system was overturned in South Africa, ending, at long last, that reprehensible system of race-based segregation and discrimination. Large parts of Africa have realized improvement in public health and gender equality, a reduction in infant mortality, and rising life expectancy. The African Union, established in 2002, has demonstrated the ability and willingness of member states to work cooperatively on a number of crucial fronts, taking a page, I suppose, from the Economic Community of West African States (ECOWAS), established in 1975.

Kenya has developed into a prominent center for the arts. The DRC (formerly, Zaire), perhaps building on lessons learned from the Ferme laitaire de Nbzanga, has made great strides in dairy farming. Conservation has become a higher priority in many countries. The DRC, for example, is apparently making progress on a program of land concessions for communities in the Congo Basin designed to encourage sustainable management of the rainforest. South Africa and Namibia are looking to revolutionize the mining industry in their respective nations through large investments in green hydrogen. Cell phones have empowered a new generation of small business owners to connect with hitherto unimagined efficiencies, overcoming many of the obstacles formerly confronting remote communities. Young inspiring voices, like that of Laiqa Walli from East Africa, advocate for a "contextualized" approach to development that looks to home-grown solutions for the problems facing Africa.

The road forward, unfortunately, has not been smooth. Of the nineteen countries and territories in Africa that I passed through, fewer than I can count on one hand have entirely escaped political, religious, and ethnic violence. It is a simple enough matter to do an online search for the places I traveled through to gain an appreciation for the level of turmoil they have endured over the intervening years. Between 2020 and 2022 alone, there have been eight military coups, both successful and unsuccessful, in West and Central Africa. The reasons can be nuanced and complex, reflecting variations on old themes, but there are also new and unexpected factors at play.

China's influence on the continent has increased exponentially, creating an uncertain dynamic. Its economy relies heavily on the extraction of natural resources from Africa, commodities such as oil, manganese, copper, cobalt, coltan, and other rare-earth minerals. Infrastructure improvements have become, therefore, a high priority. With an estimated population of 1.3 billion, it's safe to say China is also eyeing Africa as a market for finished goods. But Chinese investment has both detractors and proponents. Some argue China is forging a neo-colonial empire on the continent for entirely self-serving purposes, shackling the continent with unsustainable levels of debt and ill-suited development projects. Sour grapes, counter those in favor of the investment. Western business interests, they contend, are just put out because they're accustomed to having their own way in Africa and are now facing stiff competition from Asia.

The reality, I think, is that Africa is eager to find a new and workable paradigm and that any potential downside is worth the risk. Throughout their period of hegemony, the colonial powers extracted raw unprocessed resources for export, made no serious attempt to connect one region to another, no meaningful investment in higher education, or sincere effort to advance indigenous self-governance. Post-independence, the better part of Africa without the advantage of experience, infrastructure, or inter-regional connectivity, has naturally struggled to catch up to the rest of the world in the arenas of manufacturing, trade, and commerce. It hasn't helped that Africa has few navigable rivers of meaningful size to facilitate transportation and must contend with seasonal extremes. China, it can be reasonably argued, is the first major power on the continent to seriously and coherently address these debilitating shortfalls, including, it must be said, offering broad access to higher education. It does so, moreover, at an extremely competitive price.

Often touted as a "win-win" scenario for development by both government officials and Chinese industrialists, extensive Chinese investment in countries like Zambia and Nigeria has indeed spurred industry, created jobs, enhanced infrastructure, transportation, and communications, much of it sorely needed. On the upside, this infusion of wealth has helped fuel, as an example, the real estate and crypto currency markets in Nigeria, fostering in turn a new generation of tech entrepreneurs, fashion manufacturers, and motion picture producers. Highways, bridges, new safe and efficient rail lines, are under development at a pace only Chinese state-run industry can deliver. Cellular service is widely and cheaply available.

But the perils of unbridled investment cannot be understated. Progress may come at a price.

Low levels of transparency contained in trade agreements with Chinese firms have many critics worried. There is the considerable amount of debt that the beneficiaries of this investment are taking on, the required forms and terms of repayment, the long-term implications of siphoning away non-renewable resources susceptible to volatile shifts in the global marketplace. Not to mention the environmental toll, health issues, and cost of mitigation associated with resource extraction.

Production methods and facilities, virtual clones transplanted in their entirety from China, have undercut and displaced homegrown producers in uncompetitive sectors, weakening, it is argued, the indigenous community's capacity to shape their own destiny. What is, perhaps, more troubling is the perception, whether real or imagined, that Chinese business owners and managers lead a privileged and separate existence wielding, moreover, an inordinate degree of influence over state and local government officials. Chinese employers, it appears, are confident that the various problems cited can be ironed out with time, effort, and communication, provided there is "stability in government." Veiled speech, perhaps, for applying a firm hand when necessary. Only time will tell how this will indeed play out.

What is certainly true is that all this new investment has ushered in unprecedented levels of urbanization. In Nigeria, where the population is upwards of 211 million, millions see none of the benefits of this elevated growth, whether it derives from Chinese investment or oil extraction. The chasm of income inequality and food insecurity between urban and rural areas grows deeper. Abuse of power accompanied by growing economic disparity gives rise to criminal activity, sometimes in the guise of jihadist or "revolutionary" movements that peddle societal injustice as an excuse for their own cruel and selfish purposes. Cell phones may have empowered a new generation of small business owners, but they have also become an invaluable tool in the hands of criminal organizations that use them to organize and evade the authorities. It's a major contributing factor to the mass kidnappings of children that have bedeviled northwestern Nigeria in recent years and the growing number of attacks on the rail system.

From 1996 to 2003, the DRC (formerly Zaire) endured a brutal civil war that unseated Mobutu, but spilled over into Uganda, Rwanda, and Sudan. Unimaginable numbers of women were sexually assaulted during the conflict in an apparent effort to dispossess and humiliate them. Great swaths of the ancient rainforest that so thrilled Sara and me, were poached, mined, deforested, and turned over for cash crops beyond any possibility of recovery. A plethora of rebel militia groups, with flamboyant names like the "Cooperative for Development of the Congo" (CODECO), March 23 Movement (M23), and Allied Democratic Forces (ADF), still vie for control of the rich natural resources in the eastern Congo bordering Uganda, periodically ambushing police and military, plundering the great forests without thought or care, displacing untold numbers of civilians in the process.

The Mbuti Pygmy people we encountered, with the exception perhaps of the most isolated bands, have faced eviction from their forest homes, left to scratch a living from the soil, sell bushmeat, or enter the workforce where they receive the lowest wages and the least secure employment. Mutwanga, the town high in the Rwenzori mountains where we'd unintentionally participated in the delivery of the coffee payroll—in my experience, once one of the most stunningly beautiful places on Earth—is now home to a major hydro-electric project and a target for repeated attacks by Uganda-based ADF rebels intent on creating an Islamic state in Central Africa.

President Biya of Cameroon, who has held power since 1982, has cracked down on all political opposition and seemingly turned a blind eye to human rights abuses. Fighting has erupted between communities divided along English and French-speaking lines, degenerating into vicious tit-for-tat attacks. As if that were not enough, Islamist extremists in the far north of the country have engaged in kidnappings, thefts, and murder.

Terrorist groups have risen and splintered into a complex, conflicting web throughout the Sahel, affecting, among the countries I visited, Cameroon, Burkina Faso, Niger, Mali, and Nigeria. Advocates have raised doubts about the wisdom of a purely military response to genuine grievances, stoking fears that an over reliance on a military solution has only exacerbated the situation in these countries and may indeed be feeding the growth of insurgencies. Increasingly, there are calls for an alternative strategy that takes into account the root causes of discontent and many local and international peacebuilding organizations are engaged in this effort. Whether or not these voices will gain a sympathetic ear, remains to be seen.

Like the People's Republic of China, Soviet Russia backed a variety of liberation movements in Africa that are today, ruling government parties. President Vladimir Putin opted to reengaged with Africa, renewing these old ties, providing a cheaper and perhaps less questioning alternative to Western military assistance. The employment of Russian mercenaries with all that that connotes in countries like Mali and Central Africa is cause for real concern, but what may prove more damaging to these countries in the long run, especially given the present war in Ukraine, is an apparent willingness to act as apologists for Russian aggression at a point when most of the world is united in its condemnation.

At the time of writing, rapidly rising energy and food importation costs associated with the war are likely to have major ramifications for the continent-wide economy, ramifications that could seriously undermine what fragile progress has been achieved to-date. If the economic environment does indeed deteriorate, it is from China and the West, not Russia, that any relief is likely to emanate.

African Union forces together with France and other international allies, including Canada and the US, have been battling to keep a lid on the Sahel since 2013, where jihadist insurgents tend to garner most of the attention.[24] Mali is emblematic of the significant challenges posed by communal and sectarian tensions in Africa. A military coup in 2012 created a power vacuum that allowed Tuareg nationalists allied with jihadists to seize the region around Timbuktu and Gao, unilaterally seceding from Mali and declaring independence as the "State of Azawad." During their occupation of Timbuktu, religious extremists purposely destroyed many of the great libraries and monuments of the city's glorious past.[25] The accord between jihadists and Tuareg, however, quickly disintegrated, allowing a new government with international backing an opportunity to retake the region.

Sadly, allegations of political corruption combined with a deteriorating economy magnified societal rifts and fueled communal violence in Mali. In March 2019, ethnic Dogon militia massacred some 150 nomadic Peuhl (Fulani) from the village of Ogossagou near Mopti. I struggled, personally, to pair this news with my memories of the incredible people and places I'd visited all those years ago. Mali has since endured two separate coups. The present ruling junta has managed to alienate the international military alliance operating in Mali, in large part by hiring Russian mercenaries (members of the Kremlin-linked Wagner Group) and repeatedly delaying promised elections. France and its partners, including Canada and the US, announced in February 2022 that they will be withdrawing their security forces from the country, although they will continue to operate in other parts of the Sahel.

---

[24] Led by France, the two primary efforts are Operation Barkhane and the Takuba Task Force (specific to Mali).

[25] Thankfully, thousands of fascinating and timeworn manuscripts were safely smuggled out of Timbuktu before the destruction of the libraries. They have since been digitized and translated into several languages for posterity as the "Mali Magic" project, a joint undertaking of Google, Malienne, and international partners.

In 2021, Niger celebrated its first democratic handover of power since attaining independence in 1960, but the country continues to be racked by violence and political instability. There was an attempted coup against President Mohamed Bazoum soon after his election. Jihadist insurgents have switched to targeting civilian populations. One hundred and thirty-seven people were killed in a single attack by militants on motorbikes in May of 2021. The country is likely to benefit, however, from the pull-out of the international coalition from Mali and redeployment to Niger.

Thomas Sankara, the charismatic president of Upper Volta (Burkina Faso) during our brief transit, was assassinated three years later by forces intent upon restoring relations with the former colonial power, France. More recently, President Kaboré of Burkina Faso was toppled by a coup d'état (January 2022) and replaced by a military junta on the excuse that it was necessary to deal with the growing number of jihadist attacks taking place throughout the country.

Blessed with abundant natural resources, the Central African Republic (CAR), paradoxically, is one of the least developed nations in Africa and one of the poorest in the world (based on adjusted GDP per capita), its populace left largely destitute and subject to the capriciousness of a survival economy. The situation in CAR is almost too complicated to summarize. Since a coup that overthrew President Francois Bozizé in 2013, CAR has been racked by communal violence, coalitions of Christian militias battling coalitions of Muslim militias that have since fragmented and are now battling amongst themselves, forcing tens of thousands of refugees to flee into neighboring states that can hardly cope with their own problems. Hundreds of thousands more were displaced internally, creating a humanitarian crisis that has barely abated.

Turmoil in CAR is compounded by fierce competition over rich gold, timber, and diamond reserves and the fact that government forces under President Faustin-Archange

Touadéra control only about a third of the country. Russian mercenaries employed by the Touadéra administration are preoccupied, not surprisingly, with securing the nation's mineral wealth, undertaking their duties, it would appear, with ruthless efficiency. The fifteen thousand United Nations peacekeepers stationed in the country are hard-pressed to protect the civilian population and often find themselves the targets of insurgent attacks. Negotiated ceasefires are routinely violated.

The land border between Morocco and Algeria has been closed, incredibly, since 1994, stemming from a dispute over the former Spanish colony of Western Sahara. From a Western standpoint, this is akin to closing the border between Canada and the US or the US and Mexico for nearly 30 years. It boggles the mind.

I could go on. The tall and the short of all this is that a trans-Africa trek of the sort that I undertook from 1983 to 1984 would be ill-advised, if not impossible, under present conditions. The "New Africa" that I believed was just on the horizon in 1983 and fueled my interest, never materialized, at least not in the manner that I envisioned. Much depended on improving harmony and cooperation between communities and nations, aided, in part, by a less mercenary approach to the global economy. There has certainly been progress in fits and starts, sometimes and in some places quite impressive, but the setbacks for all that have been significant and far-reaching.

My heart bleeds for the countless people I met during my travels whose lives undoubtedly were disrupted if not ruined by the turmoil that eventually swept over them. They had hopes and dreams like anyone else and strove to make a better life for themselves and their children. In 1983-'84, they had every reason to be optimistic. I heard it in their voices and saw it in their faces. Sadly, ethnic divisions exploited or exacerbated by drought, corruption, opportunism, and easy access to arms and munitions have conspired to shatter their reasons for optimism.

Being fatalistic, of course, is not helpful. Nor is it in the nature of the people I met. Africa will undoubtedly persevere and strive to find solutions.

It is important to reiterate that I never set out to change the world I went to experience. Having encountered literally thousands of people from a myriad of cultures, social, and economic conditions, all within a few months, it would have been the height of conceit to have even tried. It is a different matter, I think, for diplomats, peacekeepers, and aid workers with a mandate to effect change and a much narrower frame of reference. I presumed going into this that nothing about my presence was going to impact Africa in the slightest. I certainly never intended to do harm. I was there simply to observe and to cultivate insight on the developing world, and maybe, just a bit selfishly, to savor the sights and sounds of the oldest human inhabited continent on Earth.

Having since read a little quantum theory I can see now that I was fooling myself—by the mere act of observing I was unavoidably affecting the reality of the very people I encountered. There was no way to take myself out of the equation. By simply choosing to do one thing over another, or refraining from one thing, yet undertaking another, I was continually acting as an influencer, shaping circumstances and altering realities. Even the act of engaging in largely inconsequential conversations with the people I met was either confirming or refuting stereotypes. I thought back to Christian, the student from Enugu who candidly asked us if we did not associate with Blacks because there were no Blacks traveling with us on the truck. How many thousands of people saw us pass by on the Pink Pig and assumed the very same thing, filing that little bit of distorted reality away in the back of their minds? It is a troublesome notion. I can only hope that my presence did more good than harm (the ribbon of squashed butterflies we left behind in Zaire will forever haunt me).

I never did get the opportunity to see Thamugadi or the Ulanga River, but there were compensations. I can rightly claim to have been to Timbuktu, the Mountains of the Moon, and the Okavango Delta of the Kalahari, although I have very few photographs to show for my effort—the single-lens reflex Olympus camera that I purchased specifically for the trip got sand in the aperture while crossing the Sahara and gradually seized up. I didn't notice the problem until it was too late. The majority of my photos came out over exposed and unusable.

If I can lay claim to a few unusual accomplishments in my life, one would be that visit to Timbuktu (I've since developed a nearly equal fascination for the Wakhan Corridor) and the other, having put a town on the map. Mobutu's eccentric city in the jungle, Gbadolite, was not marked on my National Geographic map.[26] I wrote to the National Geographic Society after my return, pointing out that a city occupying such a considerable and prominent place in that part of the world, albeit a veritable ghost town, deserved to be listed. Some months later, I received a letter from their map division stating that they had confirmed my report and that the name, Gbadolite, would henceforth appear on all National Geographic maps of Africa.

Sara made her way back to Wales via Moscow and Leningrad, eventually finding a government job as a technology transfer manager at the UK Centre for Environment, Fisheries & Aquaculture Science. We remained frequent pen pals after our return. Our conversations were often "daft" (her words) and playful. Sometime about 2005, Sara was diagnosed with myalgic encephalomyelitis, more commonly known as Chronic Fatigue Syndrome. The disease slowly drained the life away from this incredible woman, travel companion, and very dear friend.

Lila and Mark wrote to me with news of their doings after I departed the expedition. The in-fighting amongst

---

[26] To be fair and frank, Gbadolite was clearly marked on the Michelin map that I carried.

expedition members over the itinerary and expenses only got worse, aggravated by the fact that George had underestimated the amount of money required to get the group to Nairobi. After 12 fruitless days hanging about Kisangani waiting for Tracks to forward additional funds, the crew voted to move on, leaving George behind and opting to pay for expenses out of their own pockets until Tracks could reimburse them further on down the road. Passing through Rwanda, Burundi, and Tanzania, they did manage to see mountain gorillas in Rwanda and big game on the Serengeti, but the roads and bridges they encountered were often in poor repair requiring hours of exhausting labor to navigate.

After reaching Nairobi, Lila and Mark went off together to explore Mombasa, Malindi, and Lamu, experiencing a few additional adventures of their own. Lila returned to England with pus-filled blisters on her feet and legs caused by hemolytic streptococcus, a form of bacterial infection, requiring weeks of treatment and recovery. She found work with a British chemical company, met a man named Richard, and got married. Mark hitched his way around East Africa for a time, battled dysentery, then made his way to South Africa via Malawi and Zambia. Too broke for a flight home, he found work as a food scientist in Johannesburg, met a woman, fell in love, and became a dad. To my knowledge, he was the only other member of the expedition to make it all the way across Africa.

Lila kept in contact with the other members of the Tracks expedition for a time, sharing with me what news she had of their disposition soon after reaching Nairobi in 1984:

Chris and Julie found jobs as physiotherapists at London hospitals. Julie had plans to move to Australia, presumably connected to Jim, though Jim carried on traveling for a time and was last heard from in Zimbabwe; Chris planned to join Rick in New Zealand; Rick, at the time, was somewhere in Scandinavia working as a freelance butcher; Barry held out hopes of joining a veterinary practice in East Anglia; Elaine was planning to join Malcolm in East Africa where he was running Tracks safaris out of Nairobi.

Inger returned to Denmark and school, having broken off with George, who simply disappeared; Andy and Kristine planned to settle in France permanently; the last word on Hazel was that she was trying for a license to open a night club in Kinshasa, while Bernard was still tuning pianos; Gail found work as a ranch-hand in the north of England; Lynn found employment as a nanny to a very wealthy family in Yorkshire; Alison was working as an English teacher and held out hopes of finding a position in either Singapore or Japan; Ronnie, disillusioned with life in Melbourne, returned to Canada.

Any news I hear about the various places I visited can stir up old memories and emotions, but ordinary things that seem utterly unrelated can do the same, particularly personal interactions. Of all the things about my trek that I ruminate on the most are my many encounters with utterly selfless people who wanted nothing more than to help a stranger in obvious need or to enjoy a serendipitous connection. That is what truly stands out, not the outstretched hands looking for unmerited cadeaux.

I recorded in my journals the addresses of several people who inspired me by their generosity, along with any promises I'd made to send them specially requested items upon my return. I made this a priority, sending off things like water skins, soccer magazines, travel brochures, and even a couple of business introductions. With a little effort, I was able to track down the professor who had befriended the young man in Togo who had approached our truck asking if there was anyone on board from Queen's University. We both marveled at the odds. I did receive a dozen or so letters from people that had pressed me for my address along the way. These invariably turned out to be requests for money or pleas to act as their sponsor for immigration. One of the men I met in Tamanrasset even asked me to set him up with a Canadian girl "between 16 and 25 years."

I discarded all of these with one notable exception—Sylvester Edien, the waiter at the EKO Holiday Inn in Lagos who had taken a special liking to me and my stories. He had a cousin, Jacob Isang, and asked if I could please try as much as I could "to get Jacob fixed up somewhere in Canada. He is a fine soccer player you will admire when you see him play." Sylvester was salt of the earth, living proof that extraordinary people exist in all walks of life all over the world. If Sylvester felt that strongly about his cousin, I was certainly going to give it a try. I owed him that much.

So, I wrote to Jacob directly, asking him to provide me with details about his soccer skills. I was impressed enough by his credentials to follow up, asking the Toronto Blizzard, then in their second iteration as a professional team in the Canadian Soccer League, if they had any room for a talented young soccer player from Nigeria.[27] I was prepared to see my inquiry dismissed out of hand, and so, was pleasantly surprised to hear that they were actually quite interested. Unfortunately, he needed a college degree to be considered. The soccer coach at Simon Fraser University in Burnaby, British Columbia also took an interest in Jacob, but the registrar's office was adamant that he needed to take prep courses at a junior college before being considered. I was in the midst of navigating these various hurdles when a letter from Jacob landed in my mailbox. To my surprise, it was post marked Lynchburg, Virginia. He'd snagged himself a full athletic scholarship at Liberty University!

But Jacob was troubled. Liberty U, it seemed, was just as much or more interested in his education as his ability to play soccer. In his letters to me, he expressed his frustration. He just wanted to play "active soccer" and earn good money to help support his family back home in Nigeria. He urged

---

[27] This was 1987.

me to keep up my attempts to find him a place in professional soccer, preferably in Canada where the sport was supposedly better appreciated. I wrote him back in words to the effect that he was fortunate indeed to obtain a full scholarship and really ought to give his education a fighting chance. While it might not prove lucrative for him in the short-term, the long-term advantages could well surprise him. We wrote back and forth a few more times, and eventually lost track of one another.

I wondered over the years what became of Jacob. In preparation for this book, I decided to search out his name on the internet. In the thirty-plus years since coming to the States, he developed a curriculum vitae with a list of teaching, coaching, and soccer recruiting accomplishments as long as my arm. His record as a youth soccer coach is particularly stellar, but two other accomplishments stand out—graduating from Indiana Wesleyan University with a bachelor's degree in criminal justice and a master's degree in social work from Indiana University–Purdue University Indianapolis.

Jacob was not the only person that I maintained correspondence with after my trip across Africa. I sent a bundle of magazines to the young boy I'd met on a trail in Cameroon who'd impressed me with his quiet curiosity. Zaoro wrote me back to thank me for my gift and we became informal pen pals. As these things go, we lost track of one another from time-to-time but reconnected when he was in his early 30s. Zaoro had married and wanted to start a family, but subsistence farming held little promise for him.

Edi and I were also married, as it happens. It turned out that she was impressed by the flowers I sent her from Bulawayo. Many of the letters she'd written addressed to me care of the poste restante had simply gone astray in the tangled postal system. Of the letters that did make it and seemed to me a trifle dispassionate, this was merely the result of the heavy demands of her graduate workload, and nothing more. My parents hadn't been quite straight with me about her feelings, hoping, I presume, that I would cut short my trip and come home sooner. Our love for one another, in fact, survived the test. In 2021 we celebrated our 36th wedding anniversary.

Acutely aware of how lucky we were to live in Canada and to enjoy relative peace and prosperity, we were drawn to the whole concept of 'a random act of kindness.' In Zaoro we saw an opportunity to make a concrete difference in the life of at least one person, moreover, at a relatively small sacrifice to ourselves. We agreed, therefore, to help him to the extent that we were able, and only to the point where he could manage on his own, offering, so to speak, a leg up in life. We reached out to him, searching for a way forward. Zaoro wrote back asking if we would consider supporting him and his wife, Amina, through teacher's college. His argument was persuasive. As a couple, they could find teaching jobs in rural Cameroon where their services were most needed and together raise a family. We agreed, our only stipulation that they pass all their courses and send us copies of the transcripts.

Zaoro, of course, was elated. I spoke on the phone with the registrar at Écoles normales d'instituteurs de l'enseignement général (ENIEG) at Bertoua where they planned to attend school and all the necessary arrangements were put in place for the two-year program, including living expenses. We knew we'd made the right decision when we received a copy of their first trimester transcripts. What we had never given much thought to, was the fact that Zaoro, by this time, was 32 years of age. His "window of opportunity," so to say, was fast closing. We had assumed that Zaoro and Amina would focus solely on their studies, so it came as something of shock to learn that Amina had given birth to their first child. The pregnancy was not without difficulties and her grades naturally suffered. But Amina persevered, graduating alongside her husband. Perhaps it was genuine gratitude on their part, or an effort to forestall our concerns, or a combination of both, but they named their baby girl, "Edi Brigitte."

Their struggles were far from over, however. It took the better part of two years for them to secure actual teaching jobs, during which they endured many hardships. In subsequent years, we received brighter letters and emails with news about their burgeoning family and photographs of them together with their students in Yokadouma, a village in southeastern Cameroon near the border with the Central African Republic.

Life, by its very nature, provides each of us with countless opportunities and experiences. To a limited extent, we also have the option of making our own. In my case, that opportunity was Africa. I learned a great deal over just a few short months, about people, cultures, societies, and economies, but probably more than anything about myself. While I can't say that I did much to impact Africa, Africa certainly had its effect on me. I have tended ever since to think globally, much like an astronaut with the clarity of vision to see our shared planet as a "fragile oasis"—to appreciate our similarities, more than our differences. I have, ever since, also been acutely aware that more than one version of our world exists. Most people I meet don't seem to truly understand this fact, safe and secure, I suppose, in their own paradigm.

The Tracks brochure my father gave me wasn't far off the mark: "you will be one of only a handful of fortunate people ever to have had the opportunity to participate on an exploratory project such as this." It was, in the scheme of things, only a short visit, but part of my soul is clearly linked to Africa. I still "feel" Africa, both its sorrow and its joy, and neither seems to diminish with the passage of time. My journey, moreover, was as close to an authentic adventure as I have ever come in life. A National Geographic map of Africa hangs on our bedroom wall with my route traced out. Superimposed over top is a quote from The Journeyer by Gary Jennings—that book on Marco Polo I'd read about during my visit to the Canadian High Commission in Dar es Salaam:

> "Adventure is no more than discomfort and annoyance recollected in the safety of reminiscence."

Sitting here at my desk some thirty-eight years later, dredging up old memories and emotions to put to paper, I find myself thinking that I really couldn't have verbalized it any better.

ABOUT THE AUTHOR

Neil Bernard Dukas was born and raised in Ontario, Canada. He joined the Canadian Army as a very young man, serving over the years in both reserve and active capacities, including a stint on horseback with the mounted squadron of The Governor General's Horse Guards. After graduating from Queen's University at Kingston, he furthered his growing love for travel by trekking across the African continent from top to bottom. Since then, he has seen a great deal more of the world, working as a bank supervisor, Christmas Tree packer, freelance journalist, college dean, inventor, public information assistant, movie extra, and women's fashion accessory manufacturer, not to mention novelist and military historian. The focus of his graduate studies, Dukas developed a deep and abiding affection for Hawai'i. In 2011, his book on the Battle of Nu'uanu received a Ka Palapala Po'okela Awards distinction "for excellence in Hawaiian culture." The very same year, his first novel, The Spanish Gatekeeper–Empire of the Ulfair, was a Compton Crook Award finalist for best debut science fiction fantasy.

Kaladar Books
120 Ward St, Unit 5226
Larkspur, CA 94977-9024
Ph: (888) 871-1926
email: **kbservice@kaladarbooks.com**
www.kaladarbooks.com

Manufactured by Amazon.ca
Bolton, ON